Cruelest Hoax

A Day of Deception and Decades of Lies

9/11 and Recovering Our Self-Respect

An American Citizen

Contents

One: Why Write?   1

Two: 9/11   13

Three: Acceptance and Refusal   51

Four: Evidence, Facts and Stories   79

Five: Commissions, Courts and Trials
         Agencies, Obligation and Accountability   91

Six: Not Your Ordinary False Flag Event   103

Seven: Facts and Apparent Majority   121

Eight: Now, Twenty Years Later   139

Nine: Metonym   159

Ten: In Sum   183

Eleven: And So   201

Afterword: A Note From the Author

One: Why Write?

Some things are easy enough for the human mind to do. Others, much harder. We perform the intricate choreographies of creating a mindset in ourselves, or between us and others, quickly and seamlessly. Only with some difficulty, however, do we manage to think carefully and intelligently about our thinking and believing.

People among us, more than a few, say that they believe the earth is flat. Physically flat. Flat like sheet metal. Flat like a pancake. They say, with apparent sincerity, that they are not gaslighting us, not "sending us up." They present their belief as entirely genuine. A doubting reader can Google-search to find articles, discussions of poll results, and essays in explication that sum to two propositions: 1. The flat-earthers' *belief* indeed is "real," and 2. The flat-earthers support and compliment the belief by a set of other propositions about the views of other people and institutions to the effect that those "round-earth" ideas are contrivances. In short, the flat-earthers say that the round earth proposition is an "elaborate conspiracy theory."

Wikipedia, that notable conglomeration of announcement in the digital age, in an article titled "Modern Flat Earth Societies" describes the activities and views (and sincerities) of the "International Flat Earth Research Society" while also taking a moment to explain "Much of the society's literature in its early days focused on interpreting the Bible to mean that the Earth is flat, although they did try to offer scientific explanations and evidence." And "Through the use of social media, flat Earth theories have been increasingly espoused…"

The flat-earther "arguments" and allegations about "conspiracy theories" appear as if composed to give ready place to simple intuitions and seem fashioned to elide dissonance. In our experience of land, the wider the viewscape (think of driving in a car on the Interstate in the Texas Panhandle) the "flatter" the land appears so, by extension, if we could see "everything" we'd recognize the whole earth is flat. Comparably charming is the flat-earther proposition that "Earth's gravity is an illusion ... Objects do not accelerate downward; instead, the disc of

Earth accelerates upward at 32 feet per second squared (9.8 meters per second squared), driven up by a mysterious force called 'dark energy.'" And that "GPS devices are rigged to make airplane pilots *think* they are flying in straight lines around a sphere when they are actually flying in circles above a disc."[1]

That said, the flat-earth described "experiments" and "results" even more perfectly suggest what can incite us to belief. Borrowing the account of one such experiment (from among several similar accounts of other similar "experiments" and "demonstrations") we read:

> A flat-earth conspiracy theorist and YouTuber has taken a spirit level onto a plane to "prove" that Earth is flat once and for all. His 'experiment' has since gone viral, just not in the way that he'd hoped. YouTube conspiracy theorist D[arryl]. Marble took a flight from North Carolina to Seattle in order to monitor whether or not the pilot would dip the nose of the plane to compensate for curvature. Darryl and followers say his video, below for your entertainment pleasure, proves that Earth is flat.[2]

> *"I recorded a 23 minute and 45 seconds time-lapse, which by those measurements means the plane traveled a little over 203 miles,"* he explained in his video. *"According to curvature math given to explain the globe model, this should have resulted in the compensation of 5 miles of curvature. As you'll see there was no measurable compensation for curvature."*[3]

Without extensive interviews, it can be hard to know who really "believes" what, and why. The compound pseudo-scientific foolishness (there is no other plain word for it) offered on behalf of the "proof," however, is marvelously extensive. The ingeniousness of the calculation of the size of Earth performed by Eratosthenes in the third

1. www.livescience.com

2. www.livescience.com and see: https://aworkstation.com/man-says-he-finally-proved-the-earth-is-flat-by-bringing-a-spirit-level-on-a-plane.

3. With his presentation and explanation skills, Mr. Marble would doubtless be a good hire for the United States National Institute for Science and Technology, inasmuch as he and S. Shyam Sunder appear to share the "leadership" qualities cited in Sunder's 2005 Gold Medal Award from the US Department of Commerce, the Department's highest honor, and in Sunder's 2017 "Presidential Rank Award."

century BCE notwithstanding, the idea that a bubble in liquid in an enclosure, taken on a plane ride, used as described by Mr. Marble, is in and of itself determinate of geometric flatness of the globe is wonderfully mindless, on the one hand, and single-minded, on the other. The vial and bubble is proposed to be an oracle of infinite level, a kind of horizontality omniscience, that shows something made only of concept, and independent of physical feature or fact of any sort. This, to the extent that the story nearly turns romantic. The bubble becomes almost as emotionally marvelous as the early nineteenth century poetic notion of seeing all life and all living things in the rise of a single sprout, the panoplies of ecologies and species in an instant entirely become a singularly represented ideation of all.[4]

Few experiences are more welcome or more reassuring to the human mind than propositions that there exists some ultra-capable simplicity we can bring into being by means little more than our own announcement, and to which we can then hold tightly, to which we can adhere with vehemence and, from so doing, we can declare we have conquered a vast territory of arbitrary complexity. There are reasons having to do with "mental economics" we like our unifying accounts of our experience as much as we do. And there do exist certain schematics that model observed phenomena very widely and very accurately. And then there are arguably less good reasons that come, for example, from assignments of cause to forces said to be omnipresent and multiply omnipotent, and which only admit of characterizations that are astonishingly incoherent, but which have been politically useful for ages.

Unhappily, all too often we want simplifying propositions most in cases in which any apparent consistency is a mere artifact of a particular telling of the story. We zealously seek and declare simplistic modelings when they are about as real as Walt Disney's anti-gravity "Flubber"

---

4. For the movie version, try "Behind the Curve" a 2018 "Documentary," Delta-V Productions. Also see "Looking for Life on a Flat Earth," *New Yorker,* Alan Burdick, May 30, 2018 "If you are only just waking up to the twenty-first century, you should know that, according to a growing number of people, much of what you've been taught about our planet is a lie: Earth really is flat. We know this because dozens, if not hundreds, of YouTube videos describe the cover-up."

— and we will, with as great a sense of mission and determination, disdain and ignore reductive representations when they are truthful and available, accurate and extensively applicable. That Earth is a (slightly oblate) sphere, round (like a ball) is a reasonably simple truth quite helpful in observing time and the progress of days, calculating position on Earth's surface, or figuring out the velocity required for an object to orbit Earth, or to escape orbit. In fact we experience the roundness of Earth all the time. We are freely given a renewed showing at every sunrise, or GPS measurement, or at sea watching a freighter come from or go to the horizon. This presented evidence has been observed and responsibly recorded by many, many people, many, many times over many years. Uncontroverted evidence so coherent in what it presents and so extensive and so much directly and completely confirmed as this deserves regard greater than a non-scientific contrivance, and even somewhat greater than as "the result of *an* experiment." In doing a single given "experiment" events fairly described as "mistakes" can determine the results, and may wait to be corrected, but we do not help ourselves to set aside a fact, or principle or set of principles correctly abstracted from trillions of confirmatory examples, such as the round-ness of the planet Earth and the true facts as to the Earth's gravity, in response to human anxiety that stems from human emotional need to claim that a wanted simplicity ("flatness") is supposedly "confirmed."

However, many of us, indeed most of us, do not treat what we are given to observe accurately with much respect or appreciation. More often than not, we prefer to assume the constructions of others, or those of our society at large, often in return for being socially accepted by means of the fulsome implications that we offer with belief in the story told (that contradicts all evidence). Much about this preference for re-working and substituting for that which is actual would be hard to change. Socially, advantages (and many relief-providing second-order benefits, including reduced cognitive dissonance) come from changing the facts about what we see and hear and smell and taste and have the ready ability to recognize. Given a choice between the truth and the opportunity to say or suggest we have gained a certain "control" of evidence and truth — and reality — we humans will often prefer falsities we have enjoyed the prerogative to assent to, or to propose we've authored. We will consider this tendency, its various manifestations, and its consequences, recognizing its power to direct our lives and to shape our society, again in this book. There are reasons this proclivity arguably was 'adaptive' in variously 'pre-scientific' historical periods. At this point in this discussion, it is enough that we agree there are deep and consequential differences between the propositions about the world that come from actual science, conducted according to the principles of scientific inquiry, and propositions that distinctly do not.

The signal declaration of our era about the construction of "reality" and assertion of the purported advantages therefrom can be found in a well-known short speech quoted in an article in the New York Times Magazine in 2004.[5] This little lecture has been attributed to Karl Rove. (Rove has denied making it.) It is a form of words nearly perfect in its expression of an attitude about the place and role of "reality" in modern human, social, and political relationships. Ron Suskind, writing the piece, quotes a "senior advisor" to the President, explaining:

> The aide said that guys like me were "in what we call the reality-based community," which he defined as people who "believe that solutions emerge from your judicious study of discernible reality." I nodded and murmured something about enlightenment principles and empiricism. He cut me off. "That's not the way the world really works anymore," he continued. "We're an empire now, and when we act, we create our own reality. And while you're studying that reality — judiciously, as you will — we'll act again, creating other new realities, which you can study too, and that's how things will sort out. We're history's actors . . . and you, all of you, will be left to just study what we do."

The "senior advisor" is, of course, not the first person to have expressed a view about what makes for that which we say is "real." Philosophers have held a long and often technical discussion regarding what constitutes a "fact," about what makes a described "fact" worthy to be called a fact, or some thing said to be "real" (sometimes labeled

---

5. Ronald Suskind, October 17, 2004 "Faith, Certainty, and the Presidency of George W. Bush"

"ontology") and how do we come to "know" facts (more or less "epistemology"). There is an inherent "circularity," or "re-reference" to the discussion almost every time it is held. More or less, when asked "so how do we know *these* facts" we answer. "..because we know *these other* facts..." and then, or course, how do we know those...? etc.

We often arrive to the discussion with the assumption that because certain facts "underlie" or "support" other facts, there must be some headwaters to this river; there must be some truth that is beneath and underlies all others. Not necessarily in such a way, although underlying truth often gives rise to many further truths. That the relationship of supporting" or "confirming" exists does not in itself entail that there is some singular thing that truly has such a relationship to a particular given multiplicity. But this is something as hard for people to understand as it was hard for our human predecessors who had developed and implemented societal hierarchy not to say that the heavens above (and the gods in them) must be similarly structurally hierarchical, too.

Without intending to, the flat-earthers are doing us a huge favor. By their suggestions, they are challenging the rest of us to think, actually quite deeply, about how it is that we know what we say we know or, said only a little differently, what makes some representations of the world true and correct, and makes others in fact not cohere with reality, physical reality in particular.

Just as a thought experiment, let's suppose that the flat-earthers are not missing any seemingly explanatory claims. Let's say they have a way to account for every experience a living person can have, everything that can be seen, or otherwise perceived. Just for the sake of thinking about the question, let's say that there is a flat-earth version of everything of which there can be an account. (If you start a question beginning with "But what about..." to pose to our posited flat-earther, you will get in response a stream of explanation. The flat earth "theory" never fails to provide, never goes quiet.) Do we then have to say that the flat-earth "position" is as "good" as any other? If the virtue of a position, any general descriptive scheme, is that it provides "explanations," how can we say that a scheme that, as we have stipulated, provides an explanation of some kind for "everything," isn't fully as valuable as any other?

Anybody who has ever done this "five finger exercise" in philosophy in a moment of honesty is soon ready to recognize nevertheless that some explanations are much better than others. Some explanations, however "explanatory" they may seem to be, deserve to be called "false" — just because they are wrong (and often in so many ways, "bad"). The exercise in philosophy that lets us know something about the status of a merely offered account, however proposed to be "complete" in its own terms, can be done by anyone is a few minutes. The work of understanding the value and truth of accounts, explanations, models, renderings, depictions and so forth is the work of a whole human lifetime and the work of the compendium of human lives over millennia.

Some of the answers historically provided have been good answers — but not great answers. For example, one good answer has principally to do with ideas about "simplicity" (for want of a better word for the moment). William of Ockham in the fourteenth century offered a proposition (in Latin) that roughly translates to: "plurality should not be posited without necessity" or "Entities are not to be multiplied beyond necessity." A common gloss in proposed clarification has it as "… the principle that, of two explanations that account for all the facts, the simpler one is more likely to be correct." The problem with this dictum, of course, is that we have a few deeply conceptual — and potentially somewhat difficult — decisions to make before we can make any use of it. What is an "entity," and when is an entity "necessary"? And by what means of ascertainment or decision? Or, even after we have been "helped out," how do we know that an "explanation" "*accounts* for all the facts," and when, exactly, is one "simpler" than another?

If to punish an example by re-use, we can return to the flat-earthers and the airplane ride with the bubble and ask ourselves, 'What would it take to show that the bubble in the demonstration is not doing what that bubble is proposed to be doing — hewing to an independent frame of "horizontal," that it is instead responding in its position to the gravity vector in the gravitational field around the planet next to which it is traveling? The bubble is in fact not showing "horizontal" in the abstract, it is showing "perpendicularity to local gravity." And that "moves" along with the plane as the plane travels. (Just as the plane's wings create aerodynamic lift opposite to this same gravitational force to keep the plane in the air.) And to make very short the explanation, if we were to apply a "positioning system" genuinely three dimensionally orthogonal (think various forms of inertial navigational systems, or certain systems based upon accurate celestial observations, etc.) the track of the airplane would show curvature corresponding to the curvature of the Earth as the plane flew at a given altitude above it.

This comes as an example from which it is not all that easy to say that the truth is "simpler" or comes from explanation that redounds in simplicity. The screwy story about the bubble and the plane's "angle" is, by many ways of talking about it, "simpler." The virtues of the truth about the plane's path and the planet's shape come instead from coherence with a vast extent of experiment and unhindered observation, experiment that can go by a set of different names in our language, including "objective verification," "analyzed experience," "careful measurement" and the like. Truth has many properties, but among the most important are those that have to do with the way that the truth is confirmed, widely and deeply, not by anything that one or many people might say, but by existence and relationship that we can understand, usually in one or another form of "model," and have not ourselves merely put up without the concerted referendum of rationally constructed experiment. The universe, and every part of it, is full of facts, properties — truths — that are embodied in the nature of things that exist. The behavior of gravitational fields has been examined, not just by any one passenger in a plane with a bubble, but by many carefully configured sampling and examining apparatuses on many, many, many occasions. The results from all of these examinations converge to set of concise representations about the properties of gravitation, also confirmed by many experiences in practice: ascents, descents, orbiting, etc. The affirmation of these results, each for the others, and confirmation they provide regarding our understanding of gravitational properties makes it at best unreasonable to suppose that we should discard our understanding so that we can "choose" to pronounce the earth is "flat."

Even the "simplest," merest thing, a gallon of (distilled H_2O) water, weighs 8.33 pounds, has a viscosity of 1 centipoise, and a specific heat of 1 calorie per gram — not more, not less. More complicated things, a computer networking arrangement, can transmit, say, 100 million bits per second — not more, not less. More societally conventional things can be true, a pair of license plates bearing the letters and numbers XYZ-123 from a particular state is (as an ordinary administrative matter) the only pair of such plates issued. As we leave physical realities and turn toward societal conventions, the form of described certainty diminishes. Nature never makes a mistake regarding the weight of water, but in the license plate making facility could mess up and create more than just the one pair of plates with those letters and numbers. (On the other hand, if the license plate facility includes a "checking system" intended, when correctly operating, to insure that only one pair is made, and we indeed have good evidence it was working and undisturbed on the day in question, we have a significant additional quantum of confirmation.) As we move toward physical realities and processes closely involving physical realities, the evidentiary properties that extend from and connect to truth act more reliably to corroborate the factual and reveal the falsity of the untrue. As we move away from "something that the universe reliably will conclusively demonstrate to us any time we configure a sampling or test" and toward "something somebody said" we move from decisive confirmation or disconfirmation of a particular proposition to conditions of complete indeterminacy.

This is not news. We know there is no inherent connection between human utterance and factual truth. We know that in practice people tell lies all the time. Groupings of people, especially when they are official, are often inveterate liars. As the journalist I. F. Stone explained so succinctly: "All Governments Lie." The suggestion for the recent decades that Suskind forwards to us, however, is, in effect, that "things are different now." And, what is described presently "different" about things is that "reality" is now to be fresh-on "created" by the "own reality" making "act[s of] ... an empire" (which "we are now.")

To say as much is roundly to dismiss, as Suskind's interlocutor (presumedly Rove) clearly does, the notion of "reality" as comprised of a considerable part that is beyond mere creation by people, as something we can discover by and through our acts and our creations, but which, although we come from reality, and we are a part of reality, as real as every other part, has in fact as many parts as indeed it does, and that many of those other parts are things we have not created, could not create, should not propose we can create, and only through a kind of hubris, damaging to ourselves and the universe in which we live, would we suggest that by "acts of empire" we would in any way manufacture.

Both as a proposition and a guiding metaphor and prototype example I refer to "truth" and to "experiment" or "experience." It is the relationship that counts, that is important. An old guy, a friend, used to say to me from time to time, "Truth is the one strategy that always works. That is why it is and is called the truth." The saying is not perfect, but it is valuable; it helps. It tries to capture the continuity and the extended support that the truth has in the actuality that permeates and surrounds everything and all of us and everything we do, and has since time beyond memory. The ideas behind what I am here calling "experiment" are to connect our recognition of truth to a genuine understanding of the relationships that make for truth. So much of what is true is the truth because it reliably joins all the way to properties of the universe that came into being when the universe came into being, symmetries that persist through changes, principles that very reliably abstract from what has always been, is, and will be.

There is a sense in which we know what "experiment" and genuine "confirmation by a properly conducted experiment" are in a way that we do not know (and maybe cannot know) what things like "simplicity" or "necessity" are. What we can ordinarily refer to as "simple" or "simplicity" does not concern, or connect to, something we can call a "model" quite in the way that "experiment" or "evidence" does. This does not mean that we are not often attracted to ideas and concepts that are inherently very imprecise and that we do not understand well, and that we find ourselves liking, or needing, or needing to the point of addiction, or believing we need if we are to be the least bit "organized" or safe.

It takes some courage to do any experiment that genuinely tests any hypothesis upon which our lives in any part have come to dwell. It takes even more courage to consider whether a figure of mind more fully adopted than a hypothesis, a belief, either is true or false or whether it is valuable or harmful in its truth or falsity. It takes yet more courage, more than most of us have most of the time, to be willing to work from veritable first principles when we are surrounded by other people who have already bought unsupportable conclusions for which they have paid too much.

This is a book that seeks deeply to consider whether a scheme that is very certainly false that has been "created" in an evident effort to make a "created reality" which we, as a society, now have for more than two decades widely and, particularly when it was first created, generally believed and supported and taken as if true — were now better remitted to its wrongs and failures. I am just one person, but I have thought about this question for over twenty years. Therefore I write.

Two: 9/11.

The "Webster's Dictionary on-line" defines "fraud" as "intentional perversion of truth in order to induce another to part with something of value or to surrender a legal right." It is an applicable description of what the word means. By this, or any other similar definition, "9/11" was a thoroughgoing fraud.

People of the country and the world who believed the "intentional perversion of truth" of the 9/11 story parted with things of great value to themselves, to the civilization in which they live, and to the world. They unreasonably surrendered legal rights, including, in too many cases, the simple right to live.

I am aware that the truth of 9/11, and the truth that the American government and national and international media lied and lied and lied, are truths very difficult for many people just to read as written words, or to understand, or accept, but almost nothing that the United States government said or induced others to say about the events of September 11, 2001 in Lower Manhattan in New York City, at the Pentagon in Washington, D.C. or in Shanksville, Pennsylvania is true. It is not true in the same sense that a spaceship did not in fact land at Grover's Mill, New Jersey on October 30th, 1938 and there did not occur an ensuing "invasion of aliens;" it is not true in the same sense that the Reichstag Fire in February 1933 was not in fact set by van der Lubbe and other "Communists." It is not true in the same sense that North Vietnamese boats did not in fact attack the US Navy destroyers Maddox and Turner Joy the night of August 4, 1964 in the Gulf of Tonkin. It is not true in the same sense that the non-combatant naval vessel USS Liberty was not attacked by Arabs on June 8, 1967 but by Israeli torpedo boats and airplanes, that also shot at crew members in life rafts as the crew abandoned the vessel. The 9/11 story told by the government and media says that certain physical events occurred, and by described physical causes. The story as told, however, offers wholesale falsity.

The reasonable opportunity for thoughtful people of ordinary education to understand that the story the government has told in the case of 9/11 is not true, is more definite, more certain and somewhat different than in many of the other instances in which false stories have been told. As to what happened in the Gulf of Tonkin, for example, we have to rely on sources such as the Robert J. Hanyok account originally published in *Cryptographic Quarterly,* declassified and released on December 1, 2005, together with other accounts (James Stockdale's, for example, or now available documents from the U.S. Naval Institute) that corroborate what Hanyok says. There are several. They are credible for the reasons that true statements that provide truthful details generally are credible; they cohere with facts, especially facts difficult to alter, they are supported by correlative particulars; they are supported by other accounts of potentially varying (North Vietnamese) interest. Hanyok's account both in main and in its many particulars is thus highly likely true and President Lyndon Johnson's false.

Regarding 9/11, we can know a lot about the fraud without even having to decide about a person or agency engaged in a retelling. We do not have to accept hearsay or otherwise second or third-hand propositions and we do not have to do any guessing or speculating. Particularly, we do not have to make suppositions about the tendencies or capabilities of people or organizations.

In an essay posted on *Znet* by David Corn (from an *AlterNet* post), the claim is made that "The [otherwise described 9/11] plot — to execute the simultaneous destruction of the two towers, a piece of the Pentagon, and four airplanes and make it appear as if it all was done by another party — is far beyond the skill level of U.S. intelligence." What is within or beyond the "skill level" of a large and complex organization is a not a simple question, but fortunately it does not matter in answering reasonable forensic inquiry regarding the proximate physical causes of physical events. Everything "Newtonian" in the physical universe is extremely "reliable" (predictable, ascertainable) in a way that humans and organizations and human opinions and observations and the reports filed by organizations are not. A force is always required for velocity to change. F always equals ma.

An equal and opposite force is always experienced by two colliding objects. Always. Physical energy is always conserved. Momentum is conserved. Kinetic energy always equals $\frac{1}{2}mv^2$. Anyone who says that the particular capabilities (or lack thereof) of government entities can change mechanical science has a lot of supposed proving to do (or otherwise should be laughed out of any room with any thoughtful people in it). And, no surprise, these truths are not matters that anybody should reasonably get to "vote" on or otherwise decide as a matter of "popularity." A thousand earthlings can say that Newton's principles are wrong, and no one be on hand to say that they are not wrong — without thereby creating any change in the accuracy and applicability of Newton's principles. The only "choosing" that matters to the universe is that done by the many Newtonian objects in it by means of the many instances, in the billions of years so far, in which they have acted in complete conformance with those principles.

It is true that other "ballots" cast by people can affect human society; people can readily "vote" for mythologies, including stories that entirely contradict physical reality. (We will reserve for later consideration what happens to a modern society that puts much of its attention and energies into controverting fundamental science.) But the fact that the universe merely continues to act like itself both in general and in every particular makes the job of understanding the truth of what physically happened on September 11, 2001 much easier. All the chatter that offers opinions about Arabs and what Arabs might do, and that offers opinions about mistakes the Unites States would or would not make, or that makes claims about what happened based upon media accounts that claimed to describe what happened, can be set aside.

We can instead refer to physical facts and physical evidence that is very difficult to fake or very unlikely to have been faked (that, for example, World Trade Center Buildings One and Two were in fact constructed according to known plans developed by Yamasaki, Skilling, Robertson and others, and withstood all naturally occurring events at the site from the early 1970s to 2001, that a "Boeing 767-200" is a twin engine jet having an empty eight of about 180,000 pounds, a rated gross weight of about 300,000 pounds, a wingspan of 156 feet and a length of 159 feet, its fuselage and wings made from aluminum alloys, and so forth as made by Boeing and widely and accurately described in its particulars). These baseline true facts, taken together with Isaac Newton's stated principles of mechanics and other similarly certain principles of mechanical physics related to them, can bring us to truthful recognition regarding much of what in fact did and did not happen on September 11, 2001.

Considering the 9/11 Story as told by the government and media with respect to very well recognized scientific principles and truths is entirely comparable to considering the claims of The Flat Earth Society in regard to the known shape and size of the planet Earth, the very well-known properties of the physical gravity field of planetary objects, and so forth. The 9/11 Story has come from official sources and "mainstream" media in American society, but its complete disregard for very well established science and scientific truth is not less than the contempt for the longstanding and extensively verified knowledge about the physical universe than shown by the flat-earthers.

Newton published in 1687. In Latin, but what he explained is very clear. During the 314 years until 2001, many trillions of mechanical interactions between physical objects occurred (millions of millions). Not one of those many events violated or contradicted the principles Newton had set forth. These principles are not just science "confirmed by *an* experiment" (in which a mistake could, for instance, have been made by a person mis-recording data), these are described relationships confirmed over and over and over and over again by many observable events since time immemorial.

Newton's principles are no "conspiracy theory." They are accurate articulations of very observable and very well defined and inherently definite properties of the behavior of physical objects in the universe. Newton's mechanics are independent of size or scale to the extent that they apply to all objects in the known universe except quantum objects[1]. and relativistic objects[2] Newton's mechanics

1. Which are tiny indeed - think as small and smaller than the "elementary particles" – think acting in terms of Planck's constant h 6.62 × 10^{-34} joule-second.

2. Meaning those, for example, travelling very close to the speed of

apply without regard to the "internal" complexity of any given physical body, so long as it comprises a physical entity. A rock and a very intricate, elaborate rocket ship each traveling in space will each, for example, require a given force in proportion to its mass in order to be accelerated by a given amount. As will a shoe thrown, and a bolt dropped, and a pumpkin launched by a catapult, and every other thing that is a physical/mechanical thing that you might name.

The three principal "laws" and the many other derived and related very well demonstrated principles of mechanics, that forces add as arithmetical vectors, that mechanical energy is conserved, that momentum is the product of mass and velocity, that a mass has kinetic energy in proportion to the product of the mass and the velocity squared, and so on and so forth, are, all of them, reasonably simple as stated. The equations that provide statements of these principles in symbols, "$F=ma$", "$E_k=\frac{1}{2}mv^2$" and so forth, are very short and nothing mathematically fancy.

Unhappily, however, only a small part of the population of the United States, even immediately after having completed a physics class in High School which had classical mechanics as its principal focus, has an actual working understanding of physical mechanics, or scores well on a test — even one in which only Newton's three principles need be applied.[3] That fact that mechanical physics as science remains less than well understood, however, does not make its tenets untrue, particularly not the truth of which has been demonstrated again and again in plain view of all the eyes of all the world for years and years.

These things said, in our current experience the truths of physics are particularly controverted by movies and television. Physically impossible things happen regularly on screen: products leap from shelves into the hands of shoppers without any physical motive force, whirls of pixels in a twirling shape become a large man with a shaved head and one earring, promising transfixing cleanliness all about and

---

light, or for which the curvature of the space-time manifold is significant.

3. See, e.g. "Sources of Difficulty in Understanding Newtonian Dynamics" *Cognitive Science* 7 (1983).

everywhere, and Wile E. Coyote free-falls thousands of apparent feet to the canyon floor to make an outline of his body a furlong deep only to slop his way over the edge of the hole to regain a pose of astonishment at his defeat by a bird with feet so fast they smoke like drag-race car tires.

Before cartoons or movies or advertising and TV, it would have been magic shows. Sawing the lady in half in a box (without any loss of blood, of course) only to reconstitute her when she is re-covered by the drape and the drape then again removed does better than the realities of biology or physics would provide. Magic shows as such may not have occasioned an excess of societally-affecting credulousness, but perhaps that can't or should not be said about some of the "miracles" that have inspired one or another particular religion. It is in our present world, however, that we are especially given the frequent chance to try to determine whether the "created reality" of media presentation would be better understood as seriously "distorted reality." Again, this is fundamentally a book about whether certain distortions, particularly at the instance of controlling government, and as exploited by it, are profoundly harmful.

Except for created images of physical events not actually physical, and other simulacra, there is no demonstrated, legitimate record of any occurrence or interaction involving any "classical" (non-quantum) physical objects acting in a way that does not comport to Newton's principles or the other related principles of classical physical mechanics. None. Ever. Every time a physical body having mass has moved it has had kinetic energy according to the formula for kinetic energy. Every time a force has been exerted on a body there has been an equal and opposite force in the same event. Every time a body has been accelerated the acceleration has been measurable as force divided by mass. Always. And again, any described "internal" complexity of the physical object does not affect the physical mechanics of its interactions as a body. And, again, the principles of physical mechanics apply without regard to size or scale – until things change at the size of Planck's number or when moving almost the speed of light. It does not matter whether an automobile is a Cadillac or a Plymouth or a Citroen or a go-kart, a car that crashes into a wall it has the kinetic energy of its mass times its velocity squared to dissipate in the event (to use to break itself apart and, say, crack the wall). Not more, not less. An undifferentiated lump of matter of the same mass moving at the same speed has the same kinetic energy. And when a car, or a lump, or anything else crashes into a wall, the car and the wall each experience the same, equal force in opposite directions. Similarly, it does not matter whether a car hits a wall, or a wall hits a car. The force that each body experiences is the same in either case. (True, in our experience cars hit walls more often than vice versa but, do the experiment, mount a wall on wheels, roll it on rails at eighty miles an hour so that it hits a "fixed" car, observe the results and measure the forces.)

There continues to exist a substantial and significant amount of forensic evidence regarding the events of September 11, 2001. For example, there is video footage of the building collapses that is corroborated both by the frame contents and by other footage of the same subject at the same time. There is always some possibility that a given video segment is synthetic and not veridical. Video, as video, is just bits and pixels. By a careful and thoughtful examination of a video segment and all other relevant evidence, however, the possibility can be reduced to a significant improbably in circumstances in which the verity of particular imagery is borne out by all that it involves. Instances are several in which, if one does the arithmetic, one can show that the informational "depth" and scope of the required synthesis would be, with the technology then existing, beyond the relevant available technical facilities and time. Put more simply, if somewhat less exactly, there are tens to hundreds of thousands of pixels in each image frame that appear from twenty-four to sixty times a second. Even for a video lasting only a few minutes, that is a lot of pixels, or digital "bits" informationally creating them in the rendering. Redundancy or "compressibility" notwithstanding, sometimes the only practical way to get them all precisely to comport with all of the known features and details of the real world is to take an actual veridical picture of the actual real world. Reality is often the only practical source for deriving a particular set of sufficiently detailed images depicting reality (particularly in 2001— admittedly less the case now). For much of the video that shows September 11th events there is no good reason to doubt that the photography or video accurately depicts events in the real world. This, even as there is overwhelming evidence that what government and media are saying happened and is "shown" in the video is wildly untrue.

There are amusing exceptions to accurate depiction in the photography and video. There has been widely circulated, for just one "haha" example, a photo of a Hungarian named Peter Guzli standing on the observation deck of supposedly the North Tower World Trade Center Building while a Boeing jet is about to fly into it. Guzli was thereafter called the "accidental tourist" and "the World Trade Center Tourist Guy." Although the photo more or less looks "realistic" and has been put forward as if real, the plane is a 757 (not a 767); it is an American Airlines plane (not United Airlines); it comes in from the "wrong" direction, the South Tower (Two) had the observation deck, not the North Tower (antenna); the white balance in the photo has not been corrected to match the scene — and so forth. The "accidental tourist" thereafter shows up in quite a few other places, having adventures, including at Abbey Road Crossing in place of the Beatles, and the World Trade Center Observation Deck photo is changed in later images, in one instance to put a hot air balloon in place of the plane, and in another to have a large Godzilla peering over the railing.

Some accounts have it that at one point there was an effort to say that the original Guzli photo came from an abandoned camera found after the building collapses — probably not. There are also some faked photos of the 9/11 scene at the Pentagon in which the objects in the scene do not appear in the spatial relations of actual fact, which photos are said to have come from "media sources." Thoughtful people considering the Pentagon story as told generally know not to be distracted by images embodying these and other mislocations. These things said, the collapse video from-the-broadcast-air at the time of the three building collapses, as far as I now know, shows the three actual building collapses. (The footage of Building Seven collapsing that emerged publicly several years after the collapse coheres extremely well with the footage shown in September, 2001, and there is thus good reason to regard it, too, as accurate.)

Because my subject is more directly centered on whether certain lies do harm when told to a great nation and a world, and because others have done good work in considering the physical truth about 9/11, I am only going to summarize and make a list of some of the offered impossible and false propositions about buildings, planes and plane parts, forensics and physics here. Just the list should be long enough for its purposes (the falsity only gets more extensive as one delves further). I will then give most of this book to a meditation on questions in the thoughtful consideration of which it is my frank hope that you, who read this, will participate. The facts of the lying noted, the important questions are whether a government, any government, or alliance given place by government, has, or should have, the sovereign right to kill thousands of its own citizens in an act of false demonstration, or to commit wholesale fraud, to tell big, important untruths to its subjects in supposed furtherance of its purposes. Or whether a group within government, a segment of some kind, should be given or usurp the right or opportunity effectively to co-opt the offices of government as a whole in the performance of significant and significantly harmful criminal acts intended to be misdescribed in order politically to compel gross policy changes, including domestic repressions and the suppression of recognized civil rights, the pursuit of a number of large, indiscriminately violent wars of choice abroad, and the abrogation of significant international treaty agreements and conventions to which the country has been a signatory, in which it has participated for decades and which concern matters as basic to the conduct of a world of diverse nations as the mistreatment of prisoners of war and the practice of torture. Put simple, the facts are in their way painful in this case, but not especially difficult. A little bit of science, actual science, tells us a lot about what actually happened and how entirely untrue the government and media account is. Recognizing the facts should lead to a worthwhile discussion about ourselves and our country.

Said perhaps even more clearly: this is not UFOs. This is not a set of suppositions about events or causes, nor "merely statistically apparently constructed" relationships. The Popular Mechanics editors — who really have quite a lot to apologize for — have been selling alleged "de-bunking." In fact, it is just more "patter", more nonsense to confuse the audience. So far, there has been no "de-bunking" of the actual physics of mechanical objects, and it is passing unlikely there will be anytime soon. (If there were, 9/11 would be insignificant compared to a change to the universe of that kind and scale.)

Pressed, the people who actually destroyed the buildings with people in them, would likely say that explosives work is their job, and they were following orders. The same can't be said for the people who gave the orders. Nothing I know says, in a legitimate societal (or legal) sense that creating and carrying out 9/11 was "their job." A nation with any reasonable sense of self-worth will recognize the facts and serious questions raised. In the end, we must together think about our sense of self-respect most deeply and clearly. It is not easy to maintain self-respect while lying as much as we have about all the things we have lied about. In any event, let's begin with a list. Sections described in italics. Discussion to follow.

The collapses of Three Tall Buildings — World Trade Center One, Two and Seven (and Other Not-as-Tall Buildings — World Trade Center Five) in New York on September 11. 2001

— Claims have been made that a smaller upper section of a steel-framed building fell about a one story distance onto a larger section below, disassembling the building entire (Bazant, others).

Such a (nail drives a hammer) event is not possible, Newton's Third Law considered. In the interaction / collision, both parts of the building would be subject to equal (and directionally opposite) forces. A given amount of force would take apart the (in fact smaller and lighter) falling upper section at a rate at least equal to (faster than) the lower. Therefore, no matter the construction, the fall could not possibly take apart more of the lower part than the size of the upper.

There does not in fact exist any uniform solid physical object of some given length for which a one tenth part can be dropped in the earth's gravitational field a one-one hundredth's distance onto a nine tenth's part thereby completely crushing the entire lower part.

— For an upper part of a building to "fall" onto a lower that upper part must first be suspended and then fall down the distance of suspension. There is no evidence of any kind in any of the recorded video that an "upper block" of building was above and clear of the lower building then to fall down upon the lower. The highly-simultaneous removal of support to any upper block is very, very unlikely to occur in a steel grid-work building without human-orchestrated simultaneous removal of many steel structural elements by devices.

— The "suspended upper block that falls" suggestion is further unlikely because there is no lift or hanging from above shown, and there is no apparatus or mechanism to lift or hang from and be released from. In the video of the tower collapses, in fact the top part of the building disintegrates before the lower part moves down.

— The broadcast video of the South Tower collapsing shows the upper part of the building first tilting off the column of structure by an approximately fifteen-degree angle. The momentum vector of that part of the building was not, during the tilt, directed vertically downward. Therefore, and to that extent, force was not applied by the upper part to the lower part.

The fact that the building as a whole thereafter collapses directly downward can only be because the structure of the lower part of the building was substantially weakened by being rapidly dis-assembled. Were the lower part of the building intact and able to resist force, the tilted upper part would have fallen off to the side.

— Buildings One and Two, in particular, "fall from above." The shape of the collapse is that of a "descending mushroom," that is to say that any mass of material that could be alleged to push down on the structure is instead clearly seen in the video being by force pushed outward, outside of the area of the structure collapsing below. A mass on top can't be "progressively" banging the building down if there is in fact no mass atop the fall because the former constituents of the upper mass have been, and are being, ejected sideways outside the building footprint.

— An object falling downward in Earth's gravitational field has only the potential energy of the product of its mass times gravity times its height, mgh (the product of its mass, the force of gravity, and the distance to fall). It has only the kinetic energy at any destination of its fall in the amount of $1/2mv^2$ (half the product of the mass times the velocity squared). The amount of potential energy becoming kinetic energy in the fall of any of the three (One, Two, or Seven) large buildings that collapsed basically to the ground as part of 9/11 is not even enough (and not applied fast enough) to make the amount of dust that was created from the concrete and other pulverized components of the building.   Otherwise stated, even, for the moment, just considering the dust, the amount of dust that was created in the building destructions must have been caused by sources of energy other than the fall of any of the buildings.

It is a property of concrete that it takes relatively more energy to break it into dust than chunks, and it takes relatively more additional energy if the force acting on the concrete acts less than very rapidly. The same amount of force acting in microseconds from an explosion will create more dust than that force acting at the speed of dropping or crushing.[4] If, just for the sake of a test thought experiment, every piece of concrete structure contained in each of Buildings One and Two was dropped to the ground from the height it occupied when it was part of the building, the concrete would break mostly into very large chunks. With some dust, but nothing like 9/11.[5]

-----

4. A detonation wave moving at 10,000 meters/second travels a meter in a hundred microseconds (a tenth of a millisecond). An object falling from mid height of the world trade center if free falling and without any air or other resistance or "sailing" would be traveling a maximum of 50 meters per second at ground, or experience the impact force applied on the order of 200 times more slowly than an explosive. Kinetic energy being a product of the square of the velocity, a 200 times speed difference is, itself, a 40,000 times energy difference. The difference in mass moved will have an effect, true, but it is a linear effect. There are experts in the science of what is called "comminution", which is the matter of breaking apart a mass of solid material. Many of those experts are in mining. Others who have practical knowledge to the effect that explosives turn rock or concrete to dust like nothing else can are in the world's militaries.

5. In fact, it wasn't just the concrete: "I never saw a file cabinet, never saw a desk, a chair, never saw a telephone, never saw any type of office furniture.

— The fact that there was not enough energy in a gravitational fall of any of the buildings to create the dust is only part of it. The volume of dust emerged from Buildings One and Two in a very dense flow, coming out of the building at a high speed. In order to get all of those molecules of dust moving all at once forming that kind of dense cloud that spread all the way to New Jersey and left, according to Governor George Pataki, a "layer of dust 2 to 3 inches thick all over lower Manhattan" rapidly applied force from explosive devices was uniquely necessary.

— When the kinetic energy of any falling object is used or transferred to another object, the source object slows down. (The law of conservation of energy in a closed kinetic system provides that energy derived from an object is, in effect, "deducted" from that object. Kinetic energy, as noted is the product of mass and velocity. If the object remains integral, the mass of the object does not change; it loses velocity — slows down. In billiards, when the cue ball in motion strikes an object ball, the cue ball stops or slows according to the amount of energy transferred in the collision.)

If this were not true, a hammer would not slow down when it hit a nail, and transferred kinetic energy to the nail. A universe having physical mechanics which did not act in accordance with our understanding of energy conservation would be nothing at all like our universe.

Careful and thoughtful people have carefully measured downward speeds, rates of descent, of the three 9/11 buildings. The buildings descend at rates close to freefall. Deceleration that would necessarily occur if the kinetic energy of falling were used to take apart lower building structure would be very significant (bring the falling mass to a stop), would be easily observed, and is not seen.

There is no glass. It just disappeared and has become part of this fluffy white or gray dust." - Assistant Chief of Department, FDNY, Harry Meyers in Dennis Smith's Report from Ground Zero: The Story of the Rescue Efforts at the World Trade Center, Viking/Penguin, New York, 2002, p. 163. " In an office building you have chairs, tables, electrical equipment, bathrooms, all sorts of fittings and there ... there was nothing. It was all pulverized into dust." - Eddie Bowles, "Everything Was Pulverized': A New York Firefighter Reflects Ten Years On,"

— Similarly (and it is gruesome, I'm sorry), human bone fragments identified to have come from the World Trade Center buildings
that collapsed on September 11 were found (in addition to other places
to which they were widely scattered) among the roof ballast on top
of the Deutsche Bank building at 130 Liberty Street. Human bodies
trapped in a gravitational fall may be compressed into a clump, but
they are not blown to bits and scattered onto a rooftop of a 517 foot
tall building a full city block south of the Trade Center.

— The video footage of the building collapses shows large and
heavy steel parts (large sections of "grillage") hurled sideways from
Buildings One and Two during the collapses. The velocity and distance traveled cannot be explained by any gravitational collapse force.

— Official mapping of the debris pattern resulting from the collapses of Buildings One and Two also shows a large debris area that
cannot be accounted for by gravitational forces. This mapping is confirmed by many photographs of the site area, including satellite photographs, aerial photographs and local photography.

— Air samples and samples of dust from the World Trade Center
area (in addition to the asbestos from the buildings) show iron microspheres and thermitic materials. These cannot have come from an airplane impact, or from office fires, or from a gravitational collapse, but
must have come from the use of thermite or thermate cutting devices.
The amount of the thermitic material and microspheres is consistent
with the use of tons of cutting and explosive devices, a magnitude that
would be used in an intended demolition of the buildings.

— Many witnesses report the sound of explosions. The reports
describe serial explosions concomitant to the destruction and collapse
of floor structures and describe very loud single explosions low in the
World Trade Center buildings that could not have been caused by fires
burning in the upper floors at a time when the government and media
account says only that fires were started in upper floors by an alleged
airplane impact.

— Explosions are corroborated by photography, video, and by
witness accounts of their own visual observations. For example, all of

the glass in the entire lobby area, particularly of the North Tower, but of the ground floor of each building, is shown blown out in photos and video taken about an hour before the building collapsed. Firemen who walked through the area also reported "It looked like the whole lobby had been blown out by a bomb." Another fireman who went to one of the underground levels, when later interviewed on camera reported that a very large explosion occurred below and in front of him that had the rapidity and severity of a bomb blast. Multiple witnesses say that large sections of stairway and elevators in the center core of the building exploded just prior to the collapse event.

— They story that has the entirety of World Trade Center Building Seven collapsing due to the alleged failure of Column 79 (as told by the National Institute of Standards and Technology, "NIST") is not possibly a true account. The building was 743 feet tall, over 32,000 square feet in plan (a trapezoidal shape about 140 feet by 330 feet – more or less the size of a football field). The entirely of it fell straight down at approximately freefall acceleration and speed at 5:20 p.m. on September 11, 2001. No veridical model of the building structure or accurate representation of load paths shows that the failure of *any* one column could, either immediately or progressively, deny all support to the entire structure of the building. There is nothing central or unique about Column 79; it is one among many, off to one side of the structure. At most, the sudden and complete failure of one column in the Building Seven grid could lead to a local slump in one part of the building. The nature of the structure is highly redundant and the tensile and compressive strengths of the other surrounding parts would be more than sufficient to keep whatever a compromised Column 79 failed to support from falling or causing other parts to fall.

— The story, told by the government, that temperature changes caused a beam to change dimension to the extent it un-seated from Column 79 is mere fable. Among other things, any thermal dimensional change would have pulled the other (outside – free air) end of the system, the beam would not have pulled off its connection. Further, there were numerous shear studs that ran from the beam into the concrete floor immediately above it, and there were other beams that joined in the same part of the structure that would not have un-seated, even in the unusual (very unlikely) event that this beam did.

— There are several advance indications and descriptions of the collapse of Building Seven. Apparently veridical video footage shows and provides audio of a fireman who loudly announces that Building Seven is about to fall, After the announcement, we hear a countdown "four... three... two...one..." at the conclusion of which we get very loud (explosion) noises and the straight down rapid collapse of the building. It is unlikely that a massive building failure of a kind entirely unprecedented in the history of steel framed buildings would be at once an "accidental" consequence of small fires — and yet have been predicted to occur by several media sources earlier in the day, and been, at the time, "counted down" by announcement.

— BBC television reported before 5 p.m., or more than twenty minutes before it fell, that Building Seven had in fact collapsed. Part of the report was a live cut to presenter Jane Standley who "confirmed" that Building Seven had "completely disappeared." Ironically, perhaps, Building Seven can be seen standing in the opening background in the live shot before Standley is centered on the screen and again seen over her shoulder as she presents the news of its collapse. In fact, it does collapse, straight down and quickly, as shown by half a dozen videos of the event ... twenty minutes later (after Standley is 15 minutes off screen.)

Standley was asked and said, in substance, that she was just reading from the teleprompter. No doubt had she looked out the window — or waited twenty minutes — her report would have been right. Instead, her announcement was a declaration of the occurrence of an event that had not at the time had any cognizable probability of occurrence. In the entire history of steel framed buildings, none had ever collapsed "due to fire" until that morning, and the proposition that a third "had collapsed" that afternoon even when it had not, could only have come from a very particular foreknowledge, inconsistent with the observable hazard from the fires that had burned irregularly in the building during the day. [6]

6. There appear to have been three or four announcements broadcast

— None of the stories that propose to tell how the structural integrity of each of the three buildings that collapsed in New York was destroyed by fire bothers to do any substantive form of energy accounting. No story told about any of the World Trade Center buildings has any basis in any form of demonstration that the heat of combustion of the "office materials" that are described to have been burning was enough to penetrate the fireproofing on the building (and it would have had to be the fireproofing on pretty much the whole building to make it all subject to heating to failure temperatures) or to get that much steel to fail from being heated — while the heat also dissipated into the surrounding air.

In fact, the fires in all three of the fallen buildings were smoky, low temperature and without highly combustible fuel, supplemental oxygen, or induced rapid airflow that would have enabled them significantly to heat a mass of concrete and steel.

These facts are corroborated by the appearance of the fires as observable at the time and as shown on video, by the radio transmissions of firemen who walked up to the fire areas, by people who provide accounts of having walked past the fires on particular floors as they took the stairwell down and out of the buildings, by photographs of people standing in openings in the building by the fire areas who would have been scalded, whose hair would have been more than thoroughly singed and clothes would have been burned off them if in fact the fires were hot enough to weaken steel, and by measurements of the amount

over the public airwaves which said that World Trade Center Building Seven was collapsing or had collapsed before the collapse in fact occurred. One on CNN by Allan Dodds Frank at about 11:07 a.m., a second at about 4:12 p.m. on CNN by Aaron Brown, a third at about 4:57 on the BBC by Jane Standley and, part of essentially the same broadcast, a fourth at about 5:10 p.m. by Phil Hayton of the BBC. There was also comment on Fox News by Rick Leventhal at 11:55 (immediately after the Mark Walsh interview) that "there is also concern that there might actually be another collapse of *that* [pointing] building." Building 7 fell at 5:20 p.m., September 11th. Notably, not one of the sources of information provided to these presenters for the pre-collapse collapse broadcasts has been described. Every one of these reporters has been asked, and none has made any answer more specific than to say that he or she read from a text prepared by the news organization, and knows no more than that.

of infrared radiation from the fire sites.

Indeed, the collapse of Buildings One and Two happens as the fires appear to be burning themselves out; less flame is visible and the smoke is dark, indicating a lack of combustion oxygen and low temperature.

— Buildings One and Two were built with "core structures" with a rectangular surround of large box columns, indeed as strong and stronger than the perimeter of box columns at the exterior walls of the buildings. There were elevators in the cores. There were no "office materials" in the cores. Elevators are not especially combustible, but the core columns were cut at the time of the collapse and appear in the debris pile in short lengths.

— Other phenomena clearly observed in the available veridical video footage confirm the facts that explosions and cutting charges brought down all three buildings.

Numerous ejections, "squibs," characterized by the use of cutting and explosive charges appear from the side of each of the three buildings preceding the collapse and leading the collapse front. (A bogus story that some of the more significant of these are to be explained by air compression is unsupported by the fact that the relevant source volumes were nothing like sealed and by simple arithmetic regarding the potential air compression ratio.)

— There were electrical "substations" in the core on 108th floor, 75th floor, 41st floor, and the 7th floor of each of the twin towers, Buildings One and Two. In any gravitational collapse, the transformers and associated switchgear that comprised the substations would have remained intact and recognizable as what they were. Apparently, there is no evidence that they were intact in the wreckage or removed from the wreckage intact.

— An honest evaluation of the all of the evidence of the destruction of the three buildings says that the buildings did not simply "fall." Each was taken apart, disassembled, undone. What had been a building became pieces, and less, became much smaller than pieces. The complete separation of all of the three buildings into dust, individual sheets of paper, individual column and beam sections, single stairs from a stairwell, just the dial pad from a telephone is entirely inconsistent with gravitational collapse and can only be explained by explosive demolition.

The Role of Airplanes in the 9/11 Presentation.

— There is no reasonable scientific question that the video footage showing the alleged "impacts" of each of two Boeing 767 passenger airplanes into (and through) the exterior walls of the upper part of the North and South World Trade Center Towers (Buildings Two and One) is not veridical. It is not a set of actual, unaltered video images of an event that occurred in the real world as depicted. It is "constructed" video; it is what is called in the movie making industry "special effects" footage. The reasons this can be known, appearances and announcements to the contrary notwithstanding, are several.

Newtonian mechanics tells us that collisions affect both colliding objects in accordance with the force of collision. Put simply, the consequences of the collision are only the result of the actual force — and it is the same amount of force, equal and opposite — exerted on both of two colliding objects. Newton's Third Law says that for every action (force) there is an equal and opposite reaction. In other words, if object A exerts a force on object B, then object B also exerts an equal and opposite force on object A.[7]

In the case of the alleged plane and the tower, any force the plane

____

7. Apologies for 'pounding' on this point, simple as it is, and there being no good reason for controversy about it. That said, there are a lot of "threads" on the web, some having to do with 9/11, most not, in which people comment nearly endlessly about the difficulty they are having understanding, accepting, and applying Newton's Third Law. The principle is proved again and again by experiment and experience, so there is ultimately no doubt that it is scientifically correct, but we people, in our imaginings tend to project a kind of "techno-magical self-centered mechanics"'and struggle to avoid recognition when the concepts we have imagined are disproven. On the web, for example, there is at one site an unreasonably long discussion about punching a sheetrock wall with a human fist in which, among other confusions, we get notions such as that the wall only experiences a force if a hole in it is made with the fist, and the fist only has experienced a force if bones are broken. Amusing, maybe. But not true.

exerts on the steel grid-work half-a-million (many hundred thousand) ton building (moreover very well anchored to the earth) that building in turn exerts on the hundred-forty-five ton (767) airplane.[8] Furthermore, the building is held together with components and connections of much higher individual and collective total strength (tensile, compressive, shear, torsional, etc.) than the airplane.

The engines of the plane are dense and compact and could possibly go through the steel grid-work if they arrived in the gap between the box columns, but otherwise an actual Boeing 767 slamming into a World Trade Center tower would break apart on impact and principally become a scattering of wreckage below the collision site. As at other crash sites, there would be luggage, and seats, and bodies and parts of wing, fuselage, and tail — all having fallen down. When planes hit the side of a mountain the debris is strewn at the impact site. Some of it may slide down the steeper parts of the mountain. A World Trade Center Tower is basically just a vertically steep mountain, and (except for possibly a couple of dense parts that happened to arrive between columns) the wreckage would fall down into the streets below.

The plane cutting a "plane-shaped" hole in the side of the World Trade Center tower is a "cartoon" image, roughly analogous to the "coyote shaped hole" in the canyon floor we see Wile E. cut as he crashes down into the solid earth as if he happened for that moment to be made of something very much denser and mechanically stronger than the physical planet. In the case of the 9/11 "airplanes" the "dramatic" outline was in fact created by devices in the building arranged and detonated to make a "plane shaped" hole. It is not something a Boeing 767 could do. With the exception of the engines, a passenger airplane is more like a big aluminum can with aluminum sails for wings than anything else. A good size bird strike on the nose will crumple the airplane nose back to the weather radar antenna and the mount inside it. True, unaltered, video footage of a passenger airplane being run into a wall, even at relatively low speed (say, fifty miles an hour) shows the plane breaking apart completely in the collision and

---

8. 767 empty is about 95 tons; another 50 tons of fuel and passengers is a reasonable estimate.

becoming a scatter of debris. To say that the airplanes went "inside" the buildings is to describe an event not possible in the actual physical world (comparable, for example, to saying a human hand passed through the heavy metal side of a safe to take the money out — rather than, say, opened the safe door).

Photographs of the street below the alleged airplane impact sites on 9/11 taken after the alleged impact show the "airplane shaped hole" in the building at one side of the photo, show people getting away from the site, but on Vesey Street to the north, or Liberty Street to the south, or West Street to the west, show nothing like the actual "debris field / pile" that would have to be there if either or both of two Boeing airliners crashed into the side of the building above the street.

The matter of the recovery of substantially all of the physical remains of a particular airplane and any of its contents that have crashed is forensically of singular importance and significance. Supposed radar tracks of particular airplanes are easy to fake. Supposed contents of flight data and cockpit voice recorders are also relatively easy to fake, particularly without certain "header text" and type and serial number information, and without very strict custody control of the devices. (For which purported evidence there was no custodial control and no properly presented reporting in the case of Flight 93 in Shanksville, PA.) It may be said that although all Boeing 767 or 757 airplanes "look alike," especially if they are in the fleet of a given carrier, in fact both as planes and as planes-with-contents they embody features that are very distinguishing and are not especially easy to fake. Detailed construction information, testing information, flight logs and detailed maintenance logs are required to be kept for every airframe and engine.[9] Those logs contain the serial numbers that are stamped and otherwise permanently placed on many parts of the plane, from transponders to hydraulic pumps to ailerons to jackscrew assemblies. Similarly, a great deal about the events, such as the event of impact,

____

9. "... shall make a record of the maintenance, preventive maintenance, rebuilding, and alteration, on aircraft, airframes, aircraft engines, propellers, appliances, or component parts which it operates in accordance with the applicable provisions of Part 121 or 135 of this chapter, as appropriate." FAR 43.9 (b)

can be learned by trained examiners from what would appear to be just "wreckage." (Even when a crash site endures fire, or polar ice conditions, storms, other collapses around it, or sinks in deep water, if the site is properly preserved and examined, the truth as to what in fact happened to what airplane there is difficult to counterfeit without deliberate mishandling of the wreckage.)

Again, airplanes become a litter of pieces when they have a significant crash. But they don't vanish. The pieces taken together are comprised of the same metals as the original airplane; they have the same mass; and the properties of those pieces and the markings on them remain. It is not reasonable to believe that an actual plane has crashed at a described site when there is nothing like a full plane's-worth of wreckage to be found there.

— There are no wingtip vortices at all shown in the video of the smoke and flame that emerge from the buildings, despite the alleged high speed and large size of the planes and the supposed flight path exactly through the middle of the smoke and flame area. Loaded 767 airfoils (wings) do not pass through an aerodynamic fluid (air – or smoky air), particularly at speed, without creating vortices (also called a "wake" or "wake turbulence")

— The "wide shot" from the Fox TV "Chopper 5" does not show an airplane in the sky immediately before the alleged impact for a period of approximately five seconds, during which the plane should be clearly seen. (The day was clear, cloudless, weather "beautiful.")

— Careful observation of the explosion at each building clearly indicates that the blast and flames that push out of the building are not from a plane exploding and burning. Not only is it not possible to fly a Boeing passenger plane through the exterior wall of a World Trade Center Tower, it is not possible to "fly" such a plane through the core structure of a World Trade Center (and not possible to "fly" a 90° left turn inside the building in the case of the North Tower), and not possible to fly the nose of the plane out the other side. Passenger planes do not carry explosive or incendiary charges in the nose or cockpit area. Therefore, even if the nose of the plane poked through the far wall — which it could not have done and, in fact did not — it is not the plane that would have been setting off a major explosion in the far wall.

— In addition to the odd and unreasonable explosion out the east side of the building (as if the plane turned a sharp corner inside) the Naudet video of the supposed North Tower airplane shows "squibs" and other explosion effects well above the supposed airplane impact area in the top of the building.

— A few various airplane parts were found in and around Lower Manhattan, just as various bits of airplane were on the lawn of the Pentagon and in Shanksville (including dropped from the air into the waters of Indian Lake). Without getting into strange squabbles between "truthers" and "debunkers" the fact is there are 3.1 million separate parts in a Boeing 767. The plane is large enough to have seating for 180 people, to have lavatories, a galley, cockpit, flight controls, etc. Just the fuselage is 150 feet long, over seventeen feet high and over sixteen feet wide; the wingspan is 156 feet. Claims have been made that a found scrap of fuselage proves that the planes that were Flight 175 and Flight 11 on the morning of September 11, 2001 crashed into the Towers. A crumpled mass of a hot section of a jet engine that was *not* from a JT9D-7R4D engine, as would have been on Flight 175 (and *not* from a GE CF6 engine from Flight 11), was found placed on the corner of Church Street on Murray Street underneath and within temporary construction sidewalk covering scaffold and metal roofing. The surrounding structure and area show no evidence that the section of engine fell from height or fell and rolled into place. There are reports (perhaps not true) that the engine section came from the back of a panel truck which stopped, rear doors opened, and the section was pushed out and put on the sidewalk at that corner. Indeed, that is the appearance given by the photos.

The matter of the presence of a few airplane parts in New York, at the Pentagon, and in Shanksville is something we will do more thinking about in a later chapter. For the purposes of this list, we should again note that airplanes have many, many, many separately serial numbered parts in them, upon which the serial numbers are either stamped or cast into a metal body of the part or otherwise very permanently marked. In all of civil aviation since World War II, there has not been a significant airplane crash for which the crash site was located from which thousands of serial numbered parts, confirmed by logs and other records to be parts of the plane in question, were not recovered. Airplanes have been engulfed in fire and been blown up and have sunk to the bottom of deep salt water and the serial numbers on everything from landing gear trucks, to the chassis of communications radios, to propeller assemblies, to flight control units in autopilot systems have been found and identified with reference to record information.

From September 11, 2001, not any, not one, none, no single serial numbered part has been in fact identified in the customary manner, with reference to the piece or part and to the actual logs that record what parts with what serial numbers are in a given plane (of a particular manufacturer's serial number, registered to a certain ICAO "N" number, also imprinted on a permanent fireproof plate mounted on the fuselage) for any of the four airplanes that were alleged to have been crashed at the three 9/11 sites.

The usual government "line" has been that '... we knew which airplanes were involved, so we didn't have to do any identification...' In fact, from soon after takeoff, nobody knew which airplane really was which for the entire day of September 11, 2001, not Air Traffic Control, not the North American Air Defense systems, not the Federal Aviation Administration, and not even Cleveland, Ohio Mayor Michael R. White, (Perhaps also not President George W. Bush. During a speaking event in Florida on December4, 2001, Bush said he was, the morning of September 1, at Booker Elementary School "...outside the classroom waiting to go in, and I saw an airplane hit the tower—the TV was obviously on, and I use[d] to fly myself, and I said, 'There's one terrible pilot." No footage of the alleged impact was in fact broadcast at the time.)

In fact, finding the airplane parts that were "found" at any of the sites is approximately comparable to finding a couple of brake pads on the ground and saying that you have just recovered James Bond's Aston Martin. The car parts may *remind you* of a car, maybe even remind you of an Aston Martin, maybe even James', but people (admittedly a minority) who are paying the least attention will be wondering where the rest of the vehicle might be. For each of the three 9/11 sites, the answer is an obvious physical-facts-contradicting lie: At Shanksville, an FBI representative announces at one point that it has recovered "90 percent" of the Flight 93 airplane, but does not and cannot say where the recovered parts are, nor provide any documentation that they in fact exist anywhere, nor provide facts that can be confirmed regarding the alleged acts of recovery.

— The alleged "recovery" of the flight data recorder and the cockpit voice recorder in Shanksville, Pennsylvania is clearly fraudulent. Neither "recovered" recorder comes from the same manufacturer as the recorders installed in N591UA, the Flight 93 airplane; the physical serial numbers on the recorders are not confirmed from log entries; identifying data headers are missing from the record; the chain of custody was not established from "recovery;" the story told that the "recovered" recorders could not be read and therefore were sent to an out-of-custody facility which was able to read the then presented information is a tale of irregularities; the presented data does not cohere well with other information including alleged radar tracking (and the alleged cell / seatback phone calls).

— Various government statements directly and indirectly claim that the two planes, Boeing 767s, said to have hit two tall buildings and destroyed three tall buildings in New York, were being flown under control ("precise control") straight and level at speeds of five hundred fifty and six hundred, and over six hundred, miles per hour at or near sea level.

That is not physically possible. The listed maximum operating speed at sea level for a Boeing 767 (Vmo) is about 360 knots, or around 414 miles per hour. Which of the various results from overspeed a plane will exhibit first will depend upon conditions and circumstances, but the attempt to fly faster than Vmo will variously, among other things, bend the airframe, create serious flutter in flight control systems (flutter of the kind that has been the determined cause of a number of fatal accidents), cause separation of wing and fuselage parts (from inspection panels to ailerons), and change the lift characteristics of the wing airfoil in turn causing the nose to pitch down, often rapidly and uncontrollably. Further, at straight and level at sea level, with modern passenger plane "fanjets," trying to push that much air that is as dense as the air at sea level through the engines will slow the plane down and in practice prevent it attaining the speed allegedly flown. It is a complicated story about jet engines and fans and compressor stages, but the long and short of it is that jet engines that are designed for a certain maximum speed in an aerodynamic medium (air) of a particular density do not propel a plane to a faster speed in level flight.

Even if the physical facts about the plane and engines are set aside, the overwhelming likelihood is that a 767 at that speed flying at office building altitude over New York City would be something between very difficult to control and uncontrollable. The proposition that two such planes could be controlled to an impact on a selected side of a particular building, especially by inexperienced pilots, is at best very unlikely. (The alleged 9/11 "piloting crash feats" are not comparable to greasing an ILS-guided plane onto a two mile long horizontal runway at 150 knots indicated reasonably well aligned into the wind at one of the nation's major airports.)

— Everything that could possibly be wrong with the stories about the phone calls from the airplanes on 9//11 is wrong about them. (The calls are obviously very important to the story told, because there is no other evidence regarding hijacking. But for the calls, there would be no claimed evidence of hijacking. There is no 7500 transponder squawk for any of the 9/11 airplanes, etc.)

It is not possible that Betty Ong, a Flight 11 flight attendant, spent twenty-seven minutes on a cell telephone call from a 767 at altitude. Cell phones do not work at 40,000 feet going 500 miles an hour. And they truly didn't work in a plane at altitude in 2001. This is a fact widely known among flight personnel and passengers. It is a fact that remains true now, twenty years later, except in planes equipped with cell phone "base station" facilities.

The 9/11 story has been in some further instances modified to say that "seatback" phones were used. Ted Olson (Solicitor General), for one example, began by saying he had received "two cell phone calls" from his wife, Barbara Olson. (In which, among other things, she is said to have told an elaborate story about 60 passengers, flight attendants, and 2 pilots being herded into the back of the plane in mid-flight by three hijackers.) When the "cell phone" bit was noticed as not especially credible, the call changed to a seatback call "placed collect" to his office and forwarded to Ted. The details Barbara had provided, including that she didn't have her purse, didn't help the re-worked version because it would require a credit card even to get to an operator from a seatback phone. The story lost its last hope for credence, though, when American Airlines specifically officially confirmed that there were no seatback phones on the 757 airplane that was Flight 77. (United also appears to have discontinued seatback phone service on the relevant planes in January / February, 2001).

Flight attendants receive "training" before going on to work in the air. A part of that training involves what to do and what not to do in the event of a hijacking. None of the flight attendants on any of the 9/11 planes appears to do anything like what their training prescribed, even approximately. Long phone calls to the airline reservations phone number detailing the scene are not the instructed response to a hijacking or to an actual set of stabbings (the pilot, the purser, the galley attendant, passenger(s) in business class...) in an airplane in which Betty Ong says "nobody can breathe."

The calls are "out of rhythm" for conversation – even (especially) for conversation in an emergency. Simple questions get asked for reasons that don't make sense in the context of the calls. Answers that should be easy and relatively quick take time and seem hesitant or tentative, then, in instances, are corrected. At times the speaker sounds as if seeking assistance in managing the conversation from another person present at his or her end of the call. Partial / muffled / faint sounds of what seems like "coaching" can be heard. There is, similarly, an apparent radio transmission about having a bomb on the airplane that sounds like bad movie acting with an Israeli accent, and doesn't make a lot of sense for a supposed suicide flight into a building (if a terrorist has taken over a plane to go hit a building, why announce that there is a live bomb on the plane, increasing the chances of being shot down either from the ground or upon air interception?)

The background audio in the calls also confutes the official story. According to claimed flight records, at one point Flight 93 is in a very steep descent, a rate at which living passengers in an airplane would be at least be shouting or calling out or otherwise being very noisy. Nothing of the kind is in the audio. Compared to actual phone calls from airplanes, the noise isn't right, the "tone" isn't right, and the attention and reactions of the callers aren't right. The calls do not make "auditory" sense.

It is guessing, with a certain amount of corroborative information, including claims of witness testimony saying 9/11 plane landings were observed at Westover in Central Massachusetts, but the suggestion, all in all, is strong that the planes were landed and the phone calls were then created while the planes were on the ground. Perhaps indeed at Westover. Cleveland is suggested by some provided flight path diagrams, but seems less likely for reasons of timing and logistics. Perhaps the landing was neither at Westover nor Cleveland, but if they were made, the "phone calls" had to have been made from somewhere with "phone service"— likely somewhere on the ground[10].

____

10. Most importantly unresolved is the fate of the people in the various airplanes when they took off (Flight 11) from Boston supposedly with 81 passengers plus 11 crew, (Flight 175) from Boston supposedly with 56 passengers and 9 crew, from Dulles (Flight 77) supposedly with 58 passengers plus 6 crew, from Newark (Flight 93) supposedly with 37 passengers plus 7 crew. We know with great certainty they did not go through the walls of the World Trade Center Towers, nor through the "hole" in the Pentagon, nor into the ground at Shanksville. (The local Coroner, Wallace Miller, specifically said there were no bodies, no parts of bodies, no blood, nothing of the kind at the Shankville site. Quoting: "I stopped being coroner after about 20 minutes, because there were no bodies there. ...This is the most eerie thing. I have not, to this day, seen a single drop of blood. Not a drop.")

It is very likely that the planes landed somewhere and that phone calls were placed. There are some hints (that are not more than hints, and for which any follow-up evidence is entirely lacking) as to what might have happened to some (very few) of the people. But landings, followed by phone calls, do not cause 265 human people / bodies to just vanish / un-become /

These things taken together, we know with some certainty that the cell / seatback phone call story is not true. Because there are a lot of ways to create audio recordings of people saying things about planes and hijackings, and because we have no valid corollary evidence regarding the audio tracks that have been put up by the government or media we do not know the specifics of the creation of the recordings. We only do know for certain they are not what the government and media have claimed.

Application of Reasonable Forensic Principles to Understanding 9/11

— Something odd happens to everybody, to "truthers" and "officials" and "debunkers" and news "reporters" and "commentators" and editorializers when it comes to speaking or writing or making videos or other presentations about 9/11. Video producers play their favorite rock music to accompany shots of very dusty firemen's faces, or Rudy Giuliani's face, or the ghoulish outline of what can look like a monster face in the smoke from the first set of explosions. Or, in a voice that sounds a little bit as if they are still just "reading the news" they wax on (and on and on) about "unbelievable tragedy..." with still further emphasis on "believing the unbelievable." Dramatics sell – okay. But, all of the commentary and "reporting" and purported "analysis" and "debunking" and rebuttal taken together, the 9/11 story has had the "benefit" of a wondrous amount of non-information, noise, with the net effect of keeping its false claims in place — although ultimately in a place not better than falsity can provide.

One of the more interesting examples of some of this is video produced by a person who calls himself Alexander "Ace" Baker. Much of it is now censored by YouTube and not shown to requesting IP

---

vaporize.

Various speculation has been offered that the people were killed (even that they were gassed to death in the planes after landing) and the bodies disposed of (again, guessing, cremated).

When whatever it is that is "9/11" is all over, whenever that is, the government of the then United States of America needs formally to account exactly what was done, and apologize, for itself, and on behalf of the entire nation to the descendants of every one of those people.

addresses from the United States. Some of it, as of this writing, is still there. It is not likely to be to everyone's taste, but clear recognition of veritable truth is to be found in sections of his work. From amid the distractions (musical interludes, a video 'keyed-in' narrator who isn't exactly Baker himself, etc.) we get a cogent and likely explanation of the faked footage that was aired that shows the planes, particularly the "second plane" (and the various "man in the street" — Michael Hezarkhani, etc. — videos / sound tracks and photos), that includes rational, practical suggestions regarding how video masking was used, the way in which the "flash" from the building that had been (not very persuasively) hypothesized to be from a missile shot from the front of the approaching plane was in fact a way to synchronize the flying plane image with the explosion set off from the building (think of the "flash" as useful in the way the traditional "clapper board" is used). Others, too, have demonstrated the Hezarkhani and other plane impact videos to have been faked and have demonstrated that the various "second-plane" impact videos do not cohere with physics nor with each other in ways they would have to if they were genuine. Yet, Baker, particularly if one can watch the now "unavailable in country" material, can give the viewer a fairly good, if not perfect, slightly technical, and requiring nothing "magical," explanation of how the 9/11 plane-hits-building video was made. Further, probably helpfully, he also goes to some effort to think through the production choices in the result, how trying to get multiple actual suicide pilots of exceptional flying ability who could each hit a nearly-impossible-to-hit-target is too difficult and runs too many program-compromising risks, and how creating a realistic video synthesis of a plane crash that truly looks like a plane crash is not possible, so that blowing a hole in the towers and then saying the video image plane went into it became a necessary choice in September, 2001 to telling the 9/11 story.

In itself, what Baker puts up doesn't provide an excess of explanation why, in a world with many people (including many who nominally engage in analysis in what they do for work), so many are acting so un-noticing and thoughtless and distracted and bamboozled when they write or read the news or report on television or watch TV, but it does effectively demonstrate the 9/11 presentation is "work product" not so much different from other screen sequences produced for public consumption (although, considered with a bit of a critic's eye, not quite as well accomplished as a lot of other similar "special" effects).

A brief and simple re-stated summary of the effects techniques which have led to propagation of the erroneous belief that two airplanes were flown into, hit, the North and South (One and Two) World Trade Center building in New York may be helpful.

Each of the two Towers, North and South, was rigged with a device that created a small distinctive white "flash"[11] and also with devices that would create a blast "perimeter" blowing an approximately "airplane-shaped" hole in the "incoming" side of the building (at and near the "vacant" floors that had been occupied by the "Gelatin Group" / explosives crew). Particularly the South Tower was also rigged with additional devices that extended an explosion field out the opposite "outgoing" side (where the "plane" "emerges" as news anchor Peter Jennings tells us to "Watch how the airplane penetrates the building … completely in one side and out the other."[12] The Naudet later-broadcast video showing the North Tower, shows an explosion coming out the east side form a depicted "impact" on the north (as if the "plane" turned a 90 degree left inside the building).

In each case, a "stock" or pre-existing video "clip" of a plane flying in the air without visual "background," or which has been "cleaned" of any of the pixels/information in the "sequence" except for the plane, was "composited" with video of the lower Manhattan cityscape and the World Trade Center Towers. Summed together with the movement of the plane from the open sky area of the image into the building,

---

11. The "white flash" has been observed and remarked upon by everyone who has looked at the footage with any attention. To many its origin and purpose have been puzzling. Some have speculated that the alleged incoming plane fired a rocket with an explosive warhead at the building as it drew near, but without explaining why a 767 passenger plane when allegedly hijacked came equipped with a forward missile launcher, loaded and ready to fire.

12. Other commentators similarly announced: "There it is, there it is. The plane went right through the other tower of the World Trade Center" Jim Ryan, WNYW News.

it looks to the viewer "exactly" as if the plane flew into the Tower. Because the "white flash" occurs at the immediate beginning of the detonation of the explosives set to cut the "airplane shaped hole" in the side of the building, the flash is used to synchronize the arrival of the video image of the flying plane with the video of the Tower showing the explosion making the "airplane-shaped" hole. Thus the illusion that the plane "makes" the explosion and the hole appears convincing. (Except, of course, to people who think about it, and realize that a building of the kind cannot just "swallow" / absorb, etc. an intact airplane, and that the airplane should be breaking up on impact, scattering millions of parts and pieces, almost all of them outward.)

— A variety of "shows" and "stories" that are parts of the 9/11 presentation are just silly shows, but they seem to have worked remarkably well as emotional "pumps" although, when thought about, in fact discredit the government and media claims.

For just one example, the government variously said that the reason there was nothing like an airplane's worth of debris at the Shanksville "crash" site was that the ground there was "so soft" that the plane was "swallowed up" by the ground below the bottom of a (very) approximately "plane shaped" scar in the surface of the earth (something more or less comparable to the "plane shaped" holes in the sides of the Trade Center Towers). The "hole"/scar was not in fact made on September 11, 2001 and can be seen in aerial photos of the site taken and published long before. Nor is the ground in the vicinity anything like as "soft" as it would be to "swallow" a Boeing 757-222. If it were, the area would be a "swamp," not a "field," the observed trees wouldn't be standing, they would not have grown, or they would have fallen over.

Even though the alleged impact is an event more serious than Wile E. Coyote cutting through the cartoon canyon floor, the same kind of proposition — totally at odds with what might happen to a real coyote or a real airplane on a canyon floor or at an abandoned mining area in Pennsylvania — still works in the unreflective minds of the public to create a contrary-to-physical-facts physical image that becomes worked into the narrative. Real airplane crashes into the ground are really messy.[13] Offering that "the ground just swallowed up the plane" carries even more "drama" than any possible reality, and is, at the same time, so much more complete and attractive. It carries the right amount of "magic" to make us all mentally lunge for it in a hurry to believe the untruth of magic rather than the plain truth of mess.

— Something similar can be said about many of the 'items' the government says it found in and around 9/11 locations: the Koran in Atta's rented car, Satam al-Suqami's passport,[14] and so forth. We've got no inventory of serial numbered parts confirmed by genuine log entries, but we've got a story about driving to Maine to get on a plane to fly to Boston to hijack a plane out of Boston, while leaving a Koran and a supposed "Will" behind in the rental car.

Even though the supposed suicide hijackers, or people of the very same name and likeness, were, after 9/11, found to be people alive and well, mostly in Saudi Arabia, the announcements of the supposed "discovery" of the various tokens of Arabs and Arab nationality worked to help construct the intended image of the dangerous foreign / otherness that was being portrayed to have attacked America.

Very well. This should be a list sufficient to proceed to the questions we need to consider. A list, and full descriptions, of all of the false statements made about what actually happened on September 11, 2001 would take the many pages of several books, and be more cumulative than distinctive.

The facts, that actual physical facts are important. The facts stand on their own, and do not need anything other than the truth of them to be true. More important — and open to some serious consideration — is the willingness of humans to recognize and understand the facts and believe the truth, even to the degree that it deserves to be regarded and believed simply because it is true. The lies, however we may

______

13. Among the "everything" that can be found on the internet are photographs of airplane crash sites. It the reader will take the trouble to look at a few, the proposition that crashes at appreciable speed make for a messy scattering of pieces will be readily understood.

14. Or other "passports," Atta's in the Nissan Altima left in Maine, or Ziad Jarra's multiple entry and "fragment" of passport on the ground in Shanksville.

appreciate them, can never, will never, whatever else may draw us to them, have in themselves, or bring to us, the benefits of being true. Another way to understand the purpose of this book is that it is an essay to consider of what those benefits are, and what they are worth to this society in the long term. There are many among us who say truth is worth nothing for being true. A useful falsehood is, at least, useful. Truth can arrive, they say, without bringing with it the least bit of utility or value.

Collectively, we can never figure out whether the people who disdain facts and truth, particularly those who tell us that "reality" no longer works according to "enlightenment principles and empiricism" are doing us a favor or doing us harm by means of their advocacies if we do not first at least make a decent effort fairly to distinguish things true from things untrue. At a minimum, we should understand the difference the "created reality" advocates would deny and would elide. Otherwise, how can we judge what erasing that difference does? We can return to the physically impossible stories at any time. We can go back to the advertising cartoons and video mask effects and other computer generated screen events and tell ourselves something like that "well...they are *real enough* in our perception of them" any time we want to. But if we are ever thoughtfully to decide whether our national government has an obligation to our nation somewhat greater in substance than a television cartoonist or advertiser, we have first to establish some precept of recognition differentiating between actuality and synthesis, whether in a computer, or on a screen, or in our minds.

To the reader who does not recognize, even from the list above, that 9/11 is best described as a false, non-actual, not-true narrative, I can only offer the suggestion that "re-taking," in any way you can, your high-school Physics class should help. So should any noticing you can get yourself to do of Newtonian mechanics exhibited every day all around you. So should thinking patiently about how it is that we know that all the pseudo-science that is bogus is, in fact, bogus — and then applying that same understanding to all of the untrue propositions in the 9/11 story. The buildings did collapse — that is true. They definitely did not collapse because they were hit by planes (in fact they weren't) nor from office fires (the office fires were set at intermittent locations and burned intermittently — the buildings fell straight down all at once because the supporting structure was taken apart all at once). YouTube videos of backyard experiments by Jonathan Cole can be helpful. Some of the presentations by David Chandler can help. There are islands of thoughtful awareness regarding the 9/11 narrative, admittedly in a sea of absurd propaganda.

As a final suggestion, I offer the thought that knowing that something that is not true is indeed in fact not true is often not a terrible loss. The historical moment at which our civilization learned that the Sun does not revolve around planet Earth, but vice versa, and that our planet is not in the center of the solar system, (nor in the center of our galaxy, nor the universe), considered wisely, is a time of revelation and deepening understanding. Something similar is often correspondingly true regarding constructed appearances. Many professional magicians, particularly those who are the most talented, say that they know that the effects in their show are good when they find that the techniques look and feel "magical" to them, even as they perform and know more and more about what they are doing. Many very talented magicians also say that the really good tricks actually get *better* as tricks for many observers when they know how they are done, or are shown as they are being done.

A deep acceptance that things as they appear (or are made to appear) to us is not necessarily the way that things actually are, although it runs into human stubbornness about appearances offered as having been "seen with my own eyes" is, in the end, a part of progress on the path to understanding. That some of these revelations change our preconceptions and expectations about the context and size of "tricks" is also, much more often than not, educational. The magician who calls himself "David Copperfield" (David Seth Kotkin) performed a magic act in April of 1983 in front of a live audience, seated on rows of "bleacher seats" on a constructed stage, and in a live television presentation during which he "made the Statue of Liberty disappear." And then (of course, be reassured) "reappear."

I think may be fair to say that the majority of both the live and television audiences were "convinced," at least in the sense that they considered that Copperfield had indeed "made the statute disappear" — it couldn't be seen — and that they didn't then quite know how he had done it. (After the event some smart people thinking about what was done described and set out the process as in fact performed.)

What Copperfield had done, considered in all, may be said to be at least as much a piece of "conceptual art" as a magic trick. A curtain was raised between two light towers in front of the audience (between the audience and the Statue). Copperfield continued talking (performing "patter") about "...how precious liberty is and how easily it can be lost..." Meanwhile the stage on which the audience was sitting and the TV cameras were mounted was slowly — and imperceptibly in the night — turning. The curtain was then lowered. The Statue of Liberty had indeed disappeared. The audience and cameras were looking out over Liberty Island and the flat and empty waters of New York Bay. The statue was not there, either in the view of the audience or through cameras. (It was hidden behind one of the light towers. Reappearance was essentially the reverse of disappearance.)

Why would one say "conceptual art"? To think about it is probably to recognize about a dozen possible reasons, but primary among them are: a) That Copperfield, as much as anything else, staged a demonstration of human "frame of reference," and assumptive human attachment to a frame of reference. We think that when we are seated in a chair looking at something, more or less because we conceive we are "fixed," we therefore decide that the difference in what we see really is a difference "in front of us." b) Similarly, we keep a relatively naïve, almost infantile, set of ideas about appearance and disappearance throughout most of our adult lives. When we put garbage in a can and it gets carried away in a garbage truck, we (emotionally) consider it "gone", not as just moved to another place (which is actually closer to the truth) We are reflexively solipsistic and self-referent. Our eyes look out from where we turn our face. Among other things, Copperfield's show demonstrated the strength of the ideation that something that can no longer be seen, "went away." c) Several aspects of the "size" of Copperfield's show may also be understood as conceptual art demonstrations. First, on a very simple level, whatever the truth, people in audiences tend to believe more of what comes to them from "large productions." We take in many societal, social, and visual cues and then interpret and believe our experience according to them. One set of those cues is "size" (and, often enough, expense). If Copperfield had done the same "trick" on a small setup in a coffeehouse (assume with the same degree of accuracy and technical ability — just altogether smaller) would the audience have been as much persuaded — or "amazed" into persuasion? Secondly, when one begins to think about it, one realizes that many people were involved in designing and building and testing and transporting and installing the whole effect. As far as I know, none of them discussed their work "out of school." The show is in this sense a "conceptual art" demonstration of the extent and scale to which a "project," even one that has no particular demonstrated necessity connected to the well-being of the world, nation, or society, can nonetheless take on a life and adherence of notable strength of its own. To get humans "committed" to some endeavor, however odd, recondite, unusual, unreasonable — or indeed harmful — is often to get those humans to "meta-commit", to commit to their own commitment — often without regard to whether much of what they are doing makes underlying sense.

Turning back to 9/11, we, each of us and all of us together, have several choices — but they boil down into two basic groups. We can continue collectively to fail to know or understand much about the event or the narrative, just by continuing to believe a lot of propaganda tales about Osama bin Laden, and not paying attention to much else. Or, we can decide to recognize and understand the incontrovertible truth about the physical events, the fake airplane impacts, the rigged buildings, the building collapses and the airplane shell game with the non-cell-phone calls. From a fair and true representation of what physically happened and what did not happen, gained from deciding that Newton's principles were not suspended for the day on September 11, 2001, we can then think usefully about why the 9/11 events were staged. Even more importantly, we can then make informed and thoughtful decisions about who we are as a nation and what is or is not in our national interest.

Three: Acceptance and Refusal.

All would be easier if verity and virtue were simple equals, and even easier if the human instinct for either or both were a bit stronger. In practical terms in human life they aren't. No pretense otherwise is made here. Some lies are indeed justifiable. By contrast, sometimes even the outside possibility of doing something worthy gets entirely ruined by the dishonesties we deliver.

Adoption not considered, in families in which fathers reasonably know they are not the biological parent of a certain child (in addition to a tradition of ugly legal fights about child support at the dissolution of a marriage) there is a considerable history of full acceptance of parentage. A collective decision gets made that it is better for all concerned, the facts notwithstanding, to treat the child as if unquestionably the father's biological progeny. Several reasonable and sound moral arguments can be made to the effect that the family should be entitled to its representation, and that neither the state, nor any other person or entity in the society should have a right, for example, to compel a genetic paternity test just for the purposes of showing the family wrong.

In the event, often the arrangement works out. Sometimes it doesn't and, for example, a child in late teenage years adds to the not uncommon confusions of that stage of life by psychological struggle about apparently irreconcilably innate and uncomfortable differences of personality and the estrangement from the described origins of his or her being. The occasions on which the "lie" may be said to "fail" in one way or another do not, however, rise to mount a sufficient argument that the arrangement before made should be sanctioned against or interfered with. Cases that are inherently very highly particular in nature rarely admit of good general rules for the imposition of prescriptions or penalties on the one hand, and ex-post condemnation in response to acts done with genuinely good and valuable moral intent seems sour at best and typically wrongful in itself, on the other.

Before judging, it is worth asking ourselves whether our judgment is necessary. There are times when it isn't. Times when it isn't even marginally helpful. But there are times when our judgment is necessary above all else. The difference is what must concern us, especially when it comes to the 9/11 events and the 9/11 narrative. As noted, the people who created and enacted 9/11, if they are ever asked to the point of having to answer, will make arguments noticeably parallel to the arguments that were made by the people who burned the Reichstag or the people who hired guns to point at Mossadegh in Iran or Lumumba in Congo or Arbenz in Guatemala or Allende in Chile to throw democratically elected governments out of office. The arguments for the 9/11 lying, killing, and destruction will be like the arguments for other "dirty work," the claims that pretense and force, however profoundly "dirty," were nonetheless "required" to "keep the Free World free." At its core, the proposition is that the particular exercise of over-matching strength without responsibility most effectively makes and carries out allegedly required programs, preventing change in some cases, and compelling it in others, in either instance usually providing a lot of manipulative power to certain perpetrators, whether to terrify a populous or to install a "client" government. Put perhaps more crudely, with adjustments for place and era, Allen W. Dulles, Henry A. Kissinger, and Paul D. Wolfowitz or Richard B. Cheney or I. Lewis Libby or Richard Perle are, in substance, versions of the same person (as are others, like them, acting with them), and what is particularly same is that each makes claims for "the dark side" (in Cheney's particular phrase) as source for rightful or proper order (and enforcement) in the world. The "dark side" is, of course, a description of illegal and violent undertakings: bribery, rendition, false imprisonment, torture, murder / assassination, by every means from poisoning to bombing, and lying, fraud, (very) grand larcenies, and the like.

There is much to be considered and said before one has sufficiently contradicted the claim of necessity, on the one hand, or one has reason to accept the claim, on the other. Violence can be powerful in its effect. That said, its results are typically distributed disadvantageously and unequally. The perpetrator, depending upon commitment, often has the most to gain, and mostly in the present, while the victims, the society, and the possibilities for the future all lose.

9/11 is not just a set of lies. Even considered just for its untruth, it is a set of lies told about a lot of crimes, most of them suborned or carried out by government. Intentionally demolishing buildings with explosives without notice and with people in them is mass murder. The bones blasted into fragments that ended up on the roof of the Deutschebank Building are not different from the vagrant scattered bones from collective murders anywhere else in the world or at any other time in history. Nor is there any question but that the crimes were premeditated. A 110-story building does not rig itself for demolition.

This matters. It is worth a moment's review at this point, and more consideration later. In quick summary, all of the "dirty work" (crimes and lies about them) the United States, together with and on behalf of "corporate interests" and others, engaged in since the Second World War, including that used to install ruthlessly tyrannical governments in places in Central America, South America, and Africa willing to sub-jugate their people, ruinously to adopt inherently exploitive systems and structures, to sell the resources in their country for a marvelously cheap price, and to purchase United States products and "technology" upon un-affordable lending, adds up, over time and into the present, not just to "blowback," as it is sometimes called in the intelligence community, but to a cluster of eventual failures. Mossadegh said he was willing to pay a fair price for the oil assets. Does not the fact that the United States (or, more particularly, Allen Dulles and Kermit Roo-sevelt on our national behalf), did not even half-try for an agreement and chose instead, with vehemence, to install by force Pahlavi and the Savak and all that came with them (including, eventually, the revolt in 1979) have plenty to do with the present dilemma regarding nuclear-ization (which, of course, in turn, has had the United States providing the Israeli "defense" budget in addition to other aid for decades, and Israelis assassinating Iranian scientists and bombing Isfahan)?

We, the United States, acted in this summary, violent, rather graceless and disrespectful way around the world to install the Ameri-can Empire. Kennedy then sought to bring an adjustment to our think-ing and our methods, beginning with a kind of "symbol," creating the Peace Corps, and then moving on to the Nuclear Test Ban Treaty, explaining much of what he was doing and believed rightful in the speech he gave at American University. Kennedy was assassinated, more or less in response to his administration's efforts to have international relationships be not principally based upon "dark side" acts of violence and increased violence — including, yes, the attack at the Bahía de los Cochinos — "Bay of Pigs."[1] It was an attack the Cuban government had known about for years prior. Significant "air support" for it was likely, more than anything else, to be the way to have a "Vietnam War" in nearby Cuba — before having one in Vietnam.

The internal features of American politics, the "military industrial complex" and the part of the American nation that operated it had become very self-righteous and very hardheaded. John Foster Dulles (Secretary of State, 1953-59) was a constantly vocal and stubborn advocate of a "first use of nuclear weapons" policy, claiming the first use policy was required to "manage" the United States' diverse interests around the world. Whatever else might be anyone's opinion of Kennedy and his brief presidency, it is clear, on the one hand, that he was not "soft" regarding the Soviet Union, or on "communism" and, on the other, that he had thought about the issue carefully, and recognized that leadership offered the United States benefits that clandestine overthrow, destabilization, impositions of extensive systems of corruption, police state hated governments, invasions, bombing, "burning villages to save them"— the "dark side" in its many various "darknesses" — could not.

The assassination of Kennedy may be said to mark the fulfilled arrival of a countermand to elected government, a refusal and reversal developed by and through an internally highly animated, American finance/business, angrily "anti-communist," right wing, a group to which Dwight Eisenhower had, during the term of his presidency, given opportunity (and which group angrily called Kennedy an "appeaser" — and names uglier and worse). The Kennedy assassination

---

1. The Spanish word for triggerfish is cochinos, which happens to be the same word for pigs. The Bahia de Cochinos (or "Bay of Pigs" as it has been called by Americans) has lots of triggerfish, as do the reefs in the Gardens.

was organized and commissioned by the very same people who took what the CIA euphemistically called "executive action" to eliminate national leaders in second and third world countries who declined to deliver up their nation for an offer-not-to-be-refused.

Fast-forward from November, 1963 to 2001, there is then the very real, profound sense in which September 11th was the day that we, the collective "we," took the next step and did the rest and remainder of what we had been doing to second and third world countries around the world for years — but to ourselves. Crudely, the assassination of Kennedy, among other results, put a form of sponsored invasion of other countries back onto the menu, getting rid of Kennedy in retribution for not providing planes and other support to the Cuba attack. Similarly, Johnson's presidency facilitated the Tonkin fake, and thence the bombings and further military invasion that established and then fully extended the war in Vietnam.

9/11 as an exploit, somewhat correspondingly — but in particular — put wholesale control by means of "dark side" violent "created reality," which had been frequent in American involvement in second and third world countries (but not yet similarly practiced "domestically"), into the "playbook" for direction and administration of the United States itself.

Structurally speaking, 9/11 has most of the further aspects, in addition to or beyond assassination or generalized killing, that American "manipulation projects" (overthrow) of other national government characteristically had — but done to us, the United States, to our country and our government. Injury and further threat is used to compel a "response" in which a "militaristic right" takes deeper control and suppresses many of the public institutions of the prior civil society. (With some substitutions, "terrorists," more or less, for "communists", "Muslim hijackers" who supposedly participated in the scheme as a constructed drastic threat in place of hired gangs or thugs or a mercenary army "contracted" first to wreak havoc in countries we were re-organizing). The outlines, the schema, the basic disposition of forces and pressures, the consequent measures of control through "security" enactments touted as "patriotic," the use of the created hostile events for incitement (whether or not in relation to events in the country — Saddam Hussein had nothing to do with 9/11, but United States government officials were soon saying loudly he did) are all components quite like the program components for many diverse American uses of (both covert and overt, but most often at least principally covert) military and political force in other countries ranging from the Dominican Republic to Vietnam to Nicaragua to Ukraine.

Most of the countries that we, the United States, acting usually through our clandestine agencies, made subject to abusive abrogations of national sovereignty and rule by juntas and kleptocracies, had limited or no choice in the matter. The United States in its ascendancy as an economic empire possessed and controlled resources overwhelmingly greater than any other nation. With the one exception of Cuba, supervening control of the affairs of any other nation was readily handled by the Dulles CIA and its relations, accomplices, associates and successors. Different now, when the United States has been subjected to a confected terrorist threat and an elaborate set of lies about what happened, is that (although we did it in an odd — and unfortunate — partnership with Israelis) "we" did it to ourselves. In our case, there was no other large country showing military and economic strength we would be unlikely to overcome, potentially forcing us to "eat" the meal a stronger fork on a strong-arm was feeding us.

The *Project for the New American Century*, a group that included Richard Cheney, I. Lewis Libby, Donald Rumsfeld, Paul Wolfowitz, Richard Perle, Dov Zakheim, and William Kristol openly advocated 1. For coercing large increases in the U.S. military budget and military forces, 2. For removing Saddam Hussein from power in Iraq by military force, saying that Hussein "could not be permitted" to remain, 3. For continued extensive assertions of military force and control by the United States throughout the Middle East, and 4. For the occurrence of an allegedly "catalyzing event" saying that "the process of transformation, even if it brings revolutionary change, is likely to be a long one, absent some catastrophic and catalyzing event — like a new Pearl Harbor."[2] That said, the members of the "Project" were not the

---

2.   In a Report titled "Rebuilding America's Defenses" published in

only people who believed their purposes were best served by a lot of militarism and a minimum of more considerate thinking — or rational political and moral understanding.

To which usurpatious purposes, the World Trade Center buildings were, in their particular way, suited. They were out of scale even amongst a city of skyscrapers. They were the subject of big feats of popular cultural attention; Philippe Petit strung a wire between them and walked back and forth 1368 feet above the ground on an August morning in 1974; George Willig climbed the window washing tracks to the top of the south tower in May, 1977. The towers were the most recognizable built icons in the Lower Manhattan skyscape and may be said to have located images of the city in the way the Eiffel Tower locates images of Paris or the Parthenon places Athens.

They were also an outsized investment and something of a business failure. As an enterprise they did not substantially turn a profit for the Port Authority of New York and New Jersey,[3] and they were beset with a series of social and environmental problems, from the impersonal and windy plaza between them that never became a comfortable part of the urban landscape to the claims and lawsuits over the asbestos the towers contained.[4, 5] Difficult galvanic corrosion prob-

September 2000.

3.   "From an economic standpoint, the trade center — subsidized since its inception — has never functioned, nor was it intended to function, unprotected in the rough-and-tumble real estate marketplace." Business Week Magazine, October 5, 2001. See also Divided We Stand, Eric Darton, 1999.

4.   Port Authority of New York and New Jersey, Port Authority Trans Hudson Corporation (Path), Appalachian Insurance Company v. Affiliated FM Insurance Company and others. 245 F.Supp 2d 563 (D.N.J. May 2001) Affirmed on appeal, 311 F. 3d 226.

5.   See, e.g. *www.mesotheliomasos.com* "The halting of the asbestos and cement spraying unfortunately, came a year or two late. Hundreds of tons of the material had already been applied to the towers. Some of the asbestos and cement was removed through an abatement program, but not enough to constitute a remaining safe level. The beams and columns were not the only place where the asbestos was used in the World Trade Center towers. It was used in other places in the building including pipe lines..."

The asbestos was a characteristic feature of the dust produced by the collapses, see e.g. RJ Lee, *Dust Signature Study: Composition and Morphology*, 2002 indicating "Chrysotile asbestos was pervasively present in the Building. The WTC towers were built, in part, using fireproofing materials

lems with the cladding of the buildings are also variously reported.[6] Several analyses and reports over the last decade the towers were in existence gave negative reviews of the technical and communications infrastructure available in them, complaining about everything from the lack of sufficient fiber optic capacity to elevator wait times.

The number of cancer deaths among workers on "the Pile," as the rubble remains were called, for instance, being but another collateral consequence to which the empathetic among us can attend, the 9/11 event and story were created and performed, meant to leverage-move our nation wholesale to become the principal antagonist in a re-cast global "war," sought ardently by a small "managerializing" minority.

Having been done, over time 9/11 does not in fact come out better than most other created government and quasi-government "projects" that start in secrecy, proceed to lies, violence, murder and militarism, calamity and disruptions, then more lies and censorship and leveraged stringencies, whether here or elsewhere. Because we in the United States are richer, the results for us are different than what usually happens to the smaller countries of the world we "rearrange" or in which we have acted to suspend human rights and civil society for the sake of exploitation and geopolitical management. Otherwise, the damage to our nation and our wellbeing is similar enough to contemplate thoughtfully. If one were to "tally" the 9/11 results to the United States of America, one would have to account, among many other similar smaller consequences, the loss of the war in Iraq, the loss of the war in Afghanistan, both at a great cost to those countries, some significant part of which we inevitably share including in what is a largely hidden, but ugly cost to us, the continuing ramifications of other/further Middle East war, through and including the too-handy justification, just for examples, for the end-of-year 2008 and other invasions,

---

that contained chrysotile asbestos. ...Chrysotile asbestos is a distinguishing WTC Dust Marker for WTC Dust."

"The National Resources Defense Council (NRDC) report estimated more than 1.2 million tons of building materials collapsed during the WTC Event containing an estimated 300 to 400 tons of asbestos." (NRDC, 2002)

6.   See e.g, *Handbook of Corrosion Engineering*, Roberge, Pierre R.; McGraw Hill, 1999.

strikes and actions against Gaza. One would have to note domestically the so-called "Patriot Act", the burdensome, distracting and, frankly, societally diseased creations of "Homeland Security" syndrome in its various forms, an atmosphere of incoherent, random hostility (including, from time to time, to things Arab or Muslim or both), a highly increased level of surveillance, much of it notably antagonistic, even to our "friends" (so said Angela Merkle), more raw propaganda of many kinds, much of it also requiring a thickness of censorship, banning and "ghosting" used to suppress the valuable sense of human life, activity and thought. Similarly, one should recognize the harm to a not insignificant population of Mideast War veterans, most with some damage, many with serious psychological challenges. Along with them we should reckon the increased isolation of groups and assemblies within society and the many adversities of a "very deeply divided" national polity, some of it from a kind of "siege mentality," much of which begins with 9/11, some from a sense of "frustration," quite a bit of which comes from a sense of 9/11 "estrangement." from being told that so much is in the hands of government at the same time that everything the government does seems clumsy and everything government people have to say sounds merely bombastic. Acting on behalf of what we have been told 9/11 "requires" is a significant part of what has put up a vast amount of new debt, severely damaged basic financial relationships, "rescue" from which has created an entirely more striated economy that lives principally on Federal Reserve force-feeding and a new set of imbalances, other less-than-rational subsidies and winner-take-all effects. No one I know can so much as pretend to make a serious argument that we, the United States, the national "we," did not lose every one of the wars of choice we began after 9/11, military and "non-military" and "political" and "legal," and everyone I know who thinks about it recognizes that words beginning with "since 9/11" usually open but another portal on a version of failure at best, or worse provide another rendition of a dance of the devil in some particular hell. "Fighting terrorism" since 9/11 has too much of the associated actual wrongdoing of our previous rants about "fighting communism" (by infiltrating and overthrowing democratically elected government in Guatemala, etc.) for the sake of economic, political, and military exploitation, not to notice.

Although we have always told lies, saying and writing things that are unquestionably untrue on all subjects has greatly increased since 9/11. This to the point to which false propositions have become a staple of the pronouncements of public officials up to and including by the Presidents of the United States. So called "fact-checking" has become common, but is used principally to add to the lying, and has not fixed much in the environment of so-called "post-factuality" and bamboozle that is now ours.

Re-stated, 9/11 can and should be understood as a criminal act of espionage practiced by the United States as represented by U.S. organizations part of, connected to, or being extensively penetrated by the United States Government, together with others, including other clandestine entities in other nations, now directed against these United States. It appears to have been intended to have an effect similar to the effect of past instances of espionage-combat that were practiced by the United States permanently to displace and disrupt the valuable ordinary national political life in those countries, to install and encourage a corrupt or corruptible government to support military and financial schemes commended by the powers that have suborned the displacement, but which are otherwise profoundly contrary to the country's reasonable genuine national interests.

None of this is to deny that the United States has very serious and legitimate security objectives and requirements. It is instead to say that in fact staging 9/11 and the ensuing wars, and "patriot" fascisms was, in plain words, a very stupid thing to do. We will get to the interesting — and difficult — but answerable, question that asks: having nevertheless in fact done 9/11, what should we best do now. In the interval, further focus on 9/11 "dynamics."

Consideration of the 9/11 events and story also requires thinking deeply about two kinds of fear. One is fear of the sort that 9/11 was intended to inspire in people who believed the tale about the nineteen Arab hijackers. It is the fear that, even with all of the existing apparatus of our society, we, the people, are yet "unprotected," at least we are vulnerable to sudden terrible acts by "those who don't share our values." The second is fear on the part of people who can or could realize that 9/11 has in fact nothing to do with nineteen Arabs, that it is all a (very destructive) stunt, but ever to say such a thing in words that a number of people hear aloud would be to ruin their own personal career or, by supposition, would tear the society and our country apart. This is the fear that now to say or write any significant part of the truth about 9/11 would take us or our group or our society into chaos and impossibly deep doubt, not just of a kind that we might we might learn from, or that others might summon and exploit, but which would overcome us. This second kind of fear makes 9/11 the secret (that isn't much of a secret, it is "hidden" in plain-enough sight for anyone who is paying attention) that "keeps itself" to the extent that we are scared to have any part of the thin, but ideologically (and continuing in us) "terror-armor"plated cover over it slip off.

By using so much of the government to announce and reinforce the 9/11 story, by getting so many media voices to repeat so often and so vociferously that all of the hijacking and the death and destruction was the work of nineteen Arabs who don't share our values, any return to the simple truth became impossibly scary. And has stayed over-whelmingly intimidating.

People ostensibly trained in the engineering disciplines, or oth-erwise familiar with the terminology used in talking about building mechanics, have been willing to provide wildly false "analyses" of the building collapses on behalf of the government and the media. Some of these descriptions may at first seem plausible, others are obviously nonsense from the first. Most of these descriptions do not in the least correspond to what is shown on the videos of the collapse supposedly being described. (Nor, of course, do the authors introduce any evi-dence that might show the descriptions are to be taken as true and the video false.)

To a person, neither do the authors of these descriptions betray any recognition that the description they provide completely fails to match the video. All is subsumed in the mere use of the word "collapse."

The video shows a "collapse" and they say they are writing about a "collapse." The reader or audience can suppose that they are describing what is shown on the screen, and in the climate of anxiety created by the 9/11 media coverage, readers and audiences willingly convert an entirely bogus account that announces that it explains "collapse" into a treated-as-true explanation of the collapse they have seen on TV.

There are many American citizens who have more than enough understanding, if applied to the matter, to recognize that the 9/11 story as told can't possibly be the physical truth. (Even a Michael Bronner article in *Vanity Fair* magazine explains: "'The real story is actually better than the one we told,' a NORAD general admitted to 9/11-commission staffers when confronted with evidence from the tapes that contradicted his original testimony. And so it seems.") That a thoughtful American who recognized that the 9/11 story was fake would nonetheless not invite hearing it supplanted with a story yet "better" or, quite conceivably in ways "worse," is not wholly unreasonable. Even though it is now time to abate the 9/11 fraud as created more than two decades ago, we must together be somewhat careful not merely to have 9/11 as we know it supplanted with more lying, more wrongdoing, and another round of damage to the well-being of the country.

9/11 having occurred notwithstanding, one would like to think that we collectively recognize the value and virtues of some honesty in what we say and do, that we want things that are usually reasonable to want for people who live together in a country in the world, among them:

— That we see the societal and national value in justice, and in its many forms. That, although justice may be imperfect, we seek justice for its merits. Tempered with mercy, indeed, but honest and just nonetheless.

— That we want correctly to determine and declare that the perpetrators of wrongdoing are in fact those who committed or perpetrated it; we don't want to be faked into proposing to punish or punishing "patsies" or other uninvolved or innocent parties.

— That nothing is gained by having the government be

"exempt" from science, and immune with regard to forensic facts. The government should have no prerogative to deny simple Newtonian physics because it finds the results of rational analysis inconvenient.

— That we want to expose and deter criminal activity engaged in by government and governmental agencies as well as by individual people and corporate entities. In any event, we do not want the result of any mass murder of American citizens to be forced acceptance and approval because the government committed it.

— That the media should indeed be free to publish without censorship, facts and opinions both, but that is not the same as saying the media should be given license to commit criminal fraud by means of the intentional publication of false information for the purposes of substantial and detrimental deception.

The result is that we are all part of a national (worldwide, really) dilemma. It is a dilemma having to do with choice, and can somewhat be compared to what is so often, perhaps too often, called a "prisoner's dilemma." What happens for us individually is connected to what all of us do. All of us regular people on the street, 9/11 having happened, have every good reason not to want the have another 9/11-like event be staged, or another, similar, story be told about it. Again, nothing about what has proceeded from 9/11, continuous fear propaganda about terrorism, war in Iraq, war in Afghanistan, war in Yemen, war in Syria, losing all those wars — and the trillion dollars spent on those wars — nothing about what 9/11 has given place to has been good for our country, nor for regular people.

The Roman Empire and the British Empire both collapsed from a period of distributed conflict, unmanageable financial debt, and then bankruptcy. (Yes, it's more complicated in each case of extended fall in all the myriad details, Rome had its Wars in the East and Britain the protracted mess in India and the Suez Crisis, but the fights, debts and economic disembodiment are the facts in sum and broad outlines.) Even if our personal political passions are well to the right, and we consider our country delivered of God to this Earth, and entitled, our heads are not screwed on well if we have any thought but to try very hard not to have another national event, or process, like 9/11. Which is also why, right, left, center or indifferent, we should be amply concerned, for example, that we have managed our way to an entirely "post truth" public America, in which the principal communicative activity of the highest level officials and the public media is to say things that are quite untrue.

This, at the same time, that we are collectively enclosed in the lock of fear described above. Those among us who can't figure out 9/11 believe it was really about nineteen Muslims and remain scared. Those who can figure out the basic facts are scared both at what they can recognize and scared to observe the truth aloud, including for having thereafter to cope with those who will not or cannot.

All the while 9/11 is still also the name for a syndrome, a way of thinking, a way of being. After the Second World War, Nazis were brought to trial at Nuremburg with evidence and witnesses and, frankly, the relatively conscientious leadership of Robert Jackson. (Some were acquitted. The evidence regarding the convicted was substantial and public in every case. Nuremburg may have also been marked by imperfections (Operation Paperclip, for just an example, made its own decisions), but at least it was process and articulation. By contrast, after a night helicopter landing in Abbottabad, a supposed Osama bin Laden was machine-gunned to a pulp, tossed into a bag, supposedly identified by a still secret DNA test, then thrown overboard way out in the Indian Ocean — and the whole "portrayed" event was self-righteously celebrated to the max on American media.

In writing I would like to be as practical in considering events and consequences and relationships and obligations as I can be. Taking them together, I would suggest some relatively simple-to-apply principles, and enactments. They are not perfect, but they will work an improvement. Having them, if we have the courage to have them, will help us. The first of these might be called "Common Law 12 and 21 Year Rules for Stating Truth".

"Intelligence" agencies and other propaganda producing entities will continue to tell lies, including big lies. Big lies are not infrequently not good lies. "Forever lies" are almost always bad. By "forever lies" I would refer to lies that are said to have to stay in place indefinitely, and regarding which the actual truth of the matter is proposed to remain eternally dangerous. Yet for the sake of decency in practice, perhaps we should just help ourselves define "forever." So, the proposal here is: 12 or more years in the case of any act constituting or comprising a serious felony, and more than 21 years for all other accounts of personally observed facts. The time is long enough; the truth can then be told without there being any right to institute any reprisal by the government or any associated entity. The principle applied, we would be suggesting to the people who would create untruths (including as part of their job as they might be given it or they might conceive it): that they do not, in the first place, tell a lie about an act that is a serious crime that they would not be willing to have corrected by the truth twelve years from now, and do not tell a lie about any act that you would not be willing to have corrected twenty-one years from today. As a matter of acceptance and refusal, as a nation we may have to accept lying, particularly government lying, but, among other things, we can refuse to have to keep any particular set of lies in place forever. Most importantly, the government and its agents get no say in the matter. In a matter of years, they lose all right to suppression no matter what.

This may, at first, seem a rule too arbitrary, too distinct, too simple to be helpful in a complicated and context-related world. However, context is reintroduced to the situation regarding enforcement, and long experience with rules and instituting them shows that certain kinds of responsibly positioned "bright line" distinctions can sometimes act well. A society that moves in some concert with the inherent motions and effects of the passage of time will tend to succeed better than a society that refuses. Forensics often continue over time. Certain factual truths tend to sharpen. The willingness to suspend disbelief abates.

The summary proposition that "the truth will out" is not exactly right in all cases. A more accurate general statement is that lies

characteristically fracture and fail to work and often become very
"needy" over time. In part that is the consequence of the reality that a
given lie has to be "covered" with a procession of other lies (usually
many), and the facility and willingness to produce the further covering lies can reach a limit or turn to even more corruption in what it
produces. A lie that felt vitally necessary to a population of supporters
often loses its actual interest and emotional value as events happen
and time passes.

If a knowingly false statement about matters of real substance is
somehow justifiable, its justification is never eternal. If the false statement is not made to affect others, it doesn't matter, and if it is, an
inherent right to affect others with a false statement eternally is hard to
find fair reason for. Correspondingly, the social and emotional mech-
anisms, including individual excitement and social mood, that go to
work either to require lies or to support lies tend to wear and abate.
Having a rule that provides for a distinct arranged discontinuance to
the persistence of falsehood is thus preferable to not having one.

There does exist legislation in the United States, coupled to certain executive orders, generally permitting de-classification after
given periods of time (generally twenty-five years, twelve years for
certain presidential records) but for which there are, principally in executive orders, nine described (widely construed) exemptions. Written
into the de-classification legislation is some stiff-sounding language
saying that de-classification can only be postponed if it would do
clear and demonstrable harm. In practice, however, the exemptions
have it, quite overwhelmingly. The current statutory de-classification
scheme has failed to work to bring truth to the lies once told much
more often than it has succeeded. Exceptions include the report of the
NSA historian Hanyok mentioned above, as an example, although that
document, 55 pages released in 2005 (over some strong objections
from the Executive branch and after Federal Appeals Court litigation),
principally provided corroboration of information known from other
sources (including Stockdale – and, of course, what was obvious to
I.F. Stone), and the rest of the 522-page account, called *Spartans in
Darkness* (of which the August 4th Tonkin account was just a part)

was refused release under the exemption rules in Executive Order 12958 (President Clinton) and remains secret to this day.

Required in place of government selection of the material it wants to release, and not, is instead a described common law right that allows any citizen of the United States to state publicly certain kinds of true facts of which he or she has direct knowledge. Describing the facts that should fall within such a release can be set out cleanly and clearly. The release should apply to the acts of human beings, and evidence of those acts. The idea of direct knowledge is already very well understood in our system of law; essentially it is knowledge that derives from presence and observation. Hearsay and speculation are ruled out. Merely arbitrary codes and encodings, configurations of equipment, mere identities of agents still in the field, and so forth would remain as classified as they are now, with the same prohibitions on disclosure. There would be no right to tell a successor lie; the release would only apply to a true account. A further fraudulent statement, as fraud may be recognized in the law, would be punishable as fraud.

This may be thought of as a form of statute of limitations. After twelve years, secrecy law could no longer limit or sanction a person who has personal knowledge of facts describing the commission of a *malum in se* felony crime from stating the facts. After twenty-one years no form of law would prevent or sanction against a true factual account. Even a person subject to rules regarding classification, who knows what actually happened would have the right to present the true facts in public without breaking any law or order. Again, importantly, by this approach the government does not "de-classify." Instead, the government loses its power to punish the provision of true information — after having kept lies in place for just over two decades.

The principle, and the rule as enacted, are not risk free. The traditional way to maintain secrets is to kill the people who might disclose them. (Immediately, one is reminded of the murder of Mary Pinchot Meyer while taking her "customary daily walk" on the towpath along the C&O Canal, October 12, 1964.) The traditional way to keep systems of lying in place is to kill at least enough people to scare the others away from contradicting the lies in any significant way. Murder and torture and accounts told of cruelties have been shown very capable means to control information. There is therefore the risk that pre-emptive violent acts will in response greet a common law right to the truth. Rules giving protection to people apprehensive they will be murdered or renditioned, or tortured upon lawful disclosure could help, yet if the methods of violence become prevalent beyond measure, no notion of law or rule or legal right can remain cogent or applicable. Likely there is no truly good answer to the ugliest response to the existence of a right to speak. Consider, at the same time, the cost to basic societal values of the violent response. Improvements in the practice of forensics can help, and will be suggested below, but, as will also be considered in detail, self-respect, respect for others, and respect for the truth must be transcendent values — at least to a certain "major" extent for any modern civilization to propose to be civilized.

Sometimes, accidents are exactly that: accidents. Unfortunate (or tragic) inadvertences. In an environment in which deceit has become excessively acceptable, it can be hard to know. William Colby (he of the "Phoenix Program" in Vietnam) acted somewhat co-operatively with the Church and Pike committees and Colby did some talking to various authors and reporters (more than other former Directors). He may (or may not) have said something someone did not appreciate. He died in a boating accident in a canoe near his home in Maryland. Mystery deaths can also make the effect of suppression worse. Knowing, on the one hand, that a given person was definitely not murdered, or was murdered and by whom, on the other, can give clarity to those who survive enabling them more specifically to cope with the particular hazards and harms of the use of violence to control information and disclosure.

Even at 12 or 21 years, many of the matters at issue as criminal case will have become "cold" or statutes of limitations upon criminal proceedings will have run. Many, or most, of the disclosures made under the protection of the described common law right in the individual citizen will therefore not be motivated by prosecution, although the prospect of reducing first degree murder kept secret by classification probably should be welcomed. (The most reactionary blocs in certain government intelligence agencies that work in close connection with organized crime and regularly hire assassins may well complain — but such complaints can be something we observe and consider — and just regret.) Honesty regarding reputation may turn out to be a repeat motive. Some disclosures may not be better than raw jealousy or resentment by another name, but even that may serve the public interest in having the benefit, at least, of a non-fraudulent account.

It is indeed time for the cycling pressure of the "fear lock" that sham such as the 9/11 lies put into place to be relieved, at least abated very significantly. It was created on purpose by the people who organized the 9/11 events and told the 9/11 story. But left in place as created, it will continue to be a major part of the destruction of the United States as an enlightened nation of laws and human promise.

Losing wars doesn't help, either. Nor does being the principal agent of the destruction to dust in many cities in a whole group of countries do much for our world reputation. To say that we have to believe the absurd story about the nineteen Arab hijackers and must remain too scared to recognize and marshal the overwhelming physical and scientific evidence against it, and for the sake of continuing all of the obviously failed military and political and financial policies of the last two decades is, as it should be, too demoralizing even for a merely semi-aware country.

Correspondingly, the raw disrespect and disregard for facts and for the truth that now permeates our culture, and our politics, and our society is obvious to anyone with even the least ability to read the news or take notice. Clearly we need a somewhat Kennedy-like proposal for serving a different, somewhat more self-respecting, set of values. We need a change in the way we conduct ourselves as a nation — this time without assassinating the voice of the proposal and then reverting to the former, cruder, brute style — including going "all in" on the Vietnam War, or its subsequent equivalents.

Part of the present problem, however, is that the world is indeed more complicated and "difficult" now than it was, for example, in November 1963. The "dark side" is now a territory many square miles bigger. Networks of people engaged in criminal wrongdoing now have at their behest networks of other people and networks of computers to engage and act with them.

It is possible to suppose, without certainty at all, but to imagine that, had Allen Dulles not owned the "Warren Commission," evidence later adduced by the Church and Pike committees, together with other, similar evidence might have been brought forth. E. Howard Hunt might have been forced to testify a decade earlier about a matter a lot more serious than Watergate, and might have had to tell some of the truth. Legitimate ballistics (no "magic bullet") and other forensics might have been done. And the country would have, in some definite measure, had to "take conscience" of itself. Eisenhower's farewell "Military-Industrial Complex" admonition, let us agree has value for what it is worth. But the country could have been required to understand what actually happened at least in some part — to recognize , for instance, how little had, at center, to do with Lee Harvey Oswald.

Whether that could have happened in the 1960s, and what the consequences might have been, are questions to which we cannot do more than guess (maybe wildly — okay) at answers. Thinking about them can make a person wish for the chance for all of us to live in a world in which Allen Dulles, or anyone like him, and the people around him, do not get to manipulate so fully, so completely, so arrogantly, so untouchably, the account and proceeds of what they do and have done. All, always, without ever even being asked a single relevant question. Lies, particularly very big, very nasty lies cannot possibly be in fact, and are not, so worthwhile, so valuable to the rest of us that the perpetrators of them not only should have the lying continue without genuine inquiry, but have all of the things being done on behalf of and in the name of the lies continue unconsidered, with un-reviewable, overpowering government and associated institutional support.

Seventy-five years later we are also now collectively in the hands of government that is much bigger than it has ever been before, that refers increasingly only to itself in constructing its concepts and decisions, that keeps many more secrets than ever before, that is increasingly beholden to narrow, highly leveraged, self-seeking imperatives, and that in so many matters separates itself from any of the genuine burdens of candor and honesty, and from most of the inconveniences of the fair consideration of consequences. Say though one might that a bigger, more developed country entails government that is larger and more complicated, nothing about saying so offers a good reason that government should do yet so much more lying. A proposal to change the eternal immunity of government from answering for its frauds is not hostile to any of the basic notions of consent by and service to the governed nor to the values government best embodies for its own sake. In a large and complicated society, government that has some connection to the truth is indeed more necessary — even as lying has become so rampant.

Some part of the thinking comes to suggest changes in scheme. The proposal of a common law rule that, of itself, limits the government's opportunity to support lies by secrecy and punishment is specifically intended to give choices and certain power to people who know the truth and who, after having had time to think about it, would tell the truth. Importantly, this is not a proposal for another increase in administration and acts of administration. It is to confer some choices upon individual people who have truthful knowledge to make them.

The family and private example of honorable difference between the facts and rendering of them considered, the principles involved are not limited to single families. The "Operation Mincemeat" / "Man Who Never Was"[7] example, a trick played against the enemy during, and as part of, the engagement in a declared, shooting war provides another argument for the genuinely practical value of deception. Montagu's choice to tell the story is an act of pride in his invention,

---

7. A body, either that of a Welsh ne'er-do-well, Gyndwr Michael, who is said to have died in January 1943 after drinking rat poison, or that of Englishman John McFarlane, killed in the explosion of the aircraft carrier *HMS Dasher*, was deposited overboard from the submarine *Seraph* off the south-west coast of Spain. As "Major William Martin" the body carried a locked leather briefcase containing invented correspondence intended to deceive the Axis powers as to the Allied plans for landing to invade southern Europe. The papers succeeded to the extent that the Allied invasion of Sicily on July 10, 1943 found German forces unprepared, and many lives saved thereby.

self-appreciation for good luck and success, acknowledgment that group co-operation in a project without an excess of fussing, or inquiry, can be very helpful, and perhaps even something of a note about what can wash ashore. Whatever ever else it may be, even if you say it is chest-thumping, it is not, however, a betrayal. If it tells us what schemes have been in fact engaged in for what purposes in a time of war it usefully adds to our understanding. As much as anything else, a certain stubbornness in their own methods and thinking deceived the Germans. So, perhaps, may have already developed "internal" / quiet opposition to Hitler.

Plain factuality, in and of itself, important as it be, is not the only measure by which we are obliged to understand and consider words and actions. While viewing accuracy, on the one hand, and erroneousness, on the other, we must also consider position and effect. A lie that yields ameliorating consequences should not be condemned with the vehemence with which we respond to a lie that leads only to wreckage and suffering.

Understanding the great complex of differences and distinctions that, when we make our way through them thoughtfully, enable us to make moral choices both good in themselves and otherwise valuable in the end has much to do with what is accepted and what we refuse to accept. To understand refusing and accepting, as discussed here, we need to begin by thinking of information not as a something inert and "of itself," but as a proposition for a change to the condition or state of the things(s) receiving the information. Including when it is us, people, changing our "frame of understanding," our own "mental model" of reality or possibility as we receive information. Information is something that also, and importantly, exists as it acts. Thus is propaganda so often stupefyingly destructive, yet from the same set of realities and dynamics come the remedies that can come from people, organizations, and institutions capable of some honesty, some self-respect, and some great respect for other people and the planet we all in habit.

The raw 'amount' of information in a message may often enough reasonably be assessed just by considering even the simple arithmetical extent of state change the message requires for the representation involved in mere receipt. The information value of a message typically may only reasonably be assessed by considering the nature and properties of entailed change to one or more systems, often independently active systems..

For a person to consider a statement "not true" is to refuse to adjust what that person conceives to be 'actual' in accordance with the propositions contained in the statement. But there are also many other ways to refuse, or otherwise modulate, a given proposition. Information, when communicated to humans arrives to a site (the human head) with a lot of other encoding/information in it already and a living information processor (a human mind) that, depending, can do quite a bit of comparing and thinking. The media sends out a presentation in which a supposed "man on the street" figure says a plane flew into a building and video is shown of what looks like a plane flying into a building. So far, well, we (people) can readily treat, and take, the proposition about the plane as actual. Or we can consider that it is not possible that the plane flew inside the building and there is no substantial wreckage anywhere around and about the site. We can summon, also as information, all that we know about material things, crashes and wreckage, and realize that we have been shown a video image, but not a true fact about the world and — it is a very important "and" — we can think about what happens if we 'make pretend' along with the presenters in the media, and what happens if we a) don't do any pretending at all, or b) don't do any more pretending than we socially feel the need to, or c) do enough pretending to keep (what, let's say, happens to be) our job in the news media. Of course while we are making that choice for ourselves, we are also making some part of a collective choice as a society and a nation. Even if they seem initially small, nonetheless such choices can "add up."

We can use the words "accept" and "refuse" for the sake of turning up the contrast in a way that may help us observe and think about the outlines of what is happening, or can happen, when we receive things told to us, news, propaganda, advertising, gossip, etc. In the great majority of cases, we have the choice to think about what we are being told and to consider it carefully in the light of true knowledge about the world. Whether we make that choice or not can be something of a separate matter — but the choice is there.

The people who planned and caused the 9/11 events to be carried out, and who created the 9/11 story and got others to tell it, whether by alliance, or by having it put up on tele-prompters, or by issued orders, or by threats or imposed and compelling insecurities, if they are ever subject to inquiry of purpose and attention, can be expected to claim that the nation and the Western World were under "threat" and the only way that threat could be described and "communicated" was by enacting 9/11. Even on the face of it, however, such a claim is strange and unhappy. Everything about such a possibly proffered explanation indicates mere contrivance. Such people would be saying they were worried about a terrorist attack, and the cleverest thing they could think of to do in response to their concern was to stage an actual attack themselves that costs many lives, destroys several buildings and everything that is in them, turning lower Manhattan into a poisonous dust-blizzard zone. One might wonder what else they thought of trying in the way of acting on behalf of their supposed concern.

It makes no sense to say, and on a very deep level it is not true, that 9/11 was in any way a useful admonition — except as it should have given the country and the world warning about the actual perpetrating government and related entities. To say that the wrongdoers described by media announcement, 19 Arab hijackers,[8] had no right to kill the

---

8.   Not only are none of their described names included on any of the airline-maintained passenger lists / flight manifests for any of the relevant flights, no probative evidence of any kind exists that any of the described "hijackers" ever in fact boarded any of the airplanes involved in the events of September 11, 2001.

The present use of the term "hijackers" is meant only to reproduce and refer to assertions made in media accounts. The facts regarding the described "terrorists," as they are known, are swimmingly complicated — and, whatever else they do, belie the "mainstream" media accounts.

"The FBI changed the names of the "hijacker" passengers from the original flight manifests, from the first list the FBI submitted - then hastily withdrew - to the second one which it kept despite the fact that at least 10 of the 19 named hijackers it contained have turned up alive ... all the crucial government evidence depicting Islamic hijacker terrorists [who] were

people and destroy the buildings and city area they did is tantamount to saying that those who actually did the destruction and killing had no right to do it either. It will not do to suppose or suggest that the government has a right to condemn alleged "terrorists" while in fact acting itself or in concert with others to demolish buildings with people in them as would a terrorist. Not only is it not to take responsibility for the act but, especially when it is connected to the prerogatives and immunities of government, the inherent claims of exemption from investigation or sanction multiply not just the absurdity, but also the unfairness and injustice.

In addition to a common law right to state truth after a period of time, we would do well to think about news and press coverage in the present. We live in an era of large conglomerate media companies that get a large part of the "news" information they disseminate from the government, or parts of it, or people who work for it, and in which on-air reporters and commentators regularly practice common, well-recognized techniques of propagandizing, often on behalf of propositions entirely false. There new exist a few large "information moving" systems, such as YouTube, Facebook, Cable News, Twitter and Google Search, which regularly agree to "take down" or by system methods suppress information which contradicts an "official story" and for that reason alone is called "dangerous" information. (There do exist some more or less independent news providers, but without appreciable news collecting resources, and that usually receive second and third class treatment.) The theory (and law) has been that United States clandestine agencies don't practice their trade against their own country. (Radio Free Europe is established in Europe, and broadcasts

responsible for 9-11 — the videos, the photographs, the alleged in-flight phone calls, the cockpit audiotapes, and these "doctored" flight manifests — have been proven to lack authentication if not also proven, with corroboration from other evidence, to be fabrications or forgeries. A close investigation of most of the hijackers has revealed the use of "doubles," a staple of any US intelligence covert operation, especially one dealing with the forging of evidence against "terrorists," most of whom, if not all, were unwitting patsies whose doubles had to be introduced to engage in certain incriminating activities the patsies either would not or, lacking competence, physical presence, and/or motivation, could not have performed." *The Hidden History of 9/11*, Seven Stories Press / Penguin - Random House, 2008.

toward the east.) "Operation Mockingbird," and the close relationships between the Director and the Luces or Sulzbergers, as ever continually extended by more "bureaucratic" entities and means into the present contradict the stated theory.

"All Governments Lie" said I. F. Stone. All governments work hard to control as much information as they can. When a government succeeds in its efforts at falsities (again, the simplest example, having also reasonably clear comparables: East Germany in the period before the fall of the Wall) the result is distinctly bad for the nation. There is much to be said for preventing government from dictating press accounts. Although the press and the government each propose to recognize and honor a code of conduct, the uses to the government (and officials and bureaucrats) of purportedly "independent" free propaganda is too great to abstain from producing and putting it up for publication. Correspondingly, the press is quickly and completely seduced by the provision of "leaks" and other re-marketable "gets" and disclosures — especially across the purported boundaries of controlling excesses of classification and secrecy. Much of the press coverage of the political life of the nation therefore now consists in reproducing stories provided by government, its agencies, and personnel without any independent (or thoughtful, or coherent) examination or consideration of the facts or the color of their portrayal.

In the United States the collusive joinder of government and press in practical terms has reached a point at which adherence to a principle of explicit attribution should be required. If the news reporter has not witnessed the event, the source that claims the event occurred as described should be specifically named. Better that we readers tire of learning (being reminded) that a certain account is made "... according to State Department spokesperson Joseph Jones..." than that we mistakenly (carelessly) suppose the lack of attribution must mean we are being delivered objective and immutable truth.

Editors, producers and reporters similarly manipulate and modulate their accounts in order to make uncertainties become indubitables, on the one hand, and have scientific realities and definite facts become poised upon an imagined wide and indistinguishable variety of contradictory opinions, on the other. Often, as unfortunately, the reporting covers no exclusion, whether an account of the questions the source refused to answer, or note of the physical evidence that would have to be found at the scene in order to support the claim that was not in fact found, or a synopsis of the verification methods that specifically did not confirm or verify a position or assertion. "Balance" in news reporting can be understood to be the maintenance of a rightful relationship between evidence and constructed inference to produce what is written. Instead it has come to mean that the spew from propagandists from various political "teams" has been solicited and compiled.

Two decades of media coverage of 9/11 demonstrate the extent to which simple, basic facts can be completely buried in a morass of fable and fraud over and over again as a story is told and re-told, and the counter-ceremonious interment proceedings performed again and again as more, other, further stories are told. Not only has not one serial numbered part been correctly collected from any of the four alleged 9/11 airplane crash sites and properly and according to responsible forensic practice traced by reference to the actual build and maintenance logs for the airframe in question, but not one media account has directly and simply informed the public that not one serial numbered airplane part has in fact been found and correctly identified and documented.

A genuinely independent national media environment is a wholly different thing from an environment in which the media is very highly dependent upon government and the prerogatives of those in government. Complete independence probably cannot be achieved in a nation such as ours but, that said, the extent of media complicity in fraud demonstrated in the decades since 9/11 describes a dark low of servility and the lack of independent, or (even marginally) thoughtful, judgment. Whatever might be said about a "free society" notwithstanding, to be a free society is not to accept having a media landscape, however extensive, every acre effectively owned and subject to the tillage and harvest of a government or official or corresponding entity. The nation that can save itself from the mess made by 9/11 is also the nation that can, by many diverse means, court decisions, popular objection, commentary, protest, and pointed jokes on late night television re-establish some common greater actual appreciation for factual reality in news and media accounts.

Four: Evidence, Facts and Stories.

To have one or more facts genuinely demonstrated "scientifical-ly," as a matter of actual science, distinguishes those facts from other propositions we might put up regarding events in the world. Much of the discussion now comes from groups believing one particular account calling the (admittedly sometimes quite non-scientific) contrasting descriptions offered by others "conspiracy theories." It is a truly bad practice for a society to get into. An excess of secrecy, on the one hand, and lying, on the other, have increased the frequency of the use of summary contentions and dismissals without evidence, and made "conspiracy theory" a kind of catch-all label tossed at any account that is unwanted or unsettling — usually without any regard to any status, or not, as fact. To the "flat-earthers" the proposition that the earth is spherical is a "conspiracy theory." In a country that too often awards too much to repeated shouting, and too little to careful thinking, "conspiracy theories" that are clearly false are common, while, at the same time, whining and howling that calls plain truth a conspiracy theory has equally become a daily staple.

As noted, the remarkable feature of the 9/11 events is that in significant part understanding them only requires honesty — just non-self-deception — in considering well known and easily recognizable facts. There is no dispute that three large, tall buildings 110, 110, and 47 stories tall — actual buildings, not models in a tabletop shoot, not computer constructed images — collapsed straight down at close to free-fall speed. Those three buildings were physical matter, steel columns, steel floor pans, concrete floors, glass windows, aluminum alloy "skin." There is a great deal of overwhelmingly good evidence they were in fact built as designed where they stood in Lower Manhattan in the 1970s. They were big, they had many parts. They were also all stuff, physical matter.

Unlike people, physical matter doesn't really have emotions, doesn't make "decisions" about what it will or will not do, does not choose to obey or to refuse. Physical matter just does what it does

It acts exactly "physically," meaning that it acts in relation to other physical matter and forces according to certain simple, unvarying relationships. Each of those three buildings fell straight down because the building structure that held the building up was disassembled simultaneously and closely sequentially floor by floor by the application of force great enough to effect the disassembly. Thermitic cutting devices and explosive charges (of the general types that are used in building demolition) readily provided the physical means to do that. A "special effects" airplane impact (that did not in fact physically occur) would not and could not yield the required forces. Comparatively small office fires, which were ignited pyrotechnically, and did burn, showing flames and smoke, could not produce anything like the requisite temperatures or forces.

The 9/11 that we now know, the 9/11 that created a Department of Homeland Security, terrorist alerts and watch lists, and all of the other endings and conclusions to sentences that begin "Since 9/11..." nominally comes both from entirely non-physical, synthetic events, airplane "impacts" and from entirely physical, actual events, building collapses.

The airplanes were special effects, and the demolitions were in themselves unreasonable. The World Trade Center Towers were full of asbestos, but turning them into a cloud of dust and a pile of rubble just wasted resources and made for thousands of cases of cancer among the people who had to do the cleanup.

However, as we all must recognize, and must learn to acknowledge to an extent we too often now fail to, the path of societal and political systems leads not directly from events and actual truths. The 9/11 according to which we now say we look at and understand the world, according to which we make decisions, make rules, and make wars, is, in short, a 9/11 that is completely physically unreal (it is just a "cartoon show," played over and over on TV), but it has been politically monstrously potent.

9/11 comes not from actuality, but from narrative, from story, from fable – told about things that did not in fact happen. The things that physically took place in the world considered to any degree rationally, scientifically, standing by themselves (before even in the most minimally rational inquiry) could not manage to yield the narrative that was so readily produced.

In this the 9/11 story is not so unusual. Throughout all of history, many have observed the eagerness with which great mobs will believe tales supposedly told about facts in the world that are indeed plainly untrue. The proposition that a woman gave birth to a child while remaining a virgin is not unique to Christianity, for example. Like much of what became Christian gospel, physically very unlikely events, such as angels descending from heaven and providing announcement, (and virgin-magical pregnancy and childbirth),[1] and resurrection appear to have been borrowed or re-positioned from the story inventions of preceding religious sects and cults.

To say that human society has incorporated and embodied a highly developed facility, for as long as there has been human society, for converting the actualities of things that happen on this planet into impossible mythologies, while true to say, however, doesn't provide a particularly satisfactory account as to why 9/11 was created nor why it was able to take such hold, nor why it has left a broad wake of national failure. It is not hard to note, just as an example, that astronomy without instruments would lead to other methods that are not so much astronomy and not science. The night sky could be a zoo of creatures, bears and dolphins and dragons. They are charming. Without telescopes and observatories, and an entire culture of understanding from them, it can well be because Helios has completed a chariot ride across the sky that day turns to night. The soup of any explanation is cooked from the vegetables of observation, impression, and mental modeling that we have collected in the baskets of our culture and our experience, and in our imaginations and in the imaginations of others entered into us.

---

1. "Attis was the Good Shepard, the son of Cybele, the Great Mother, who gave birth to him without union with mortal man..." King, Martin Luther, Jr. (Crozer Theological Seminary) *The Influence of the Mystery Religions on Christianity* (1949-50)

Explaining a choice, specifically and drastically to avoid science when science is fully available and entirely relevant, however, is not as ready, nor plain, nor facile. What happens when we say now in the 21st Century that we have just invented a new apparatus that perfectly shows the sun actually hitched to the chariot and the horses? We make a movie that shows the procession across the sky? Crowds can turn on their TV and see it. That said, the chariot remains missing from the actual sky. It isn't there before the lens of an optical telescope, just looking upward from anyone's back yard. What, then, do we accomplish that we before did not? Greater attendance at the movies? Emotional attachment and motivation among a large group of people? Life on Earth continues – and do we have a new version of an old (and capricious?) god to whom we must now daily pray?

9/11, as such, does not exist in nature (in the same sense that other special effects footage is not a depiction of naturally occurring events — this, even though the building collapses are real). Whether 9/11 (the story as told) is "real," to use a quick phrase, in our "intellectual culture," or, for another form of words, according to our "developed understanding," becomes a question somewhat more subtle, involved, and (maybe) uncertain. It is hard to say what a society does or doesn't "know" when its politics asserts as physically real and preeminently significant that which its physical science unambiguously recognizes as not real, and "knows" and indeed should know is faked.

9/11 does not withstand the only genuinely significant test of any theory: experiment. If we had a large supply of Boeing airplanes available for the purpose, and a similarly large supply of World Trade Center towers, we could fly the one into the other (even at an impossible 500 or 600 miles an hour) many thousands of times, and not once would the airplane fly through the building, and not once would the building wait an hour and a half and then in ten seconds collapse to a pile of rubble in its own footprint, spreading an enormous cloud of hot dust. Comes then the question of the "status" of an event that is not possibly an actual event, but which a government, media, and large society propagandize to treat as if it were.

Before, and in some ways separate from, the media blitz saying that

America is under attack by people who don't share our values, 9/11 starts out as, and is as synthetic as, a Wile E. Coyote "cartoon event," — our common susceptibilities to which are worth some consideration, especially while keeping in mind some of the common effects of "exaggeration" and "inductive following."

In Wile E.'s case, there on our screens, with a sort of 'slide-whistle' noise at descending frequency, we see Wile E. fall through what appears to the viewer to be a thousand feet in the middle of the canyon, and then to the accompaniment of a big 'klunk' noise Wile E. crashes into the solid canyon floor, making a coyote-outline impression in it that looks deep, even from side angle. Every sense-perception part of the presentation has a simplifying and 'mental convenience' effect to offer the observer. The slide-whistle noise, for example, reinforces a concept of speed and rapid descent. The coyote-shape of the hole immediately persuades us that the coyote just made it (we don't have even to think about the material the canyon floor is made of). Similarly, we tend mentally to "convert" (by implication; it is not something we usually do "actively") the exaggeratedly long distance Wile E. fell — which should have broken his body into pieces, especially if he lands on material that can be cut-out in one bang into an exact coyote-shape — instead into *the "reason"* he manages to cut the coyote shape in the canyon floor.

The point of view shifts to looking straight down from above into Wile E.'s penetration of the solid earth, and we can barely see Mr. Wile, apparently way down. Point of view back to side angle at the canyon floor, and after an interlude, we have Wile E. raggedly, but miraculously, slopping himself out of the hole onto the ground above, and, after another short interval with a rising slide trombone accompaniment, the re-constituted coyote resumes the prior chase. Etcetera.

People of a certain young age, particularly boys, having seen screen depictions of unreal events, are sometimes wont to suppose they can do very unreal things in the real world, and they are ready to jump from canyon walls, or from the top floor of their apartment building in just their pajamas and a "Superman Cape." A minimum gain in maturity — as well as their survival — requires at least that they overcome suppositions of the kind and, in the great majority of cases, inspires a pretty deep appreciation for reality — exactly for being real — and as full a recognition that unreality is not real and never will be. The same kid who was jumping from the arms of the living room sofa, his arms outstretched forward, cape sailing behind, will usually, at a comparably young age, come to agree that it is "make pretend, and not really."

As people more fully mature, learned over a much longer period of time is a great deal more knowledge about many of the distinguishing properties and features of reality. That, for example, many of the things that happen occur at certain characteristic rates, the transitions and speeds of which are the effects and consequences of the thing happening. That many events and sets of event are cyclical; the moon waxes and wanes. That many things that happen have physical causal connection to others; that the gravitational force of the moon raises the ocean tides. Reality becomes not just different, across a dividing line, from unreality, there is an entire set of distinct kinds of relationships and distinct relationships which characterize it. The more true science we learn, the more we learn about these relationships and the more readily we observe them.

At the same time that we learn about the structure that attends physical reality, we learn about other realities and other structures. For example, we learn about purely abstract things such as logic and mathematics and representational structures in other symbolic systems, such as languages. We learn what might be called "meta-principles" about when and how abstract schemes apply and do not apply to realities. (We start to understand "systems." We classify them, not entirely unfairly, as, for just a crude example, "analog" or "digital." No classical physical object can be in two places at the same time, but — fascinatingly enough — there is a sense in which a quantum object can. The dynamic relationships between a physical thing and a copy of it are different from those between an informational thing and a copy of it. And so forth.)

This additional learning, not just about reality, but about modeling it and investigating it, including the use of working models to make further models, can lead us, in the better instances of it, to a maturity otherwise hard to achieve.

A certain aspect of 9/11 then, inherently asks us how we would collectively treat a certain variety of distinct intellectual *immaturity,* that consists not so much in liking, or being entertained by, or wanting, or fearing what is entirely more synthetic than actual, but in the strong (although usually unwitting) decision not to notice, not to regard, not to recognize the reality difference, especially in a particular, large, right "in your face" instance. This is a "decision" with respect to all of the "component contents" of which, planes, flying, buildings, collapses, dust, pile, etc. generally speaking, all of us are fully "conscious," but which almost all of us "decide about" essentially completely unconsciously. In which *un*-consciousness is our fundamental immaturity. In effect, we think about "everything *except* what we are doing" when we take on our belief in the "9/11 story." It is not that we don't think about "ourselves," we do that — it is that we are not aware of, and do not consider what we are doing, particularly when we choose, almost without considering or choosing at all, to believe.

This is a pattern of combined attention and indifference that is common, even to the extent of being frequently socially leveraged. Even at the societal level, the unmindfulness is more often exacerbated than alleviated. 9/11, like other stories (but arguably more so) plays for our close-to-complete lack of attention to features of distinguishing effect and that make for the consequential differences between things that are actual and not.

It may help also to take some note of a related proposition that is commonly held up as if it were fundamentally accurately descriptive, as if to ratify, again without due evaluation, a similar proposition about credence.

The Arthur C. Clarke adage to the effect that advanced technology is indistinguishable from magic is a very interesting proposition to think about and consider — but it isn't true. There is a very clear distinction in fact to be observed: technology relies upon actual properties of the actual (and physical) universe; magic, as magic, proposes effects that rely on dynamics that are imagined in and by the observer, and do not necessarily cohere with the properties of the actual universe. Although we can call physical phenomena we don't particularly understand "magical," if they are physical, they're not. If we assemble a battery and wires and a switch and light bulb and turn on the bulb with the switch, we can say doing so is "magical" — but really it isn't. The physics of electricity and conductivity, etc. models and — it is not an unfair word to use in the context — "explains" what is going on in a way that is in any event more coherent, systematic, reliable, and detailed than just saying the illumination of the bulb is "magic."

Saying that this distinction does not exist is unreasonable. There is no known scheme that can fairly be called a "technology" that does not cohere with physical reality or the dynamics of physical reality. In all "technologies" energy is conserved according to energy conservation principles, and so forth. In "magic" the phenomena, as experienced, do not cohere with real physical reality. They cohere with a scheme of mental and emotional "drama events." The lady, who we have first confirmed to be a flesh and blood being, is sawn in half without any loss of blood. Within the "magical" occurrence, of course, there is always a hidden actual physical set of events and sequence. The woman's lower body is tucked into an unseen compartment, and then a box-like structure that is in fact physically empty is cut in half. It may seem to us remarkable that radio waves propagate or that trillions of bits can be encoded in minute semiconductor devices within a plastic envelope of modest size, but atoms and molecules are stable as organized into state devices above the Planck size. That is a fact. It needs no illusion worked into our understanding that isn't true in the actual universe.

Then may come the question whether the distinction between technology and "magic," although it clearly exists and is not an uncertain difference, is what matters to us. Given what we are like as people, our "human nature," are we, on the whole, characteristically unable to recognize the difference, unable to appreciate the difference, unable to model conditions and events in a way that fairly distinguishes reality from supposition? Are we condemned to believe that we are observing real events when we are in fact "observing" events that are not real that are constructed by our imagination, including by means of inducements to particular imaginings provided to us by others?

It is not a completely simple question, because every act of perception is, in a certain sense, an act of "construction." In order to see "things," tables, chairs, books, we are, in every instance assembling the receipt of reflected photons onto our retinas into the things we perceive. There is no perception of any kind, by man or machine, that is not in some sense a creation, however mundane. Again, however, there is a substantive difference, that cannot be said not to exist, between a particular act of perceptual creation and another. The analysis isn't especially simple, and there may be no way to make it simple, but when informational contents represent some thing, informational or physical, there are particular ways to evaluate and characterize that representation as more accurate or less. Whether a certain model is "better" or "worse" in described conditions is not simply a subjective apprehension, it is a determinable circumstance. (Again, it isn't simple, and what it takes to evaluate or test a model is an involved subject, but the important point is that evaluation is by no means impossible.)

After we learn that reality and non-reality are genuinely and consequentially different, and we learn about modeling reality, and we learn about evaluating models. At the same time, we learn more sophisticated ways to distinguish reality from non-reality, and we learn how to use and manage the differences and distinction constructively. It is to generalize widely, but the education as to what reality is and is not and how to understand and live well with things real and unreal is basic to human maturity. Growing up may be a matter of loss and gain, but almost universally appreciated as we advance is the developed ability to overcome unnecessary and unhelpful confusions, particularly to know enough to avoid being "suckered" or defrauded.

In a very important sense, accepting 9/11 is thus also an enormous act of widespread extraordinary *cultural* immaturity. The hucksters have taken over, told us all a nonsense story, and rather than think about it at all, and rather than telling them that their tale isn't really very funny, or clever, or helpful, we've just "bought" the whole pile of stuff, Arab hijackers knocking down buildings, and all. With this "sale" to us, to the people of this country (and this world), 9/11 has created a lot of mistake and mess and failure.

Even more importantly, however, ours is also a collective immaturity quite unsuited to a country and a realm that, among other things, plays with powerful and dangerous toys (atomic weapons, hypersonic missiles, large computers, horizontally and vertically hyper-extended banking and financial structures, gene editing, an extensive satellite co-tenancy in the outer space around the planet, and logistics systems capable of moving large amounts of one part of the planet from one place to another.) 9/11 isn't just about 9/11. If it were, the argument could make some sense that we might just ignore our collective mistake about the real facts as an error probably better if not made, but now in the past. 9/11 is actually and rightfully more about very big issues, and only the less important matters have to do with Arab hijackers as such. 9/11, whatever answer we chose to make, or not, asks all of us whether we, the people, in fact have any responsibility for fraudulent and criminal acts which we collectively grossly misunderstand and misrepresent and to which we collectively act in assent. Do we get to be fools, now and forever, without any apology to ourselves and to each other for our foolishness? Or correction? Is this a nation of the people, by the people, and for the people, but in which the people can, at scale, act in complicity with fraud with every immunity and no responsibility?

Which in sum can tell us something about (another) form of typical failure in our educational system. Even to the extent of having students do "exercises" in discerning representations that depict possibly physically true events from those that do not, the education of consciousness regarding components, connections and context can do a lot to develop a society in which most people, anyway, are not deluded.

In the instance of many lies, it principally matters that the lie itself is not true. Of more consequence and importance with respect to other lies is the fact of the lie was told, by whom, and who believed it, why and to what effect. In many ways, the 9/11 lies are of the latter type. The most important things about them are that they are the way the government treated the nation, that a large majority of the nation subscribed to them, and that anyone who noticed the lies were untrue was completely shouted down and cast away by a howling media propaganda storm. The 9/11 lies have defined or re-defined the relationship between the government and nation for two decades, and forever, not so much regarding Muslims and terrorists, but regarding trust in the character, motives, decency and honesty of those having power, and in the uses of power. The underlying, but most important change "since 9/11," with respect to making war and the purpose of war, regarding surveillance, the civil and constitutional rights of citizens, the nature and measure of "security," and extent and scope of required adherence to central and governmental control, is that confidence in the acts of government in this country is at serious risk of being entirely misplaced. Whatever the truth of other political notions we put forth, it isn't too hard to propose that "deficits don't matter" (in substantial disregard of the eventual relation between credit and credibility), but it really takes a lot of thoughtless and harsh denial to propose that the fraud that is 9/11 doesn't matter.

Maturity of many kinds arrives as solipsism abates, as the human consciousness extends outward and recognizes how many other living things there are on this planet, how wide are the oceans on it and how wide the oceans of the universe in which our mere, tiny in the universal scheme, millions of miles of solar system turns. With all that is minute is much that is enormous. With all that is singular is all that is infinitely multiple and just plain infinite. The self in not the only thing that can be known, the word "known" being used in a worthy, relevant and meaningful way.

Karl Rove's proposition (that he wouldn't quite acknowledge to Ron Suskind, but which seems to have been fairly attributed) is not the first utterance of the sort. The idea that "we create our own reality" if meant to be a commentary upon the responsibility we have and should take in producing the results of what we do can be a usefully guiding maxim. As the altogether strong if implicit suggestion that we can substitute random inventions of ours, however meager, for the nature and truth of actual reality, the proposition is dangerously delusional.

Especially as used to create 9/11, the delusion is a long acting poison sprayed wholesale by media and "leaders" of a country who, despite all that we might have learned from our history, would propose that now is the time for the maximum disregard for reality and for a hazardously immature and most self-centered and disrespectful manufacture of false stories from arrogant premises.

It isn't. The sooner and more honestly we recognize that, the better off we will then be.

Five: Commissions, Courts and Trials, Agencies, Obligation and Accountability.

If there were thoughtful beings living on Mars, and a small group of those thoughtful beings visited The United States of America either in the period after the assassination of President Kennedy or in the period after 9/11, had the group of Martians enough time to gain even a summary understanding of available Earthling methods of inquiry, they would be nothing less than astonished that in either case the matter of ascertaining the facts was turned over, with the acquiescence of the nation, to a politically appointed Commission. They would be further amazed, no gobsmacked, that the Commission in each case was put fully in the control of government people the very least likely to be in any part honest in their work as Commissioners or Staff. If there is a word in English that yet better combines astonishment and being flabbergasted (maybe choking with disbelief), the observing visitors would apply it to witnessing Philip D. Zelikow, Staff Director for the 9/11 Commission construct the "public myth"[1] of 9/11, controlling the evidence before the Commission (suborning perjury), and creating the (broadly fraudulent) Commission Report.

Much of the astonishment would come from background awareness that we Earthlings have spent over two thousand years, slowly and painfully, but persistently, developing schemes by which conflicting claims regarding factual truth could be aired and reviewed, and the review be responsibly considered. These schemes include the cross-examination of witnesses in forums we may generally call "hearings" or "trials," qualified (peer) reviews of propositions about the physical world and physical events (loosely, the making of models that comprise "Science") or regarding mathematics or logic, and examinations in the nature of "auditing" (following a system of representation to confirm or disconfirm offered results) for examples. None of them are strictly perfect. On balance, however, the more attentive among us,

---

1. Zelikow's phrase from his college thesis and a 1998 article in the *Miller Center Report.*

and thoughtful visitors from other planets, would agree that any of these methods separately, and the uses of them as a group, enable us to ascertain truth more effectively than a propaganda "Report" produced by manipulative politics. Why, then, when it comes to making societal decisions about how we will treat a financial statement, or an individual violation of law, or the announced result of a science experiment, do we engage the schemes we have developed for checking and confirming truth (imperfect, but much better than mere hazard), and yet when thousands of people have been killed, when highly unlikely and unreasonable allegations and propositions about events are flooding the news, when proposals for "emergency" suspension of longstanding cornerstone legal principles, from international law regarding torture to constitutional law regarding search and seizure, are being insisted upon, do we put up a "Commission" with a manipulative and entirely over-controlling Staff Director (or "Executive Director") who (together with Ernest May)[2] will write a false narrative Report even before hearings are held and will orchestrate witness testimony according to the terms of the false narrative?

It is an embodiment of a view of our collective welfare as plainly irrational as if we committed to putting out any small campfire as an "all alarm" event, bringing out all the equipment in the Fire Department, while we meanwhile declare we will only deal with huge fires in the city by having a few drunks piss on the flames.

Among the foibles of our human nature is to be found our proclivity for being told things we want to hear, and without particular regard to reality or truth. "Lie to me, I promise I'll believe..." We can be forgiven, for example, to the extent we thus might get help being talked into becoming better versions of ourselves. As not-always-strong individual beings sometimes we find we have to "fake it until we make it." Nothing of the kind justifies turning the nation and our collective fate over to the 9/11 hoax, or to believing the biggest building freefall from office fires story or the myth of the hijackers who crash 225 seat passenger planes with no identifiable wreckage. There is not to be

---

2. Former professor (Harvard) when Zelikow a student and co-editor of a book about the "Kennedy Tapes"

made even the smallest part of a claim of "making" to it. It is all destruction — of people and buildings and the air being breathed — that only leads to destruction of the trust environment, of civil society, of human rights, of armies, of national credibility of purpose. Why, if we ever thought about it, would we want to succumb?

And not just capitulate, but capitulate without summoning such means as we have for living in a country that holds to some form of reality and reasonableness?

Twenty and more years after the 9/11 event no court in the United States (and none in the World) has held an actual evidentiary hearing in which the considerable physical evidence that the three tall buildings that rapidly collapsed in New York were brought down by demolition was presented, nor presented the considerable evidence about everything from the phony cell phone calls to the actual helicopter footage from September 11th, to a frame by frame analysis of the CGI "airplane impacts," to the impact of the light pole in the windshield of Lloyde England's otherwise spotless taxicab. Our court system went completely to politics, without any rational consideration of actual evidence.

Judge Alvin K. Hellerstein of the Federal District Court in the Southern District of New York, case managing, as judges do, and working closely with Kenneth R. Feinberg, Special Master of the Victims Compensation Fund, saw to it that each of the 96 cases brought by and on behalf of 9/11 victims was settled without trial or any other evidentiary hearing. Hellerstein also presided over other 9/11 lawsuits, and, for example, dismissed the Consolidated Edison action against 7 World Trade Center Co. L.P., Silverstein Development Corp. and Silverstein Properties Inc. saying "...the events that led to the tower's destruction were 'too farfetched and tenuous to sustain a claim of negligence'..." Hellerstein is further quoted by the publication *Business Insurance* explaining: "Con Edison, in order to succeed, must overcome the improbability of a long chain of events, one acting upon another," then adding that the utility would "need to demonstrate the predictability of the entire set of circumstances that caused the building's collapse, including the hijacking of aircraft, the strike on the twin towers and the probability of resulting fires spreading to the 7 World Trade tower." Recognizing that the so-described "entire set of circumstances" not only wasn't especially predictable, but did not in fact happen, and could not in physical fact have happened as described, and that the Towers were leveled by very intentional actions, appears to have been beyond the notably limited capacity of the Court.

A commonplace among lawyers has it that as the pleadings in a lawsuit are filed, the actual, plain truth of the matter "falls to the bottom of a bottomless pit." The nature of lawsuits considered, the gibe will always be apt. That said, the true facts are in different cases pushed downward to, and past, that bottomless bottom with different degrees of force, and to varying effect. Although our court system becomes involved in too many cases, our system also fails to hear cases that, for the well-being of our society, it should hear. Judge Hellerstein, who had very serious conflicts of interest which should have precluded him from any involvement of any kind in any 9/11 case, kept saying it was all and always about money anyway, and kept forcing money on the plaintiffs, while managing — rigorously — to avoid any form of analysis or disclosure. But there are no good substitutes for accurate analysis, and disclosure is sometimes worth much more to the well-being of society than money.

A worthy system of justice, having some strength in its structure, Hellerstein and his failure to remove himself from a large group of cases he should not have been sitting notwithstanding, at a minimum would have flushed the PNAC people, government event planners, Larry Silverstein, and those with them, out of their Osama bin Laden / "terrorism" cover. To think about it, perhaps a bit optimistically, is to imagine the cross-examination of witnesses who would claim that the building knocked itself straight down at nearly freefall speed by falling on itself. A transcript of that cross-examination, if done even half-capably, would have become required reading for every law student from now until forever. Similarly, no expert on airplane flight and aerodynamics could have sustained a claim that a Boeing 767-200 flew straight and level under control at sea level at five or six hundred miles per hour under further questioning, couldn't have cited to one example in which this had happened, even in all test flights, in any emergency conditions, ever, could not propose even to calculate, much less cite to actually measured lift, drag, and thrust values for the plane that would make the alleged flight conditions possible. No mechanical engineer could have sustained a claim that an aluminum wing section could have cut through big steel World Trade Center perimeter box columns, much less core columns, and no kinetics calculation could even come close to news media's Peter Jennings observation that the plane went "completely in one side and out the other…"[3] Even if a witness could take the stand and describe seeing video footage of one or two airplane parts being recovered from nearby sites, there remain the determinative problems of wrong type parts, no serial numbers, not matched to logs, and — where are the other many millions of parts?

Again, whatever else it does, 9/11 shows that, even as we overuse and abuse our legal system, we are missing some very important legal principles and features in our society. There are lots of cases that should not go to court, and lots of cases that should not go to trial. Courts are sometimes good about keeping those matters "…from consuming the resources of the judiciary." On the other hand, there are also certain cases that, provided reasonably capable people are working on them as lawyers and experts, should, no matter what, be tried with great diligence and thoroughness. Court trial in such matters is often the only practical way society can avoid the damage it sustains by giving over enormous prerogative, resources, money, and other valuable leverage and rights to bullshit, to fakery, to nonsense. Court trial can also provide an example to the other institutions of society that have less well developed, less responsible, rules regarding evidence, and fewer opportunities to ask questions of the claimant about a given claim, or to present facts a claimant has tried to shadow, until the inquirer agrees to rest.

Court trials are very far from perfect.[4] One can well imagine that if

3. "Watch how the aircraft penetrates the building … go ahead … completely in one side and out the other. … It just disappears like a bad special effect…" (Interview with Evan Fairbanks ABC News "Newswatch" September 11, 2001)
4. The example of the W.R. Grace case in Woburn, MA, discussed in

Judge Hellerstein sat a trial in which the 9/11 "planes" and the building collapses were at the center of the evidence to be presented, the government and government-associated parties would be winning motions in limine and motion after motion to the bench in mid-trial to prevent the provision even of simple answers to simple questions about blueprints and building construction and force and mass and velocity and debris piles and microspheres and human remains on the Deutsche Bank building rooftop and comminution and distance and time and maps and FAA, NTSB, and airline procedures, on the grounds of "privilege" and "national security" and who knows what else.

Nonetheless, many of the people of this country, including many of the people who took money and signed non-disclosure agreements (which those who received money are said to have done), having been told it was what they were going to get, in their heart of hearts know that the failure to bring the 9/11 matter to a public examination is another, not insubstantial, part of what is a national and public disgrace that no amount of war-making or flag-waving will amend.

Without in any way intending to force an unhelpful flood of new cases into the court system, I would strongly advocate that there be added to the Rules for our federal court system a form of motion by which the moving party would say that a dismissal [12(b)(6)] without trial in a particular case could only come from what would be, or be tantamount to, a fraudulent rendering of the nature of the central facts in the matter, and that such motions (hopefully very rarely required to be made) would be tried to a jury of impartial / disinterested experts in the relevant factual subject matter. In determination of the motion, the jury would be instructed that its result should not depend upon where the fraud had its origins. If it is the government that says the moon is made of green cheese or that the air in Lower Manhattan that is now full of asbestos is not harmful to health, it would not matter. The case would still go to trial. If the trial jury doesn't make an award, fine, but the testimony and evidenced adduced during the trial would stand as

---

the book *A Civil Action* is a story, among many, of basic failure in a court process, just as an observed example.

the public record. Again, it could be peppered with many more lies, but each one of those liars would have sworn to tell the truth and would have had the privilege of responding to inquiries by all of the parties in the case, limited only by reliability and relevance. Propaganda stories that run so mind-numbingly dramatic in the media, and often work altogether too well in legislative hearings, can sometimes sound a bit out of place in a courtroom, particularly under responsible cross-examination — and that can be a very fortunate thing. Therefore, let's give ourselves the chance to have a motion brought before an expert jury which, upon the jury's decision regarding the state of the alleged facts, can prevent dismissal without trial. Not to be overused, but to save us from ourselves when we need to.

The lack of any useful analytic proceeding is also impressive considered in the light of our often stated ideas about the basics of criminal law. We say that we have attorneys general and their offices, and that it must be they who prosecute crimes because, although the victims of crimes, the people who are stolen from or beaten up or murdered, are badly affected, crimes are more importantly offenses "against the community." And we say that by reason of the paramount community interest in prosecution we must have government maintained prosecutorial offices respond to any act of crime. (At core, the usual chronic government anxiety about having and exerting control arguably has as much as anything else to do with the systems that are established. Nonetheless, I and everyone I know would rather live in a society in which criminal acts are investigated and tried and met with reasonable sanctions, than in a society in which people clobber each other freehand.)

Whatever else can be said about the 9/11 events, acts of crime are basic to them. People and property were, with intent, mashed, murdered, turned to rubble, and otherwise injured by other people in the course of those events. A "nation of laws" however cannot, consistently with any of its principles, have the beholden news media tell false stories about the proposed perpetrators and what supposedly happened while it effectively suspends, forecloses and prohibits all other investigation, examination and inquiry into the acts of harm and those who in fact did those acts or otherwise caused them to be done.

Laws are imperfect and legal systems are very imperfect. Nevertheless, they are based upon ideas that are an improvement over fiat or mere thoughtlessness. Every fundamental notion that we have ever had, and every claim we have ever made about the nature and processes of criminal and civil justice in our country is contradicted, however, belied by the strange and total usurpation that 9/11 represents.

If 9/11 has taught us not to expect the judiciary to sustain once claimed principles, a comparably pervasive disappointment in foundational promises once made and the continuing fair expectations of the community is provided by Executive Branch agencies, particularly FEMA[5] and NIST.[6] Nothing turns the observer's stomach quite so distinctly painfully as watching and listening to video footage of S. Shyam Sunder of NIST at a "presser" as he introduces the World Trade Center 7 Study to the media and public, and says in explanation of the collapse "... anyone who has run a tight jar lid under the hot water to help loosen it up knows that metal expands when it gets hot." If we sit through a video of John L. Gross of NIST angrily denying that any significant explosions occurred in connection with the three large World Trade Center building collapses, only to be immediately followed by highly demonstrative screen testimony of one and another and another firefighter, and policeman, and building worker describing explosions, and footage of press reporters who experienced loud explosions and who say straight to the camera how large and loud the explosions were, we get a further unhappy sense of the insistence and scope of the "created reality" betrayal we have suffered from government agencies and their representatives.

The National Institute of Standards and Technology is responsible for certifying the validity and value of the most important encryption methods which secure, for example, digital banking, for doing foundational experiments in atomic physics, for the conduct of highly sophisticated measurements of distance, time, and other physical properties and parameters. Its job is most definitely not to say things

---

5. Federal Emergency Management Agency
6. National Institute of Standards and Technology

that are nonsense at the behest of corrupt political forces.

The extent of the overall fraud and the large number of "component sub-frauds" (lies within lies) engaged in and perpetrated by NIST considered, a reasonably full discussion that would cover even a sufficient sampling of them would take more than a whole book in and of itself. A sample of a small part of just one comment, and a quote from a NIST response to a FOIA request will have to serve as a sufficient enough example here:

> The **NIST** investigation of the World Trade Center 7 collapse is even worse than the Twin Towers. Not a single piece of steel was retained for analysis; not even the reported "vaporized" steel **FEMA** recommended additional analysis on. As a result, the **NIST** computer model for WTC 7 is 100 percent theoretical. Now, if this model behaved realistically and answered our questions, that would be one thing. But it's actually so bad that it's hard not to get physically upset when watching **NIST**'s WTC 7 collapse model. After a single failure, which happened with fireproofing fully intact and relatively little damage to the building, the entire interior of WTC 7 just flows apart like a waterfall. It's as if **NIST** forgot to insert all input data for the steel connections between the columns and floors throughout the building. The animation looks utterly disturbing and seems to make little sense. How can the entire core of the building fail while leaving the exterior fully intact? Unsurprisingly, when pressured with a **FOIA**, **NIST** blatantly refused to release the vast majority of its crucial files:

> *"We are, however, withholding 74,777 files (approximately 80% of all responsive records). The NIST Director determined that the release of these data might jeopardize public safety. This withheld data include remaining input and all results files of the ANSYS 16-story collapse initiation model ... all input and results files of the LS-DYNA 47 story global collapse model, and all spreadsheets and other supporting calculations used to develop floor connection failure modes and capacities."*[7]

NIST official S. Shyam Sunder carried on at length when promoting the NIST Building 7 Report about the "months" of "continuous"

---

7. *New WTC 7 Findings: NIST Manipulated Computer Input Data; Explosions and Extreme Heat Ignored; Key Videos Cut Short*, 911 Study Center, van der Reijden, Joel, (June 6, 2016, November 11, 2016)

computer processing on "fast linux computers" required to produce the Building 7 event simulation. Which, as noted by every attentive observer, does not in the least comport to the observed collapse event, but upon which NIST relied for its conclusions regarding the causes of the Building 7 collapse.

To say that a certain process produces a certain result is, in its substance, a claim of fact, that, like other claims of fact is subject to verification, or not, by objective analysis. In the case of computer programs and simulations, there exist in the (rather) abstract certain ultimate limits to the analysis,[8] and there can be a lot of work involved, but for the cases we have reason to be interested in, if we have the software in question and a clear claim as to what it is supposed to model, an effective and meaningful objective evaluation of that claim can be made. NIST, however, in its own words, in substance claims that a fair and honest evaluation from the actual computational information used "might jeopardize public safety" Baffling enough, one might suppose; if they "told us they'd have to kill us" — all. Obviously, rules and policies that fully and completely discount claims based upon an offered result of a completely obscured computer process are required.

If we can think of a reasonable rule that could be implemented, we should seriously consider adopting it. Ours is a world of too many rules, but it is more significantly a world of too many rules that directly facilitate the corruption of our institutions, that have the principle (and often singular) effect of giving place too secure to harmful and wrongful behavior.

Is there a way to have scientific standards and genuine good faith, rather than cheating, concealment and corruption, decide the nature and contents of NIST work product, not just some of it — all of it? Structurally, can we give the right amount of control (or power), to the right people in and associated with the NIST organization so that the motives to do honest science and valuable experiments and analyses, inherently quite strong in people who want to live a good life and

---

8. Having to do, for example, with what is often called "the halting problem" or "entscheidungsproblem" (decision problem) which concerns indeterminacy even in defined state machines.

have meaningful careers, effectively displace the schemes that led to the NIST Building 7 Report and the — there are no other words for it — vast amount of bullshit that NIST representatives put forth to the press and the public?

Because we have fairly good meta-societal methods for distinguishing statements and other information that relate "facts" from those that provide "opinions" we can do fairly well to protect NIST to every extent it says or writes true facts. We can also subject it to being corrected — by methods a bit more effective than are available at the moment — when NIST work-product misstates facts. Rather than have NIST bureaucrats accept or reject appeals regarding wrong claims of fact, we can have an appeals process referred to the community of capable people in our society who know the facts. For example, the physical properties of structural steel are very well known to a fairly large community of metallurgists and engineers. We don't have to wonder about the Young's modulus of a particular section drawn from a given alloy. It has been measured. It is known. It can be measured again with great care and accuracy. There are people among us who have acted scientifically and who know how and can be asked to act scientifically again.

An institution such as NIST does not serve the country unless it holds itself, and is held by the country, to an obligation to stick to the truth. Better not to have an institution such as NIST unless it is willing, in every instance, to refuse to lead to or produce results that are fraudulent. In turn, that obligation must be supported by an obligation to NIST that the rest of us undertake and honor to support it when it declines to engage in fraud.

Ours has become a country in which we need to say aloud and to each other that we are not going to do certain kinds of cheating. This is not to say that humans do not have certain basic impulses to lie, cheat, steal, beat up other people, and otherwise act very nasty. The issue is whether we will descend to lying, cheating and stealing for the sake of a relatively small group of people who have little regard for the rest of us and for the actual consequences of their scam. This while realizing that preventing or recovering from bad behavior is often not easy and not simple. No suggestion that wrongdoing could just be stopped, by fiat, is made here. However, every suggestion is made that the future well-being of this country and the world depends profoundly upon overall societal management of wrongdoing much more thoughtful than we are now accustomed to.

9/11, if it does anything, shows that the corruption is too close to the center and too tightly tied to the fundaments of our government and our institutions. Although most of us do not yet realize it, to recognize how wrong and stupid and damaging to the 'health – body and mind' of our country 9/11 has been and continues to be is the most important thing we can now do for the sake of our own, and our children's and grandchildren's futures and for the future of our nation — which is a lot closer to failure and "fall" than most of us understand or would recognize. Commitments to meaningless wars and an unreasonable excess of debt have been basic ingredients in the collapse of empires for millennia, and 9/11 is a kind of big "pin" that has been installed into our society to lever us into the messiest military involvements and to create fissures and ruptures in our financial system, diplomatic relationships, and national capabilities. Agreed, the average "millennial" who would like to buy a house can't figure out what has happened to make her jealous of others her age who have rich parents, rather than just a salary from work, and can't see what that has to do with being in a "post 9/11 world" — ever since 9/11.

Presidents and other officials act and say things as they do, as do all of the other mouthpieces of government, but now the next station-stop for all that's said are jokes on late night television about the relative supposed "truthiness" or not of any public statement. Which should tell us that, to every extent we have means to do better than merely churn nonsense when we speak, we will all be better off in dealing with serious subjects if we engage them with some form of honesty. False reports, one after another, whether by Commissions, Courts, or "Standards" agencies, in particular, have to become things of the past.

Six: Not Your Ordinary False-Flag Event.

And ."..not your father's Oldsmobile" either. Mocking tone, nevertheless it is worth taking the difference seriously. The "magical" disappearance of the Statue of Liberty mentioned, and the further developing and expanding regime-nouveau regarding facts and truth and "reality" observed, the Presidents whose speeches sum to the refutations provided by overtaxed, and never good enough at their job, "correctors" and "checkers" registered in our attention, it is yet worth considering further why 9/11, although it has its antecedents, is entirely in its own category.

The 9/11 presentation is also a dare to all the world. 9/11 does not just say "We can lie to you." Governments have long claimed the prerogative to lie. 9/11 does not just lie at the same time that plain evidence of the falsity of the lying is being constantly re-broadcast to the whole world, along with, and as part of, the propaganda messaging. Although not on this scale, plain falsities have been globally shared before, and the clear indication of fraud has before been included in the pronouncements made. 9/11 does not just lie about physical, mechanical facts. This is not the first time that simple mechanical, facts have been lost to wayward religion, cheap politics, or false patriotism before. 9/11 does not just work by instilling fear in a population. Implementation of policy by getting ordinary people to be irrationally scared has been a regular feature.

9/11 does all of these things with a defyingly absurd, enormous, hyper-aggressive — and yet flimsy — compound and extended self-righteousness. Absurd self-righteousness isn't new either, but the 9/11 version of it has been truly special. 9/11 tells the world that building demolitions that clearly and provably were done and could only have been done by demolition teams (who occupied space in the buildings and rigged them over a period of months) were the work of "airplane hijackers with box-cutters" and that therefore terrorists are...(we must suppose) hiding under every bed throughout the nation, from where they are ready to spring forth to commit uncontrollable acts of mass murder and mayhem (which are said can only be abated by global war, concentrated in the Middle East, yet more absurd in its "bomb them" / "drone them" military "strategies" than those practiced in Vietnam, and with conflict schemes even more gratuitously vicious, while ruinous and feckless, than were the Phoenix Program and the Provincial Internment Camps.

The thoughtful may even get a chance to wonder why, if very large building demolitions can be done with such simple facility, and the results can be so complete, turning a once very large, very strong structure into a thick layer of dust over miscellaneous chunks in and around the once footprint of the structure, does anybody ever bother with the usual process of hiring an expensive demolition contractor? Others, doing some thinking, but not having a full set of evaluative resources, may wonder, or speculate, what other structures are ready to crumble to bits in consequence of a small impact. Surely any house, or mansion, however grand, should turn to crumbs with a whack from something like a baseball bat. But that is a big — perhaps the biggest — part of the 9/11 idea: an op run by an angry guy who lives in a cave in Afghanistan takes over four of our large passenger planes at once with box-cutter blades, then "pilots" who briefly went to flight school and didn't do well in the smallest single engine prop planes are nonetheless flying these airliners at impossible airspeeds, pinpoint into and "through" buildings. Even the least capable entities with the least resources are astoundingly able to reduce our tallest buildings in the center of our largest city to dust and rubble.

The other least capable entities with which we are fully familiar aren't capable of doing any of the other things we regularly recognize they are incapable of. But 9/11 tells us that of course we shouldn't distract ourselves to consider whether societal inadequacies, matters regarding climate, or housing, or politics run by lobbyists and money, will be corrected by other least capable means, great big solid things we have built that stood tall can be leveled when attacked by — what is really just the image of — a bogeyman.

We must be very scared, therefore, scared enough to suspend thinking. Especially, we should radically change what we consider vulnerable and not. Our places of living, working, and travel are all ready to be taken to ruins, anyway. But our very expensive militarism "complex" typically leading to hapless outcomes, unaffected, shall intensify eternally.

And while we are emotionally distraught, and not reflecting clearly upon what has actually happened, and not examining and considering the evidence, 9/11 then says everybody should act as if nothing particularly special happened, so yes please, just keep shopping whilst we convert domestic society, upon "Patriot Act" and similar terms, to have full body imaging in the waiting lines at the airports and blind disregard for a made-mostly-invisible new heavily subsidized culture of financial wrongdoing, foolishness and excess.

As a core feature of which, we have one of the most astonishing, or amazing, or dumbfounding things about 9/11, that the building collapses were not just shown on public television, but given many repeat performances on the air, and even the repetitions contributed to having the world (with but a comparative handful of exceptions) more ardently believe complete nonsense, announcements that were not, and continued not to be, even partly true. Cognitive psychology lab studies have illustrated many facets of "confirmation bias," the (often strong) tendency to consider *any* evidence of any type, even if it in fact contradicts a person's beliefs (even if the evidence is very clear and unambiguous) as confirming the conceived truth of those beliefs. The effect is not shown only in the lab. For just one example, the reports from military units on the ground contradicting the claims made in Secretary Colin Powell's speech at the U.N. that Iraq was in possession of many weapon of mass destruction, were shown by several surveys to have been considered instead to have been confirmation of those claims by a significant segment of the American population. When it comes to 9/11, the extent of the effect is particularly spectacular, however. To a first approximation, *all* of the belief in the 9/11 story is the result of confirmation bias. There does not exist any root physical evidence that confirms the story in any way. The story is only proposed to be confirmed by telling of further versions of the story that the audience has been, by the story, earlier enjoined to believe.

Nor is there much of an argument that the population has, or in any way should have, its own separate interest of some kind in having and repeating and believing the 9/11 story, however untrue. It is not actually an especially "inspiring" tale, even if the Flight 93 "let's roll" drama is included and the encomiums about "heroes" in New York, firefighters who walked up seventy-five flights with equipment, only to be themselves pulverized in the demolition, are repeated. Even if some of us figure out how we might understand why some overwrought, but adapted, psychopaths in and around New York and Washington, who have political and economic power, wanted to get rid of some huge not-quite-commercially-successful real estate laden with asbestos — and do quite a few other seriously dirty tricks at the same time — ordinary people living in this country have no particularly good reason to enjoy or to support any part the story, including the part about "terrorists."

The public traction and overall national adaptation the 9/11 tale gained may be, as much as anything else, due to a phenomenon similar to the "What's the Matter with Kansas?" circumstance. People can be conditioned to accept notions that are very unworthy proxies, analogous to developing an addicted taste for cheap fats, sugary, salty non-foods, mono and diglyceride emulsifiers, artificial sweeteners. We people think a lot about ourselves, but almost always by and through notions, often not relevant or not true, almost always not actually our own notions, but brought to us more or less like "processed non-food, but sold as food items." Even if we think about ourselves a lot, we typically don't genuinely "think *for* ourselves" in the actual active "thinking" sense, for even a millisecond (even when we think we are thinking for ourselves).

Yet 9/11 isn't just about the regular displacements of societal attentions and formed identification, rooting for sports teams and the like, totem proxies such as flags and anthems, or even the popularity of inherently paradoxical slogans and concepts (only when also the last, least bit of us have our own small-arms guns can we say we are all "free"). The transference in the case of 9/11 doesn't just avoid "inconvenient" facts, it takes the palpable fiction, the nonsense, the absurd crap, and "converts it" (if one can say that) into exhibited, pseudo "(non) scientific proof." (The greatest known similarity to this conversion comes from the way proponents of the claim that the earth is flat take sciencey-sounding inventions about "refraction" and "electro-magnetism," that aren't even close to being supported by any experimental results, and use them to "prove" that the earth is a flat horizontal disc.)

This transference to the Muslim hijackers who are said to have taken over several passenger airplanes with box cutters and flew two of them, at impossible flight conditions, into and through very large, thick steel walls, setting fires that knocked down the three tall buildings in New York "works" remarkably, astonishingly well — at the same time it doesn't work at all.

Arnold Schwarzenegger can be voted into office as Governor of California, that's one thing, but this is more like everybody marking the ballot for *The Terminator* — because they "know" that cyborg is so much more *real.* And there are apparently so many other "important" voices in society, from Senators to "debunkers," forwarding, advancing, "confirming" how "real" the unreal is on the screen. Even while telling the population to "keep shopping," 9/11 goes completely "in your face — in everybody's face" and "metaphysically total" providing a full gamut of not-true (quasi) "postulations" ("Muslims," "they don't share our values," "learned this in flight school," "left a copy of the Koran in the rental car") in "support" of the definitely not-physically-true claims about events.

In fact the North Vietnamese did not attack the Maddox and the Turner Joy on the night of August 4th, 1964, but such an attack was not a rampant impossibility. The faraway Gulf of Tonkin lies off the coast of Vietnam. The North Vietnamese had torpedo boats in their (small) Navy, the American destroyers were on "patrol," the Americans were "stimulating" radar and other responses and mapping them with obvious purpose. The Tonkin military engagement that did not in fact occur, at least by some form of argument could possibly have happened.

The 9/11 story, in contrast, is a panoply of impossible nonsense. And, even more significantly, the fact that the story is completely untrue is repeatedly, obviously, in-your-face blatantly shown to the country and the world as and while the story is being told and re-told. Its very untruth, its fundamental and complete nonsense, is basic to what, in our society at large, "confirms" it.

9/11 isn't just a "false-flag" event or a "state crime against democracy." 9/11 is a "false everything" event. False terrorists, false hijackings, false impacts into buildings, false "merely gravitational" collapses due to office fires, false physics, false mechanics, false forensics, false reports about the air quality over "the Pile," false cell phone calls, false discovery of a non-matching jet engine section, false discovery of a hijacker's passport, false claims about no sound of explosions, false proposition about ground swallowing airplane in Shanksville, PA, false story about the light pole being "clipped" by plane and into the windshield of Lloyde England's taxicab, false story about what images from the Citgo station show, indeed many false ("photoshopped") still and moving images, false/premature reports of Building 7 collapse, false radar screen images at the NORAD facility in Rome, NY, conceded false accounts told by military representatives to the 9/11 Commission, false computer simulations created over months on "many fast Linux computers" by NIST... the list... endless.

As much as by anything else, the 9/11 story has maintained itself over more than two decades by the extraordinary collateral extent of its falsity. Even the "truth" groups that produce careful studies which accurately and extensively document and conclusively demonstrate that the building collapses occurred not due to "ordinary office fires" but due to demolition, twenty years later still talk about the "hijacked airplanes" and the "Arab terrorists" who purportedly flew planes "right through" the two Towers (yes, as described, such that three tall buildings fell). In fact there were Arab "terrorists" of a "sort" who were followed around the world and around the United States prior to September 11, 2001 by American intelligence agencies and by the Mossad, but they did not fly Boeings through buildings in New York, or in Washington, or bury one upside down in the ground in

Shanksville. And yet the "opposition" groups (if that is what they are) now in our society saying the 9/11 story can't be true regarding the building collapses and the alleged cause of them, still will talk about an event staged by Arab terrorists "who flew airplanes into buildings." Those who have thought to pay attention to the physics of collapse have been quite distracted from paying responsible attention to the physics of collision.

The 9/11 story reifies (doubled up) the maxim that for those who don't sufficiently appreciate one lie, the best thing to do is to provide another (and usually bigger) one (and, of course, still another one after that). 9/11 is also, and indeed, a state crime against democracy, yes, but actually against something larger and more important than democracy. It is a crime against civilized societal organization, against any requirement that government serve with fiduciary responsibility to the nation, against acting with faith, reasonably ethically, and on behalf of the people of the country. It subverts many founding and constitutional principles, comprises profound violations of oaths of high representative office (Vice-President, President, Congress included) and constitutes an extensive betrayal of the values and purpose of institutions intended to embody values requisite to the workings of an actual democracy (Law Courts, the National Institute of Standards and Technology, etc.). The nonsense is so much, and so widely and loudly spread, that one might as well call 9/11 a "state crime against reality."

The 9/11 events and story overflow with paradoxes, but the inversion by which the volume and extent of untruth apparently combine to cause the story to be believed rather than recognized as fraud deserves our attention. It is just guessing, but suppose there were no "Muslim hijackers with boxcutters" part of the story. Let's think about a story instead that says an ordinary airline pilot made a mistake, or a number of mistakes, and flew into the side of just one of the World Trade Center Towers. For the moment, let's keep the parts of the story that say the plane flew through the building, and the building similarly collapsed top down, ejecting matter out the sides, into piles of dust and fragments, after an hour from office fires.

Quite possibly, the NTSB would have to actually investigate the crash, in theory more or less as the NTSB ordinarily does. Although the Transportation Safety Board has been very wrong in a thankfully very small number of other cases,[1] more often than not they do responsible forensics, issue a preliminary report, and then a final report with a probable cause finding and a reasonably worked out and credible account of the actual event sequence. Considering also the number of cases in which accident investigators all over the world (including from high speed midair collisions and explosions) have accurately and carefully inventoried, examined, validated and reassembled wreckage, we might suppose that had the NTSB investigated the alleged airplane crashes at the World Trade Center, or in Shanksville, or the Pentagon, there is at least an even chance they would have had to admit they couldn't find any of the wreckage of the plane, and in fact had none of the serial numbered parts verifiable by reference to the logs.

Similarly, we can make not unreasonable surmises about what might have had to happen if there were no "airplane impacts" and instead the story was that office fires started in the upper floors of both World Trade Center Towers one September morning, and that a little less than an hour later, in the one case, and in about an hour and fifty minutes in the other, each building, huge sections of grillages and box columns ejected our sideways, and in a dust "avalanche" that blanketed all of Lower Manhattan and the Hudson River all the way across to New Jersey, fell straight down into a pile of rubble. The NIST report, and Shayam Sunder at the press conference, said that the supposed jet fuel burned away, mostly outside the building, and that the precipitating cause of the collapse was "office fires." So, take the same office fires and the same, straight down, rapid, collapse. Leave

---

1. For an example, the demise of TWA flight 800, which went down in Long Island Sound, from the bottom of which substantially all of the plane was recovered and reconstructed in a hangar at the former Grumman Aircraft facility in Calverton, NY, was falsely attributed to an errant spark in the empty center fuel tank. Some tampering with the reconstructed plane in the hangar at the small hours of the morning occurred, more likely by FBI people than NTSB officials. Relatively minor tampering notwithstanding, the evidence in the case shows clearly that the plane was in fact shot down by a missile. That said, much more often than not, the NTSB has done honest forensic work and produced real and factual accounts of airplane crashes.

both the terrorists and the planes out of it.

This, thus, more or less, reproduces the situation of Building 7. But if Building 7 is any guide, we know what happens; the most bogus of bogus reports gets written and, more or less, "defended" by officials. Yet let's suppose that there were in the story, in effect, three Building 7s in New York in one day. After what they have done, we could say that NIST can, and will, do anything, no matter how false, irresponsible or unreasonable. Yet to suppose that NIST could have made false claims for three of their reports for one September morning might actually be a stretch, even for them.

Similarly, it would be interesting to know how many Americans would readily believe an account of a long (say 30 minute) cell phone call from a Boeing at 40,000 feet in the middle of the country in 2001, with no story about hijacking or Muslims with boxcutters attached to it. Suppose a court trial were in progress. An opposing witness takes the stand and is asked where she was at a particular time on a particular day. She answers, let's say, that she was sitting on a bench in the town square in some town in New Jersey. And she is asked what she was doing there at the time. Let's suppose she answers: "I was just talking to my friend Oscar. He was on his cell phone on a United Airlines flight from New York to LA, over Western Pennsylvania and Ohio. We talked for half an hour. He said the weather was clear and the view from 40,000 feet was great." That gets no cross-examination from anybody? And no witness then gets called to the stand who actually knows something about cellular telephony? And the proponent gets to use it as un-contradicted evidence of fact in the case as to where the witness was and what she was doing and where Oscar was and what he was doing? Possible — maybe. Lawyers, even when we call them "smart" can sometimes be very dumb. Nevertheless, when lies of the kind involve matters of consequence they are often scrutinized and, with some frequency, shown to be false.

Perhaps examples that have to do with technology that everyone uses and very few people think about or understand reach only to a collective difficulty recognizing what entails what else that too much extends all around and beyond 9/11 to be helpful in understanding and thinking about the 9/11 story. For just one further thought of this kind, however, we might nonetheless consider some of the very many 9/11 failures of systems, descriptions of which are bound in to the 9/11 story. The failures of things, people, organizations and institutions are so many that I am just going to make an admittedly much less than full list, and then consider what we might reasonably have expected from ourselves in response to these failures.

Failures then:

-- Flight data recorders and cockpit voice recorders are said to have failed to survive, to be recovered, or to have the information recovered according to the recorder "registration" at a rate never before experienced, causing many of the recorders to be reported as lost, data to be reported as lost, and data to be reported as "recovered" without any part of the ordinary verification of genuineness. Data recorders are designed and built with much consideration given to their endurance, and there are specific measures implemented meant to ensure the verity of extracted data. ("The storage medium of each recorder is located in a protective capsule, which must be able to withstand an impact of 3,400 Gs (3,400 times the force of gravity). Additionally, each must also survive flames at 2,000 F for up to 30 minutes, and submersion in 20,000 feet of saltwater for 30 days. Typically, to increase their chances of survival, the recorders are located in the tail section of the aircraft, which usually sustains the least impact in a crash.")

-- The radar and other similar information coming to NORAD in Rome, New York was very inaccurate. For example, none of the alleged subject planes are said to have squawked the 7500 hijack code, yet personnel later stated that, during a period of time on September 11, 2001, they were "working 29 separate hijackings." Put plainly, if the various information about what was in the air that was displayed in the NORAD Rome, NY "cab" on September 11th is in any way characteristic of the capabilities of the systems in use or the information regularly displayed, the facility cannot, and should not, be called an "air defense" facility

-- The fighter plane interceptor response, if it could have

accomplished anything, nonetheless notably failed. The supposed Flight 11 (American Airlines "hijack") refused to follow Air Traffic Control instructions and deviated from course at 8:14 a.m. turning off its transponder at 8:21. "Panta 45 and 46" (fighter aircraft) from Otis Air National Guard (Air Force) Base were "scrambled" at 8:46 am, and apparently actually arrived over Manhattan at about the time of the second Tower collapse. (10:28 a.m.). The recognized standard for alert response is less than "five minutes." An F-15 can fly at about a thousand miles per hour, and it is on the order of 150 air miles from Otis to New York City. "In January 1999, the 1st Air Force air sovereignty team, which, as part of NORAD, is responsible for the air defense of the continental United States, scored an unprecedented "grand slam" in an evaluation of its effectiveness. The three air defense sectors responsible for protecting U.S. airspace had their command and control skills tested in the Air Combat Command Operational Readiness Inspections (ORI). All were rated "outstanding," which was the highest score possible on a five-tier scale. Brigadier General Kenneth Stromquist Jr., the 1st Air Force vice-commander, commented: "There's never been a grand slam [before] in the history of this outfit."[2]

Two fighters from Langley Air Force Base, similarly, appear to have flown out to the east (out over the Atlantic Ocean) for an unreasonably long time before turning back toward Washington supposedly due to mission control confusion.

-- At least six air traffic controllers who dealt with two of the "hijacked" airliners on Sept. 11, 2001, made a tape recording a few hours later carefully describing the communications events that had occurred, but the tape was destroyed by a supervisor without anyone making a transcript or even listening to it.[3] This is one small example of a very large number of significant failures to preserve substantive evidence in several forms regarding actual 9/11 events.

-- Similarly, anything like proper site forensic work appears to

---

2. "Outstanding: CONR Sectors Receive Highest Inspection Ratings." *American Defender*, 3/1999.

3. ... "the Transportation Department said Thursday." *N Y Times, May 7, 2004*

have been deliberately failed to be done at any of the 9/11 sites. The excuse, for instance, in New York, that some part of the debris was in the streets and partially blocking them is nothing like a sufficient reason to have failed to set up a site survey grid, failure to do forensic documentation of locations, failure to do anything like responsible forensic photographic documentation, failure to measure parameters such as temperature or composition or volumes (for example, of the molten metal under and within the site that was reported and can be seen in videos), failure to select and test a reasonable set of rubble material samples, and when samples were collected and they clearly showed the use of thermites, failure to examine for, and to examine, cut profiles confirming thermite use and enabling further forensic determination of the effects thereof. Similar failures at the other 9/11 sites include similar failures to conduct reasonable forensic analysis, including neglecting to do actual careful examination of the debris, to rationally describe why plane debris fell into Indian Lake outside of Shanksville, miles from the alleged Flight 93 crash site, or to reasonably determine why there were no bodies and no blood, nothing having to do with a human body, at the 93 site, or why the alleged Flight 93 data recorded (carried in the tail of an airplane) could have been allegedly found 15 feet underground while a supposed engine had rolled a thousand feet over the ground and into the woods – all from a supposed nose-first impact.)

Another way, simplistic, metaphorical, crude, but which may help just by images to begin to think about 9/11 would be to consider as pattern a story line in which a guy with something of a simian profile stands somewhere in the middle of a roomful of ten thousand people near where a miscellaneous but suspect, bonfire burns a poster of Uncle Sam's hat. Incidental arsonists, casually messing around with their nearby handy supplies of gasoline and C4 also turn the building and its contents, including bearer bonds and unique documents and records, to splinters and cinders, as well as shorten the lives of, and cremate, some of the crowd who were unlucky enough to be at the fire site and couldn't get out of the way. Then a "bullhorn sermon" is preached to / yelled at / ranted before the crowd to the effect that *jungle monkeys* ignited the terrible conflagration (Uncle Sam's Hat, building, bodies — the whole mess) just witnessed. In the peroration, shouted in the echoing sound and with a video show that covers the entire walls and ceiling of the venue, the "delivered" voice announces that all present must cut off their right arm, then grab that bony bleeding mess in their left arm and immediately run off (into the jungle) to use this configuration of their limbs to beat to death any and all monkeys they can find (while also soberly noting how important it would also be for other parts of society to make sure not to interrupt their game of cribbage, nor lose position of any of the pegs in the board) ... and, even more impressively, nine thousand nine hundred ninety of that audience become overpoweringly excited, shouting "Yaaay! Revenge!" salute vigorously (left arm, we can suppose) and stampeded to go slaughter monkeys, bloody messes of arm in arms raised high.

Not to make light of it, but on September 11, 2001, somehow the American nation, and the world, lost the last vestiges of its collective ability to discern regarding reasonableness and ridiculousness; the 9/11 presentation and story, and the "Response to 9/11," so-called, are that much "displaced" or "offset," and make just about that much sense.

Except emotionally to millions Americans, and, more or less, billions of other apparently acquiescent people in the World. Indeed, that is altogether-too-significantly what the perpetrators of 9/11 accomplished. Entirely basic to the displacement achieved, for something that is readily capable of rational, forensic analysis, has been to forestall, prevent, suspend, and, by a huge, multi-layered, multiply self-referent, multiply amplificatory, media propaganda blitz effectively prohibit any form of rational evaluation, and a shockingly remarkable degree of emotional adherence and political leverage exactly for doing so. 9/11, thus recognized, is comparable to a government and media declaration that Earth is really flat — like a pancake — which is made into a primary article of adherence, compliance, allegiance and citizenship (and the grounds for inciting armed conflict with the moon) not permitted to be contradicted by the truth of obviously applicable scientific principles in any way, and all of this is enforced and reinforced by censorship, name-calling, ostracism, false and piled on "debunkings," extreme universal worry about falling off the "edge" of said flat earth, and, in the case of the 9/11 event itself, contextually encircled also, of course, by a considerable number of miserable murders.

As thoughtful, rational, and considerate as may be the works of Mill and Locke and other seventeenth and eighteenth century progenitors of our civilization, as much as those thinkers and authors may have tried to consider deeply the psychological frailties in the population for which they sought to develop principles of knowledge, beneficial government, and enlightened society, the (relatively few) suggestions they made for overcoming collectively destructive primitivism seem to have been, at best, much too limited. 9/11 has again shown us that a society that had once progressed by discovering and respecting truth in a somewhat organized way can quickly become overwhelmed by an insanely ferocious attachment to fraud.

This said, the fact that the perpetrators of 9/11 were so much "emotionally on" in what they accomplished with their scam and the presentation of it is also the reason that the future of the United States of America as a worthy nation depends upon the substantial repudiation of 9/11 and of the people who orchestrated and conducted it. We will have righted the boat in which our society and nation sail when anyone you meet on the street says "9/11 ... yes, big fake by big government — unfortunately it confused us; we did a lot that was wrong and harmful to ourselves and others. But we are no longer the same country that believed that story. We will never again be overcome because a scheme compiles one falsehood with another and another."

Otherwise, there is no limit to the wrongful exploitation and expropriation of our country.

Our culture has for too long told us that punishment (of someone) uniquely and sufficiently answers wrongdoing. Especially in this instance of multiple fraudulence, punishment is not at all most important. Exposing and declaring the fakery and the shame that those who brought us 9/11 should bear, and resolving that our future comes not in frauds, however, is ultimately valuable to the country. Especially in response to those who would say that governments and nations are "entitled to do whatever they can get away with doing,"renunciation of things they have done and said, (even though now decades ago), is by far the best possible present course, and even though any repudiation may not be readily understood or accepted by the perpetrators or their allies or fellow travelers.

From time to time we say (in John Adams' phrase – as borrowed from others) that we are "a nation of laws, not men."[4] Especially now, it is as important that we be a nation of verity and knowledge, and not of unreality and frenzy. There are far too many serious matters that we as a nation must deal with. The 9/11 event and the 9/11 story are ridiculous. While deadly, also risible. And yet, in the end, the situation created and maintained is serious. The most salient "problem" with 9/11 is the particular and peculiar way that 9/11 makes responsible cross-examination of Richard B. Cheney out of reach and impossible. That is the "displacement" created from the use of the fraud itself and the repetition of it, using a lie to "support" another lie, connected to another lie, and putting it so much "in our faces" as "proof" at work again. That displacement thus is at the core of what is truly dangerous. The nation as a whole, and the world, was specifically (further) "trained not to think" at the same time it was told the 9/11 story, in the instance that "training" became a secure prohibition against science, rationality, and physically certain facts. Over the ensuing decades, that training has become a hydra of (sometimes seemingly unrelated, but with relation that can be recognized and understood) features of our lives, a (further) fulsome stream of bombast and nonsense, "things you can't say" rules, "cancel culture," many military proposals, including for "artificially intelligent" weapons, in order to move trigger pulling decisions back from the field to "policy" (false "reality") makers, and so on.

Not to over-state the matter, 9/11 really is different. Many false flag events have taken place in history. The Greek "Trojan Horse"

---

4. Cf. Massachusetts Constitution, Article XXX .".. to the end it may be a government of laws and not of men."

episode takes place as a false flag event (or perhaps a "misrepresented gift event" — but the idea of presentation of a deceiving identity is there). As long as deception works, as long as victims and their allies will blame countries or groups other than the actual perpetrators for the bombings, murders, and the like, false flag events will continue to be staged, particularly by countries that have particular national beliefs as to their own entitlement and national disdain or disregard for other nations or peoples. (In a world of a high degree of technological amplification and elaborate weaponry, from drones to micro drones to kill darts to hypersonic missiles to atomic weapons, however, the consequences of unconsidered "intensity" of provocation has to be a matter of national and international concern, especially in conditions of displacement.)

Anyone paying attention has to recognize that 9/11, considered with the benefit of two decades of hindsight, turned out not so badly in certain very narrow terms (certainly not as badly as it could have), and yet has turned out very badly when broadly considered. Those of us who notice some of the below-the-fold items in the news keep in our grateful prayers thoughts of appreciation that General Curtis LeMay did not get to drop nuclear bombs on Cuba, and appreciation that the apparently ordered nuclear bombing of Cairo, Egypt by planes from the Sixth Fleet on June 8, 1967 was called back reportedly three minutes before bomb drops. To these we can add appreciation that 9/11 did not precipitate much larger and more sudden economic failure and thankfulness for some of the accommodating choices made by adverse foreign interests not to exploit 9/11.

9/11 is singular among false flag attacks because we (a very small, but empowered, group of "us") did it to ourselves (with some help) — but not for that reason only. As with the Kennedy assassination, we have to lie a very great deal, and tell lies about the lies, even more after the event, in order to propose to maintain a myth once central to our sense of our identity. (A "democracy" is not a democracy when the secret intelligence apparatus assassinates the President. A responsible government is only crushingly irresponsible when it attacks its own buildings and people in its largest city.) A nation does not live by the "rule of law" when "terrorist" crimes are the murders and frauds of an entangled set of hoax events suborned by government. 9/11 forces many millions of people who otherwise have no reason to want to repeat nonsense stories about collapsing buildings and airplane "hi-jackings" and drama cell phone calls and crash sites without actual crash remains to "believe," and to believe the "whole package" of the lying, and the follow-on lies, because the alternative involves also recognizing a very great (even greater) deceit, because the alternative is threatening to others in ways that make those others threaten, because the extent of the lies has become a network that responds with excess penalty to actual reality, and because even in a world with many resources, the game isn't being played for truth (no one trusts truth for any value), but for the aggregation of resources and leverage.

With respect to false flag events, noted, mis-attribution is what the "false" part of the committed violence is about. Not uncommonly, however, especially after the event, there is widespread factual recognition as to who in fact did the attack. The world knew, even at the time, who had shelled the village of Mainila. Most of the Israeli / Mossad operations during the twentieth century are, by most aware people and institutions, accurately attributed. 9/11, however, is about trying to force forever-continued mis-attribution, compelling, by every assorted propaganda and other bullying means, the most non-credible fraud story to be permanently treated as truth.

Moreover, in the instance of most false attacks, a single "provoked" response will do (although the prospect of dropping nuclear bombs on Cairo gets a prize for being singular). 9/11, by its terms, intends to become a longer-term war policy and national policy, both to institute "War on Terror" politics in what is suddenly being called "The Homeland" and to turn a region (and more) of the world, already known for conflict, into a generalized war zone. Even more dangerously does 9/11 become a, eternal "created truth" policy. In order to do all that, the fraud needs to be, and gets, amplified, even to the point to which saying things that are not true and bullying insistence upon them becomes an unlimitedly generalized practice, even in much public discourse. Similarly, military acts and theatrics achieve a newfound

merger and we have, for instance, the "Osama bin Laden" in Abbottabad event. Many of the profound economic effects are latent, and have
yet to become manifest. The extent to which they will is not certain,
but it is very unlikely none will occur.

If 9/11 were just a false flag event, knowing we will not bring
the dead back to life we could with some reason let it become a past
mistake. Our attention could focus just on doing better — as we can.
9/11, as intended by those who did it, has become too official, has
become too much integrated into our political ideas, our government,
our practices, or requirements, our habits. The "terrorist, terrorist,
terrorist" sing-song isn't now heard as often, but the truly damaging
propositions about irrational response, false investigations, failed forensics, lying, secrecy, and suppression have now become our confirmed creed.

Seven: Facts and Apparent Majority.

A story, perhaps apocryphal, has Adlai Stevenson, running for President, told by an encouraging supporter that "every thinking person will vote for you." Stevenson is said to have replied, thank you, but the offer is "...not enough — I will need a majority." Stevenson was a politician, sensible of the wiles of political behavior and events, quite capable of later delivering the "... don't wait for the translation ... yes or no... I am prepared to wait for an answer until Hell freezes over, if that is your decision. I am also prepared to present the evidence in this room..." speech to Soviet Ambassador Zorin and the U.N. General Assembly during the Cuban Missile Crisis of October, 1962 next holding up enlarged photographs of launchers — an interesting historical example of bullying in a time of predicament that, in the event, proved helpful and useful. (Arguably to both countries, and to the world. Worth carefully contrasting to Colin Powell's 2003 presentation. Noted, Stevenson's words had the benefit of truth as to the facts.)

The results of Stevenson's presidential campaigns indeed bore the practical results of open-handed thinking while Dwight Eisenhower gave the voting public more proposed comfort, satisfaction with itself, and simple reassurance — even in a world building large atomic arsenals, and in which Cold Warring led us to invasions principally destructive, stalemate in Korea and later failure in Vietnam, and on to riots and assassinations to emphasize our national discomposure. Thinking, clarity of thought, and consciousness regarding national conduct and purpose did our country well when Abraham Lincoln was President, turbulent and nasty time though it was, and often not badly during the also often complicated and challenging presidency of Franklin Roosevelt, but it is hard to say that thinking in good faith on behalf of the country has made a significant contribution to a rise to political success since. Along with Stevenson's losses may be observed the political defeats of many instances and examples of decent thinking — and sanity — in the decades since, from the conduct of the

House Un-American Activities Committee in the 1950s to the repeal of Glass-Steagal and related banking regulation in the 1990's.

Together with an extensive and extensively servile media, Karl Rove and the administration he was part of did "create their own reality" — which while doing, somewhat more particularly, produced the "exhibition," the "show" in New York, NY, Arlington, VA, Shanksville, PA, and, most importantly, on national television, a show that was presented as "news" full with urging that it was all "real" and crucial. Societies, to an extent even greater than individual people, do not relinquish the hold of falsity and fraud easily and gracefully. Once a society has been generally bamboozled into a non-scientific, non-rational account, the change from the false story to the facts is perceived as impossibly contrary, profoundly burdensome and as fearsome unwelcome as torture.

But there are three hundred twenty-five million people in this country. Even if only one tenth of one percent of us are people well enough educated to know and apply the principles of mechanical motion articulated by Newton three hundred thirty-four years ago, that would nonetheless be three hundred twenty-five thousand people who have every reason to know for themselves and explain to others that the 9/11 story told by the media and government is a nonsense tale. That is also approximately the number of full-time, active full and associate professors at accredited institutions (among over one and a half million college and university teaching faculty members and over four million United States citizens who hold PhDs). Notwithstanding the observation attributed to P.T. Barnum that "You can fool most of the people most of the time" (and W. C. Fields' addendum "…and that's enough to make a living") in the face of claims that are obviously wrong as a matter of physical mechanics, some percentage of the audience, however small, has the "mental equipment" and has a good chance of knowing, with great certainty, that the story that has been told is nothing like in fact true. As to physical science as such, majority votes don't (and shouldn't) count; only confirmations of stated principles by correctly conducted and understood experiments qualify. Physical scientific reality does not in any way come from the illusions of, however many, people; it can only come from the honest and accurate development and application of scientific knowledge.

In a nation of three hundred twenty-five million that does lots of mechanical engineering and makes millions of mechanical contraptions, including machines of hundreds of thousands of kinds, including automobiles (there are about 280 million motor vehicles registered in the United States, about 17 million new cars put on the road annually, and about 9 million of those are made in the U.S. — they have collisions subject to Newtonian mechanics) and rockets delivering satellites to space, and in which lots of analysis of mechanical performance is undertaken in professional journals and in popular magazines and failures and collisions and other accidents are investigated and reported on it is passing unlikely that, although to many people any mechanical object exists only to be declared confusing and incomprehensible, there would not be not at least some part of the population that can think about the 9/11 story clearly and scientifically enough to realize how little of it is the least bit true.

Taking Isaac Newton himself as example or prototype of sorts, in matters of physical science, in which theory is proved by honestly conducted experiment, if but one person publishes a true set of principles the entire rest of the world can verify the generality and correctness of those principles, testing them to the fullest extent measuring techniques and technologies allow, and can thereafter know the mechanical facts of all of the very many events to which the principles apply.

Although it may seem an utterly naïve question when asked, it is worth asking: Why, then, should our entire nation (and the world) continuously, since September, 2001, spout nonsense and more nonsense about physical, mechanical events? The science involved is simple, and certain, and very well proved through hundreds of years and a very large number of tests and examples, all of them confirming the science. Why should our nation, and the world, tell and believe all the lies?

The reflexive answers are many. Social memes are so much more important to social beings than science or scientific truth. Membership has practical value in excess of the costs of personal adherence to a story told, facts notwithstanding. "Created" reality has all of the benefits of control and sponsorship in its "creation" and none of the hazards and detriments of being real. Status matters; truth can thus only matter to the (subordinate) extent it might confirm status. Science is a recent and "thin" proposal about the world compared to the strong and deep primitives of the human psyche. One of the greatest "displays" having paramount societal effect, and for establishing rank, and place in a power structure, is an exhibited show of superiority over facts, and an apparent "practical" ability to change, to manipulate and manage, features otherwise understood as facts. Something similar can be said about "limits and limitations." Humans cede or award power to displays that show actors and actions, whether merely conceived or actual, that do something that was before considered unlikely or impossible. "Superheroes" are revered because "they do what can't be done." Such figures ('figurations" we might call them) almost automatically are immediately upon receipt mentally and emotionally insulated from testing with respect to known basic properties of the world and universe. Overall, most of the time, in most of our lives, truth is well down on the list of our interests.

Rove-style "created reality" has come to mean that described "majorities" are "major" in an entirely different sense than referring to actual greater numbers of people who give genuine political support to actually representative candidates. "Majority," from at least the time that Nixon used the term "moral majority" in the 1970s has come to refer to a rather abstract concept of persuasion in effect. Reference to "majority" in practice at present is to a state in which belief and opinion have come under control. "Majority" is no longer about numbers or counting, it is about a condition or state that might as well be called "fenced in," similar to the way cows are kept in post and wire enclosures. Put even more crudely, the current meaning of the suggestion that "we" (for some social or political group) have a "majority" in "support" now actually means something closer to the proposition that "we can get away with saying such and such if we think it serves our interests." Or, even more crudely, a "majority" proposition is a statement, however false or fraudulent, that the organized society has the resources to repeat and reinforce and any opponents do not have the facilities, institutions, or resources to analyze or understand or correct. Examples of instances in which politics and political figures have told lies about simple scientific and physical facts in such conditions are many, not few.

This, even as "majority" of any kind or not is not an especially valid matter, not really an intrinsically relevant question. The 9/11 story has at its center a set of lies about which there are not possibly divergent true versions or opinions. F equals ma. F does not equal something else, m times a over two, or m times a times h, etc.. Without application of a force the velocity of a mechanical object does not change, etc. 9/11 has also frequently been veritably said to be at the center of our national and political world in our time. Mechanics being certain in its relationships, the propositions at variance tell us only about our politics and culture.

Rove's "created reality" is but a modulation on what is now a longer-running and larger theme. For some years now, the United States of America has led the world in the conduct of animated broad opposition to plain facts and the suppression of cognizance regarding actual reality among great majorities of people, almost all of us increasingly effectively addicted to "info-stuff" – a synthetic replacement for actual, relevant, true information.

It is hard to know quite what else to call it. It isn't just "propaganda," at least not in the traditional sense. It bears a resemblance, for example, to what the East German government told its people that wasn't true as that country compounded its miscarriages and the invasions against its own people into a general failure of the nation. But American "info-stuff" of the last half-century is not just delivered by "the government" or not just "official;" it comes from what seems to be every place and portal; it is more "fueled" than it is "controlled" (as in "controlled media"); it is hyper-output, delivered as by a very large hose; it talks fast in order to connect to the parts of the receiving mind that operate more quickly and responsively than thought; it is repetitious and repeated, drummed; it "beats" and is "beaten into" the country and the world; it is programming of the scene and of the recall, of the computer and the user, of the words and of their meanings, formulations and conclusions, complex extent and synoptic reduction, that arrives with a relentless insistence — and near zero actual self-respect.

I would offer four instances and examples of brief descriptions that four well-known, sane, thoughtful people have provided that, in a certain sense "triangulate" to explain parts, each different, of what I am for want of a better, more generic term, calling "info-stuff," information that, however "extensive," isn't true, "information" that isn't even meant to be genuinely informative, or is put out to be noise, information that is really just pushed out "stuff."

First, from the September 1964 issue of M.S. Arnoni's *The Minority of One*, a piece by Bertrand Russell, British Philosopher, Logician, Mathematician:

> The official version of the assassination of President Kennedy has been so riddled with contradictions that it has been abandoned and rewritten no less than three times. Blatant fabrications have received very widespread coverage by the mass media, but denials of these same lies have gone unpublished. Photographs, evidence and affidavits have been doctored out of recognition. Some of the most important aspects of the case against Lee Harvey Oswald have been completely blacked out. Meanwhile, the F.B.I., the police and the Secret Service have tried to silence key witnesses or instruct them what evidence to give. Others involved have disappeared or died in extraordinary circumstances.
>
> It is facts such as these that demand attention, and which the Warren Commission should have regarded as vital. Although I am writing before the publication of the Warren Commission's report, leaks to the press have made much of its contents predictable. Because of the high office of its members and the fact of its establishment by President Johnson, the Commission has been widely regarded as a body of holy men appointed to pronounce the truth. An impartial examination of the composition and conduct of

the Commission suggests quite otherwise.

Second, from an interview with Carl Sagan, astronomer, media figure on matters of science, in 1996 (with Charlie Rose):

> And if we don't understand it, and by "we" I mean "the general public," if it's something that, "Oh, I'm not good at that, I don't know anything about it," then who is making all the decisions about science and technology that are going to determine what kind of future our children live in? Just some members of Congress? But there's no more than a handful of members of Congress with any background in science at all. And the Republican Congress has just abolished its own Office of Technology Assessment—the organization that gave them bipartisan, competent advice on science and technology. They say, "We don't want to know. Don't tell us about science and technology."
>
> Rose: Surprising. What's the danger of all this? I mean, this is not the thing that…
>
> Sagan: There are two kinds of dangers. One is what I just talked about. That we've arranged a society based on science and technology in which nobody understands anything about science and technology, and this combustible mixture of ignorance and power, sooner or later, is going to blow up in our faces. I mean, who is running the science and technology in a democracy if the people don't know anything about it? And the second reason that I'm worried about this is that science is more than a body of knowledge. It's a way of thinking. A way of skeptically interrogating the universe with a fine understanding of human fallibility. If we are not able to ask skeptical questions, to interrogate those who tell us that something is true, to be skeptical of those in authority, then we're up for grabs for the next charlatan political or religious who comes ambling along. It's a thing that Jefferson laid great stress on. It wasn't enough, he said, to enshrine some rights in a Constitution or a Bill of Rights. The people had to be educated, and they had to practice their skepticism and their education. Otherwise we don't run the government—the government runs us.

Third, from a piece by Sean Illing in *Vox* (originally published in

November, 2019)

> ... No amount of evidence, on virtually any topic, is likely to move public opinion one way or the other. We can attribute some of this to rank partisanship — some people simply refuse to acknowledge inconvenient facts about their own side.
>
> But there's another, equally vexing problem. We live in a media ecosystem that overwhelms people with information. Some of that information is accurate, some of it is bogus, and much of it is intentionally misleading. The result is a polity that has increasingly given up on finding out the truth. As Sabrina Tavernise and Aidan Gardiner put it in a New York Times piece, "people are numb and disoriented, struggling to discern what is real in a sea of slant, fake, and fact."
>
> ... We're in an age of manufactured nihilism.
>
> I call this "manufactured" because it's the consequence of a deliberate strategy. It was distilled almost perfectly by Steve Bannon, the former head of Breitbart News and chief strategist for Donald Trump. "The Democrats don't matter," Bannon reportedly said in 2018. "The real opposition is the media. And the way to deal with them is to flood the zone with shit."
>
> ... This idea isn't new, but Bannon articulated it about as well as anyone can. The press ideally should sift fact from fiction and give the public the information it needs to make enlightened political choices. If you short-circuit that process by saturating the ecosystem with misinformation and overwhelm the media's ability to mediate, then you can disrupt the democratic process.
>
> What we're facing is a new form of propaganda that wasn't really possible until the digital age. And it works both by creating an apparent consensus around false narratives and by muddying the waters so that consensus regarding true facts is no longer conceivable.
>
> Bannon's political objective is clear. As he explained in a 2017 Conservative Political Action Conference talk, he sees Trump as a stick of dynamite with which to blow up the status quo. So "flooding the zone" is a means to that

end. But more generally, creating widespread cynicism about the truth and the institutions charged with unearthing it erodes the very foundation of liberal democracy. And the strategy is working.

Fourth, from Hannah Arendt's 1951 book *The Origins of Totalitarianism* (three distinctly separate, but in their way related, well-known observations:

> Before mass leaders seize the power to fit reality to their lies, their propaganda is marked by its extreme contempt for facts as such, for in their opinion fact depends entirely on the power of man who can fabricate it.
>
> ... The ideal subject of totalitarian rule is not the convinced Nazi or the convinced Communist, but people for whom the distinction between fact and fiction (i.e., the reality of experience) and the distinction between true and false (i.e., the standards of thought) no longer exist.
>
> ... In an ever-changing, incomprehensible world the masses had reached the point where they would, at the same time, believe everything and nothing, think that everything was possible and that nothing was true. ... Mass propaganda discovered that its audience was ready at all times to believe the worst, no matter how absurd, and did not particularly object to being deceived because it held every statement to be a lie anyhow. The totalitarian mass leaders based their propaganda on the correct psychological assumption that, under such conditions, one could make people believe the most fantastic statements one day, and trust that if the next day they were given irrefutable proof of their falsehood, they would take refuge in cynicism; instead of deserting the leaders who had lied to them, they would protest that they had known all along that the statement was a lie and would admire the leaders for their superior tactical cleverness.

The 9/11 story is not the only pack of lies ever told. It is not the only act of murderous faithlessness ever committed by any government, or by the American government. It is but further fraud after a few decades in which bamboozle and nonsense and "evidence doctored out of recognition" have been regular features.

A further, and perhaps helpful, way of thinking about the problem may be to consider what the "flat earth" proponents have been able to achieve (at least on the internet) and by looking more fundamentally at the systemic resemblance between what the flat-earthers say and the 9/11 story told by the government and media. The flat-earthers say that they know the earth isn't curved because they took a bubble level up in an airplane and watched the bubble. (This is just one among a group of several very similar "experiments"— that are not actually experiments because they have no analytic relationship to hypotheses and are couched in presuppositions that are unfounded. But, to their own audience, the flat-earthers get them to "work" in ways that "create" response and adherence as if they were.)

The 9/11 "debunkers" say that the collapse of Building 7 was a fully anticipated event from the early afternoon, in the "reasoning" of Deputy Chief Peter Hayden from a correspondingly similar sort of disconnected "presuppositious observation":

> "...also we were pretty sure that 7 World Trade Center would collapse. Early on, we saw a bulge in the southwest corner between floors 10 and 13, and we had put a transit on that and we were pretty sure she was going to collapse."

That gets the "Wow!" award (to share as a prize with the bubble on the plane and weird claims about gravitation and curvature — and all the others). You "put a transit ... on a bulge" you say you saw between floors 11 and 13 on the south-west building corner, and from that you say you knew that the whole 47 story building of 1.9 million square feet was going to collapse straight down in seconds, with the penthouse falling into the roof line, sequential emissions evidently from devices running up the facade, and the whole building sinking straight down into its own footprint — and all this elaborately as reported by NIST to have been from a girder supposedly unseating from Column 79 — which was in the *north-east* corner of the building, several hundred feet — the whole building's distance — from the "southwest corner"? Gadzooks, perhaps we should say — or maybe something a little bit more literate, maybe something somewhat more "salty."

Both 9/11 and the "flat earth" story derive, quite similarly, from wondrous assertions about what "proves" what. About "evidence." Yet even more importantly, about "models and modeling." And even more importantly about the isolation of modelings from responsible sources of confirmation and disconfirmation. Perception of any kind is in fact always comes from, or is "informed" by something. There are several different words in English we regularly use to name or describe that "something." "Recognition" of the thing perceived, an "understanding" of reality / the world in front of the perceiver / objective conditions, etc., "cognitive mapping," a set of "orderings of the perception" etc. As a general term, we can use the word "model." It is fair to say that perception inevitably occurs according to one or more (often many inter-related) models. In simple terms, we have mental "models" of what a dog looks like, and when the lenses of our eyes focus upon our retinas an image of a horizontal furry creature in a certain range of sizes with a dogish head and snout and a dogish tail, we *see* a dog.

A similar sort of "modeling" is also involved in perceiving collections of things, including collections of "events," or "sequences," including perceiving relationships in and among such collections, such as, for instance, "cause." Or "demonstration;" or "proof." When ordinary human understanding gives way to false propaganda, when people come to believe things that are otherwise obviously untrue, modeling is created or changed that either partly or completely fails to cohere with other models or other parts of the model or with available perception. Again, put another way, perhaps more simply: lies are by their nature inherently inconsistent with other propositions that are not lies, and "propagandizing" on behalf of lies is fundamentally the matter of inducing people to ignore, or create excuses for (or, best, admire) those inconsistencies.

Many of us would like to think that there are truths we're fond of that can be independent and nunciative — and that for the truths we don't care about, no matter, we can substitute lies and frauds we like or find convenient. The majority of truth, however, is true also by and through its coherence.

The flat earth "debate" has, of course, moved along on the internet and to YouTube. In particular, still posted at the time I write is another "back and forth," miserable from the point of view of scientific understanding, but very interesting as an illustration of human cognition, its specific failures, what accommodates and accompanies them, and what we humans feel the need to say as we fail.[1]

Perhaps the most indicative moment in several hours of video overall, is the moment at which "Professor Dave" notes that recognizing that Earth is a sphere and rotates upon an axis about 23 and a half degrees from the orbital plane while orbiting, together accounts for day and night, annual seasons, observed angles of the sun, the existence of an astronomical "pole" and "pole star" (and precession of the axis, etc.) ... all at once. There are several such demonstrations regarding "model" in the exchanges, of course, but this one is done in about three clear sentences in English, and it is only the very daft who would not be struck, impressed, face-up fully reminded by the scientifically explanatory value and efficacy from the way the explication coheres.

There is perhaps a difference that may be noted between "appearances" and "observations." An "appearance" has, somewhat more closely attached to it, an ideation, an interpreted associated position,

---

1. The comments section below Farina's video provides its entertainments as well:

Never argue with an idiot. They will drag you down to their level and beat you with experience.

Y'know, they make a "good" point. There is no evidence, so long as you ignore it.

You cannot reason a man out of something he never reasoned himself into." -Dean Swift Thanks for trying, but it's impossible to use logic to convince a flat earther that the earth is round because they didn't use logic to convince themselves that it's flat. We just have to live with them being wrong.

What ... makes me utterly uncomfortable is the sheer confidence in which these men talk about their claims. The way they spit out insults. Not only are they dumb, but they're bullies, and utterly confident in their lack of understanding.

It's like playing chess against a pigeon. Doesn't matter how good at chess you are, the pigeon is just going to knock all the pieces over, shit on the board and declare itself the winner and fly away.

brought to the situation by the person. A way to point at this would be to say that we can (sometimes, often enough) observe things as they "look," but they often "appear" to us what we decide they "look like." An "observation" usually describes something more "objective," more kept to being "simple information" and less nudged, poked, jostled by our interests and anxieties, as part of the perceiving, toward a "conclusion." Even beginning with the word "flat" itself. The emphasis in this context emerges from appearance — "appears flat to us." Doesn't have to cohere with anything, except perhaps our sensations. "Observations" regarding "flat" have more of the quality of making a set of equal or closely equal measurements with respect to a geometric line — which, or course, have at least to cohere with the arbitration of the measuring stick.

The modern matter of propagandizing has everything to do with getting large numbers of humans, one way or another (but usually anxiety is involved) to abjure the reasonable human interest in facts (and science) and a coherent understanding of the world in favor of an *in*coherent set of emotionally driven attachments to appearances, in other words to get humans to excite themselves to interfere mentally with our own observations before having observed to the extent of giving ourselves opportunity to sensibly apply concepts.

In a world of relatively "low" technology, plowing the fields with a mule, incoherence and the emphasis on appearance will not get a group of people into too much trouble. In a world of elaborate and complex tech, in which nearly all of the controlling entities in the important control systems, from genetic material in viruses, to computer code in a computer, to microwave information links, in no particular way "appear" to the human "eye" but instead show up as they are in front of coherent understanding, the fundamental program of dissociation involved in propagandizing can be extremely harmful. (Karl Rove seems to have had nothing to offer as to what the "downside" of his "created reality" program might be, but that should not keep us from thinking about what changes, and how it does, when "reality" moves from being, to being "created.")

All that noted, 9/11 is unique. And it can be astonishing to anyone doing a nickel's worth of noticing and thinking. No other false flag event is constructed in attempted reliance so completely upon the inability of the deceived to recognize plain incontrovertible facts in plain sight. 9/11 works by means of something like an unmodifiable convention requiring wholesale acceptance / credit of a repeated media / television story (if its on TV it is true...). Said another, similar way, no other false flag event relies so completely upon the deceived to deceive themselves so much more than they could be deceived by being misled by a conceivably possible, but misleading account, as compared to the factually impossible account that gets believed. No other false flag account repeatedly offers such a "wide bandwidth" and compositionally complete a rendering of its fraudulence. To no other false flag event is media "coverage" (think "wall to wall") so fundamental to perpetration, nor for any other similar governmental scam has fraudulent "debunking" of descriptions that are truthful, and heavy social shaming waged against those honestly saying and writing simple factual truth, been in such widespread use as much relied upon means to further the scam.

All of this on top being a) completely self-inflicted (as noted, Osama bin Laden in fact did no part of 9/11), b) gross violence directed at "civil society" office buildings and people, not soldiers, not military bases or installations, not even energy or resource facilities (demolition of large landmark structures in the largest, arguably most "cosmopolitan" city in the nation), and c) a complete breach of the fundamental trust between a nation and the government that purports to serve and lead that society. (Citizens do not pay taxes and serve in the army in return for having the government contrive to blow them up at their daily workplace. One may argue that some of the worst acts done in the Soviet Union during the Stalinist period are of a comparable murderous faithlessness and as profoundly abusive, but, except for those, the betrayal that creating and telling the 9/11 story comprises is singular.)

To which list one must then add a more convoluted, many-part, complex, imprecise, unfathomable, and yet very powerful, item d). What does it mean to say, as several commentators in parts have, that

9/11 is, in one set of words, "the all-the-way-from-the-ass-to-elbow fraud that keeps itself from being in any part recognized"? The Israelis soon afterward admitted that their Irgun (disguised as Arab workers) bombed the King David Hotel in Jerusalem on July 22, 1946, killing 91 people and injuring an additional 46. Neither the Israelis, nor the Americans, are now about to admit the truth regarding 9/11 (and each appears to cling to the notion that no one never will). Similarly, many of the people who do know a bit of basic physics and are otherwise capable of looking at evidence and thinking, retreat to denials of plain facts or to absurdities that are offered features of the official 9/11 story, even when given, as non-threateningly as humanly possible a chance to have even the merest outlines of an honest consideration of the subject.

The truth of 9/11 is dreadful, too dirty, too much of a perfidity, and departs so much too desperately much from our self-image (going back to the propositions that we "saved civilization itself" in each of two world wars and that we then worked tirelessly for the myriad graces of "freedom" for all the countries of the world threatened by the scourge of "communism"). Every one of us in some (often pretty deep) way wants the truth of 9/11 not to be true.

If it can be called that, the "genius" of the people who staged 9/11 would be to have anticipated the extent to which most of us will eagerly "program ourselves to persuasion" from made-available sources, without thinking about what we are doing, if the programming can be driven by enough anxiety over which we sense we do not have control and deep and multiple uncertainties (or raw fear, even if — actually, especially if — the programmed subject matter is apparently scary). Thus, without analyzing the content, without consideration of what is propositionally entailed, and without reflection regarding further inconsistencies and impossibilities, we will "choose" to be "frightened of terrorists" rather than face the serious real burden of recognizing that our government has profoundly betrayed our nation to stage an episode of destruction in order to leverage a thereby instilled fear of "terrorists." Screwy, but that is the way most of us work emotionally. We choose an unconscious, and compliant, response, if adversity is pointed to and "outside" ourselves, rather than become conscious (in some sense bring "within" ourselves) that we are in fact being abused. We surrender our self-respect to a false premise of external assault that takes the place of the more painful truth that we thus become contributors to the fraud by which we are then less than citizens in a country that is remade as, to use the mafia phrase "Commission territory."

To the observation that most of us will actually help to put the 9/11 fraud in place in our society, that we will "assist" in becoming duped and being deceived, seems to get been added notice that most of us, having done so, will hold on tightly. We will not be talked out of what we have done to create the (false) certainties we now conceive *we* have "realized" because we have attended the choice of them.

The actual "majority," to use the word again, that afterwards surrounds and protects the 9/11 story is the number of us who are existentially frightened to try think about the story for one moment more once we realize how really ugly, at core, the 9/11 event and story are. In truth 9/11 is so much unjustified and unreasonable that we decide, without actually thinking about it, that continuing to deny the truth, and thus keep the fraud in place, even though also an unreasonable thing to do if considered rationally, is required.

No other set of lies in the history of this country (except colorably the lies about the assassinations of the 1960s) has had anything like comparable "protection" from fair rebuttal, refutation or refusal. Yet if we are save ourselves from more abuse, more scams and deceits indeed worse, turning back the 9/11 story is our only choice. We must do everything in our power to make any similar sort of "completely glued in" fraud no part of our future.

Perhaps one of the best proposals made to ordinary people about dealing in practical terms with institutionalized lying comes from Aleksandr Solzhenitsyn. On February 12, 1974, the day he was arrested (to be sent to the Gulag), he published a short essay titled "Live Not By Lies." It is short, only a few pages. It is summary, but directly stated. After rounding the problem, including features of the relationship between violence and fraudulence, he says what we can do:

For violence has nothing to cover itself with but lies, and lies can only persist through violence. And it is not every day and not on every shoulder that violence brings down its heavy hand: It demands of us only a submission to lies, a daily participation in deceit—and this suffices as our fealty.

And therein we find, neglected by us, the simplest, the most accessible key to our liberation: a personal non-participation in lies! Even if all is covered by lies, even if all is under their rule, let us resist in the smallest way: Let their rule hold not through me!

And this is the way to break out of the imaginary encirclement of our inertness, the easiest way for us and the most devastating for the lies. For when people renounce lies, lies simply cease to exist. Like parasites, they can only survive when attached to a person.

Our relationship with what we are willing and able to hold as true, on the one hand, and to recognize as false, on the other, is indeed as personal as described. Credit, belief, tribute, homage, however they may be extended to others, all begin as facets of an inalienable power originally held even by the most societally powerless. Too often we are browbeaten or seduced or cajoled or manipulated into surrendering or disclaiming sensible plain truth in exchange for some (often small) privilege or prerogative controlled by others or institutions and metered out to us in exchange from doled.

Yet if we have any form of courage, and any amount of self-respect, we never lose the chance to realize that our participation in the fraud has not been worth it. Some few have gained leverage against us they have used badly, and by which much has been forfeited and nothing worthy gained.

Eight: Now, Twenty Years Later.

9/11 was a really bad idea when it was done. Further pretense and piles of debt heaped up since then notwithstanding, 9/11 has damaged America and the world, not only by what has been wrought in Iraq, Afghanistan, Lebanon, Syria and throughout the Middle East, but by what has happened to the societies and politics of nearly all of the Western nations. America's fraud has lead us and our allies to divisions, distrust, disrepute and to a myriad of compounded failures and distraction. Not only has the National Institute of Standards and Technology in the United States emerged as corrupt, but so has the European Central Bank, although, admittedly, in a different way.

As challenging as the prospect of telling the truth about 9/11 and as much as renouncing the fraud may be altogether too daunting to many people, doing so is the only good choice we can now make. As a society we have already "doubled down" on the 9/11 story, insisting that anybody is a "crazy conspiracy theorist" who notices aloud or in writing that the 'terrorists with box cutters hijacking airplanes as discovered by cell phone calls from 40,000 feet who then flew pinpoint at sea level going five or six hundred miles an hour into and through buildings constructed of many very large steel box columns' tale could not possibly be true. We have already "doubled down," and more, on blaming "Osama bin Laden" and "al Quaeda" and proclaiming the extreme risk and danger of the "terrorist threat" to the Western world. We have already in substance doubled the extent of corruption and the reliance on corruption in the federal government. As a nation, we have already spent, not just many trillion dollars on 9/11- based "imperatives," from war abroad to "control measures," domestic spying, "rendition," imprisonments around the world, "security consultants" and mercenaries (Blackwater contractors), but used up much of our status as a leading nation and much of the good will in the world we had earned in earlier decades.

Honest thought about whether and how we can help ourselves, even now that the 9/11 fraud has done so much to "lock itself in," implores us as a nation to figure out how to let go of the false story, no matter what the government may think it wants, nor what the officials in the government may want to do, what plans they may have for continuing to re-tell the same or similar falsehoods, or further dramatize them in TV "specials" or propaganda movies, or make them part of another advertisement to the world to the effect that we have supposed reasons to start sanctions and wars to lay waste to other countries. Continuing 9/11 will only make for more failures.

That noted, there is no way to get even partially free from the fraud that will not be difficult for the country and, with some very few exceptions, the people in it. Getting out from under 9/11 will also be a diplomatic and a legal (or perhaps better described as a legal and political) challenge more extended in nature than other comparable challenges we have faced.

As thoughtful observers have noticed and said, despite all of the follow-on stuff produced by Popular Mechanics magazine, and in Hollywood, and on television, and by propagandists, and by NIST, once they consider the false claims, impossible physics, the lack of substantial airplane wreckage where big airplanes are said to have crashed, the lack of verifiable log and recorder information, and the ascertainably faked properties of particular still and video images, people who once believed the official story often realize the official story isn't true, but it never happens that people who have recognized the fraud return to the claims made by the official story and change their minds then to believe that the tale told by the government and media is true. Despite the continuing propaganda and the continuing contrived diatribes against "conspiracy theories," for this reason as much as any other, millions of people in the United States alone, twenty years after September 11, 2001, to varying degrees do not credit what the government and the media have said and, no matter what, it is unlikely the number will decline in the next decade. While only some Americans have a thorough understanding of Newton's principles or of physical mechanics as a whole, collectively we do seem to have a sense about a story featuring a bearded guy who has past connections to the CIA from an earlier "secret" war, who fires an automatic rifle in the air, who is living in a cave in Afghanistan marshaling multiple simultaneous airplane hijackings that knock three really big, tall buildings straight down in New York, have an airplane crash fireball event that half an hour later collapses a just-rebuilt section at the Pentagon, and crashing a plane into the Pennsylvania countryside, again without, among other things, reasonable crash remains.

More and more propaganda tales are not going to help. Similarly, the approach of refusing even to notice obvious and clear events and facts doesn't work well either. (I have personally had the experience of running each of the two clearest video clips of the collapse of Building 7 in New York on a large computer screen for an otherwise obviously astute, well-dressed, well spoken, middle-aged gentleman who had been identified by social acquaintances at a highbrow dinner party as "having a relationship with the CIA" who, upon observing the two video records, stated flatly that he saw "nothing at all unusual or remarkable" in them. Mentioned to him that these were record video of the collapse of Building 7, he did not then ask what Building 7 was. Instead he acted entirely as if he knew. The only thing he said, which he was helpful enough to repeat, was that the video *definitely* showed *nothing* interesting or noteworthy. The ultimate effect of his denial, of course, was to propose that he was unable even to offer any form of polite or possible suggestion in any part that any the demolitions in New York, sufficient facts considered, were even conceivably understandable as anything other than gratuitous.

Especially as time goes on, an ultimately disturbing vacancy, something that should deeply discomfit everybody in this country, high and low, involved and estranged, fortunate and hapless, appears at large in what we learn about the activities, "projects" and schemes of the agencies and people acting in secret whether as and for government, or in de-facto associations connected to or in place of overt government. The plans are elaborate. The resources are extensive. The developed relationships are many and intricate. But the purposes are often harmful, at best vacuous, the intentions unworthy, motivations tawdry. "Hamilton 68"[1] is a list of people, not Russian, not bots.

———————

1. Created by former FBI Special Agent Clint Watts, the project was

Over the last several years, reasonably reliable information from several sources that matches notably well has let those who read and understand pretty much know who killed President Kennedy. Names are named (many of them are unpleasantly familiar). There are lines to draw, for instance, from Cord Meyer's organizings to the described gun of Lucien Sarti, (apparently through E. Howard Hunt, among others — and lines up from the storm drain at the curb near where the President's limousine stopped) but, aside from some suggestion that the assassination in November 1963 enabled the Vietnam War in main to begin in August of 1964 (after the Gulf of Tonkin "attack" that did not in fact happen), the propositions regarding why John F. Kennedy was killed appear to have to do with reasonably denied personal claims to extended terms in office (Dulles, Lemnitzer), contracting for military hardware, personal liaisons and jealousies (re ex-wife Mary Pinchot Meyer), and bickering in the ranks (including, but by no means limited to, Lyndon B. Johnson v. Robert F. Kennedy). We know that Oswald was "dipped in soup" (in agency slang) in Mexico City and in New Orleans and that the Warren Commission and its Report would much more accurately be called the Dulles Dupe Group and their multi-volume output called hyper-padded-distractionalizing, but we know essentially nothing, other than errant propositions that Kennedy was not "anti-communist enough" — by any reasonable measure untrue — that could possibly be cause for the assassination among people not out of touch with reality.

It is now, more or less, sixty years since the Kennedy assassination, and the "worst" that has come to public knowledge regarding him and his presidency is that he had some extramarital affairs. Among many other significant suggestions of probity in fact in the conduct of office, one may note that Kennedy flatly refused Operation Northwoods (an airplane switcheroo fake meant to be launched in accusation against Cuba proposed by Lemnitzer).

---

supported by the Alliance for Securing Democracy and the German Marshall Fund. That means a host of powerful former government officials with long histories in and around intelligence agencies promoted the shoddy research for years. *Federalist (website)* Emily Jashinski 23 January, 2023

Viewed also as an effort by a very few people forcibly to enact changes to the conduct of the affairs of the country and the world, something comparable, although even more serious — and somewhat "diagonal" — can be said about the 9/11 scheme. Even if one were to say that 9/11 was a putatively rational way to foment a "War on Terrorism" among a public that showed no particular interest in waging one, that is not to say that a "War on Terrorism" is a rational thing to intend to set off. "…foreign-born terrorists have killed roughly one American per year" and "… the typical American is … 29 times more likely to die from a regional asteroid strike."[2]

The 9/11 scheme and story can also be considered as possibly another part of a compound form of "threat explanation" or conceived demonstration of the "need" for pre-emptive attacks — for commencing aggression for the projected alleged sake of "American safety"— including as "justification" for the 2003 invasion of Iraq (although lacking any actual nexus).

The employers of Kennedy's assassins apparently sought to replace him for some policy reasons as well as personal complaints. On the other hand, they weren't at the "9/11 level" trying thereby to deceive an entire nation about facts, specifically threats, purportedly determinative of the state of the world and nation, by physically enacting those menaces locally at extended scale, falsely and under false pretenses. Even twenty years later, 9/11 is singularly different from any other known attempt to compromise the consciousness of the nation, to play "rough" or "murderous" with everybody, and to steer what is purportedly a democracy by the yet more un-democratic

---

2. Business Insider, www site. By contrast, an article published March 19, 2018 in *Salon* (and on the Salon web site) begins: "March 19 marks 15 years since the U.S.-UK invasion of Iraq in 2003, and the American people have no idea of the enormity of the calamity the invasion unleashed. The U.S. military has refused to keep a tally of Iraqi deaths. General Tommy Franks, the man in charge of the initial invasion, bluntly told reporters, "We don't do body counts." One survey found that most Americans thought Iraqi deaths were in the tens of thousands. But our calculations, using the best information available, show a catastrophic estimate of 2.4 million Iraqi deaths since the 2003 invasion." To say that the "war" that has been waged is against "terrorism" is a proposition unsupported by the facts.

means, by actually staging an attack repeatedly fraudulently portrayed to have been brought by a very committed enemy, all with grandiose indifference to the people of the nation, their lives, and their deceived understanding.

Analogously, 9/11 is a worse, much more lethal and more physical, version of a stunt, for instance, proposed to "prove" that a "system" (such as a computer system, say) is dangerously, threateningly "insecure," because the people who exclusively operate and control it, who have instituted the security provisions and who know all the codes and passwords, and in whose secure air-conditioned room the machine runs, can themselves stage a completely compromising "penetration" or "death hack." Of course they can. The fact that they intentionally manipulate the system to resulting destruction at their own hands, while doing lots of lying, proves instead and above all else that the people in whom we have placed our trust to create and operate the system are not worthy of our confidence. The problem with the "system" is, in fact, the people (and groups / institutions) managing it.

When only half thought-about, or as considered in some detail, the 9/11 story also contains and projects too much failure even to suppose the conceivably effective basis for any form of past, present, or future risk or threat explanation. We don't have especially good information, for example, about the compound air defense failure of that day, We do know, however, that the job of the people responsible for successful air defense is to actively defend against serious harms as and when they come to exist, and no part of their job is ever to "play along" with anybody's building demolition "project," nor is it actually to lie about much of anything in response to legitimate inquiry as or after it has happened. Even only minimally recognized and understood, 9/11 should be said to let us know, even twenty years later, that if we are to worry, we should be worried about the accuracy and honesty and national loyalty of some kernel part of our air defense facilities, about the complete compromise of our investigative and forensic institutions and capabilities (as well as, of course, worried about anyone ever again appointing a government Commission to accomplish anything that is in the real interests of the country).

It is also worth doing a significant amount of further thinking about matters regarding "threat," whether as "perceived" or "explained," particularly in conditions of secrecy. Obviously, the assertion of a particular proposition that depends upon specific evidence in order to ascertain whether it is or is not true, while the evidence is proprietary and kept entirely concealed, or obviously lied about, becomes merely a demand for acquiescence. In the case in which a government says a country is "threatened" but further says only "secret intelligence," which "cannot" and will not be revealed, would support the claim about the "threat," the people of the country are inevitably deprived (usually intentionally) of a reasonable authority in response.

The nature of humans and our proclivities and associations considered, no matter the purported or actual source of "threat," people and organizations dealing in a given threat, real or imagined, whether created by them or created by others, tend to find purpose in manipulating the threat. A successful modern society, even in a world in which there exist dangerous weapons, therefore cannot give over the power of discerning, assessing, and responding to threats to an enclosure of secrecy without expecting the acquiescence that can be forced therefrom to be abused to the greater detriment of the country.

This is particularly true in circumstances in which the "threat" is easily and readily synthetic, and a powerful and amplificatory system that will "follow orders" is directly connected to important presented information. 9/11, like the Gulf of Tonkin matter, again, somewhat metaphorically, but descriptively, is another case in which the "radar screen" has been "hacked" and a gross national response begins and continues (for decades) without meaningful audit. As metaphor, the "29 hijackings" the Northeast Air Defense Sector says it tracked on September 11, 2001 at the "input" to the 9/11 "machine," become something like 29 of the cities in the Middle East where buildings became bomb-strewn rubble at the "output." The "planes" that were mere overlaid video images "flying into and through" Buildings One and Two become "shock and awe" detonations in Iraq and Afghanistan, more or less as the "blips" on the radar screen, that were not North Vietnamese navy boats out in Tonkin, managed to turn into B52 targets over North Vietnam. All without thoughtful consideration of the actual facts; the relevant details sealed in secrecy.

Even twenty years later, 9/11 is not "over" until we either amend what 9/11 is and what it has done, or (we could dismally suppose) yet more fully succumb to it. The 9/11 show and story needs now to be judged by human beings who had no part in perpetrating the scam, people not engaged in "government security" and neither troops nor officers in any government "war on" anything like "terrorism" (or a collectively so-described "Islamic" "State" or "Caliphate," or the ordinary habitants of any country or region somewhere between the Mediterranean and the Pacific Ocean), nor people in "finance" (the matter, if stated in terms, honest if perhaps harsh, of "playing with dollars," being the informational symbols introduced by the computational systems of the Federal Reserve into the systems attended to by "money center" banks) who, unhappily, also have an inherent interest in exploiting opportunities provided by a lack of realistic representational accuracy of information. Similarly, none of the rest of us now need to hear more from those who are officially, economically, financially, or unofficially, in the business of sycophancy or propaganda or creating gratuitously fake "debunkery" in response to plain facts.

The people we so greatly need must come from among the "greater us." They exist. Some of them are podcasters who, once a week, for weeks at a time, think and talk honestly, genuinely scientifically, accurately and with good heart. Some of them are experienced medical doctors who have enough training in science and the practical matters of disease and recovery to be very "reality based" and thoughtful, at the same time that they understand a lot about other people, about what helps us understand the truth, to be honest with each other and with ourselves, and to live well and fully. Some of them are mechanics and machinists who have seen function and failure in so many guises and variations that they don't particularly take to crap about what caused what.

The least amount of "politics" of any kind involved, the better. This can't be a fight for power or office or votes now or in the future, or for further political reimbursements from tax dollars or from "financing." It has to be a struggle to achieve some honesty, credibility, and real attention to real things that matter. Political statements are exaggerated and inflammatory; they also often focus on distractions, often exclusively.

In preference, we would hold a serious and exceptionally well conducted public evidentiary proceeding, a trial, a full inquiry into all of the events of September 11, 2001, into all of the statements thereafter made by officials, or anyone acting or speaking on behalf of officials, to the media thereafter, and into each report regarding 9/11 that was thereafter made by the government or any person connected with the government.

No person would be exempt from being called to testify nor from being sworn in and required to answer truthfully any question, under the pains and penalties of perjury. Witnesses could avail themselves of the protections of the Fifth Amendment, but could thereafter be referred for impeachment or indictment for discovered serious crimes, testimony or evidence they declined to provide notwithstanding. At the trial, nothing having to do with obtaining or adducing evidence would be done by any government officeholder or official or person appointed by any governmental person or entity or appointee. The trial could principally be run, for example, by 51 Examiners, one from each state at the nomination and selection by the people of the state and one from the District of Columbia, and be held at a suitable location within the United States having suitable technical facilities and network access, outside of New York City, outside of Washington D.C. between the two and readily accessible from either. Examiners would receive a reasonable stipend, be prohibited from holding or running for any governmental appointment or public office for twenty years after the conclusion of the trial. Examiners would be subject to punishment for serious wrongful acts according to terms described in the Judicial Code of Conduct, or the law of contempt, or of impeachable offenses, as understood by the terms of the law and rules applicable in the District Courts of the United States, but further would receive a specifically described national Medal of Honor if they have served the trial (without committing any wrongful, corrupt act, or act of falsity.)

In the conduct of such a trial, the citizens of the United States would be invited to submit requests for the production of documents and other evidentiary things of any kind, and for the examination of witnesses, be invited to submit requests for questions to be asked of any given witness. Each request would be indexed and posted in a secure form on a Trial Network site. Requests that are substantially identical would be consolidated, either by the citizen(s) submitting the request or by the Examiners, and the consolidation shown. Wrongful consolidation could be reversed upon a written motion. Questions genuinely irrelevant would be declined to be asked by the examiner, the database record regarding the proceedings showing the question and the determination regarding relevance.

Plainly wrongful refusal to ask submitted questions that are clear and reasonable in the circumstances would be reversible upon a written motion allowed or denied according to the recorded vote of the majority of the Examiners. An extended pattern of wrongful refusal of clearly reasonable questions would be punishable as wrongdoing on the part of the Examiner.

The public record of the trial in video and typographic form would be broadcast contemporaneously with the proceedings and the examination of witnesses.

Any claim that the answer to a particular question required the witness to divulge classified information would be taken to an inquiry of record in a completely secure location, either at the time the question was posed or as collected with other similar objections to other questions, at the discretion of the Examiners. The Examiners would be required to provide for the trial record the full answers made regarding any question for which a classified secrets privilege was claimed that provided credible evidence of the commission of a serious criminal act. By their two-thirds vote, the Examiners would also have the power to de-classify any matter whatsoever, and to compel the answer to any question for which a classified secrets privilege was claimed.

President Nixon is, among other things he said, remembered for his opinion of April 6th, 1977, provided to interviewer David Frost. As recounted in a *History Commons* review:

> … Frost has a difficult time with his subject, former
> President Richard Nixon, in the day's early questioning.
> Frost attempts to recoup with a line of questioning sug-
> gested by his adviser James Reston, Jr., one used in the
> trial of former Nixon aide John Ehrlichman. Were there
> no limits to what a president can do, even if the president
> wants to do something plainly illegal? he asks. Could he do
> anything despite the law? Burglary? Forgery? Even mur-
> der? "If the president does it, that means it's not illegal,"
> Nixon retorts.

Some of us would argue that the purpose of the prolonged hearings regarding the "Watergate" matter held by the Select Committee
of the United States Senate in 1972 and 1973 was to consider whether
there are and should be legal limits the nation should regard in respect
to what a President does, and that the conclusion of the Committee,
the Senate, and the nation was, indeed, that there are. Specifically, that
neither the President, nor any of the people who act on the President's
behalf or are members of the Executive Branch, should act in ways
that are inherently criminal or grossly wrongful, or which redound
to the most fundamental discredit of the Office of the President or of
the nation. Although we may never know with any more precision
what an "impeachable offense" is than that it is what a majority of the
House of Representatives says it is, the Select Committee managed to
get us to notice that a president who ran a break-in gang in the base-
ment of the White House was not necessarily working for the benefit
of the country.

The findings and conclusion of the Select Committee, however,
were, in actual practice, soon lost upon us, and have remained missing
since. Once absent, the fundamental aversion to significant criminality
was then further encircled by extended secrecy, and by added and ple-
nary enforcement of extended claims for secrecy and privilege, even
against those who held no commission and had made no promise of
keeping the secrets of a government that, by its own acts, had revealed
them. (At this point, it is supposedly the settled law that even after
facts have been made public, the government can "reclaim" them as

classified information merely by its later statement that the facts are "classified" — a proposition that had never been supposed during the prior decades regarding classification.)

Although such a trial by the ablest members of the national public would do the most to renew our sense of reasonable regard for legality, justice and good conduct, modern politics considered, it is not going to happen. Not even close. The argument would immediately be made that our Constitution does not provide for any such direct event in which no representative body has the opportunity to interpose the interests it derives from its position — and, indeed, our Constitution does not.

Nevertheless, we collectively face a serious challenge to get ourselves to act as something better than irredeemable fraudsters. More realistically, we can conceive and develop a transition that has some resemblance to and follows, for one (not infrequently cited to) instance, various parts of the example of German reunification (beginning with people going through the Berlin Wall without anybody getting shot, moving to closing down the Stasi and opening the Stasi files, and proceeding to rejoining an imperfect, but less autocratic and oppressive member of the community of nations). Other examples of national transition that we might do well to consider in the process of creating conditions in which our country can alleviate some of the burdens of wrongdoing may be found in the Truth and Reconciliation Commissions in places such as South Africa, East Timor, Rwanda and Guatemala. The United States has historically taken political positions rudely antagonistic to every of form of International Court and every form of inquiry and result derived internationally. In so doing we have often sounded like any other noisy bully whose only thought is to provide for its attacks unfettered. Even if the particulars of our national character would have us chafe at any review of the 9/11 fraud by an international entity, we would do well to consider what has worked restoratively to any appreciable degree in other nations.

We Americans share a cultural tendency to conceive "fighting" an essential activity. We often talk about pugilism as if it were most essential to any consequent result. We even talk about "fighting," for example, "for justice." Justice, of course, can also often most readily be achieved by declining to act unjustly or deciding not to leverage or extend injustices. Greater results are sometimes better accomplished by preventing fighting than by engaging in it. By contrast, maximizing damage is commonly a first order battle imperative. Nations of people, if not prevented from helpful co-operation, will sometimes act collectively in ways that genuinely benefit the nation. The best remedy for many lies is the honest truth; the fact that the liar was lying "asserts itself" and, by and large, does not need to be contested.

Various forms of social resistance to lies and liars are worthwhile and, no doubt, a serious review and rejection of the 9/11 fraud from the outset would have been to our common advantage. Even though that should have happened and did not, at the center of our attention, more than anything else, now must be substituting sanity for the insanities developed by the fraud. Exactly what constitutes sanity may require some discussion, but the very fact that "truther" has become a derisive epithet, a way of calling another person bad and wrong, shows that we have inverted our values too fundamentally.

As most of the people know who have been principal to the propaganda offensive and the "flooding the zone with bullshit," and who have kept doing what they do for twenty years on behalf of the 9/11 fraud, the lies must be maintained by a fairly constant stream of additional lies[3] and propaganda. Those people aren't likely to get tired easily. And if and when they do fatigue, there is a ready additional supply of them, continually replenished from who those who instinctively and readily treat other people as mere objects, who have more ambition than they have moral sense, who culturally more or less agree with Karl Rove that reality is something readily "created," who

---

3. From Sissela Bok *Lying: Moral Choice in Public and Private Life.* "It is easy, a wit observed, to tell a lie, but hard to tell only one. The first lie 'must be thatched with another or it will raid through.' More and more lies may come to be needed; the liar always has more mending to do. And the strains on him become greater each time – many have noted that it takes an excellent memory to keep one's untruths in good repair and disentangled. The sheer energy the liar has to devote to shoring them up is energy the honest man can dispose of freely."

do not miss the coherence with reality that actual reality contains and benefits from, and do not know or understand enough science or truth, or enough about science or truth to have and hold reasons to favor honesties or to disfavor deceits.

That which the 9/11 fraud can conceivably run short of would be the people who accede to the fraud in response to the "bullshit flood" and the rest of the propaganda. It is a bit like the then government of East Germany not running out of corrupt officials so much as running short of East Germans who sufficiently accept the country as it is in 1989 (or who are soldiers willing to put a bullet through one of their fellow citizens who wants to cross "the Wall"). That many have stood with the liars and the lies notwithstanding, it can, and sometimes — if rarely — happen that a nation of people will throw off a harmful regime of falsity.

A significant majority of Americans now have many very good reasons to be unwilling to accept that our country should continue under the burdens of the 9/11 fraud. The fraud has made us less powerful rather than more powerful, limited our possibilities rather than giving us opportunities, inspired us only to insistently waste great resources we need for other purposes, make implored strategy decisions that were nothing like strategic, been part of what has damagingly set us against each other and fractured many of the underlying relations and connections that live under the surface of society, but become immediately invaluable when trust and co-operation become essential.

Were it to take place, the formality of a public event in which the public received testimony and other evidence so that facts could be set forth, understood, and evaluated is desirable in and of itself. There is a great deal of further information that, if made available to the public, would help ordinary people scientifically and rationally to understand the data and the unequivocal facts that exist. Some manner of true accounting that has at least certain formally descriptive properties is likely to be essential.

Even twenty years later, and even though probably about half the country knows that the 9/11 story is incoherent, and doesn't "add up" as a matter of basic physics, ninety percent of the country, with some reason, fears the consequences of treating the truth as it is, in fact, true.

Even without any further examination in the form of any kind of trial, there is more than sufficient incontrovertible evidence now publicly to say and to write that what the government and media have said for twenty years is a string of lies. But nobody quite dares. Talking frankly about 9/11 is on the order of openly discussing the Gulag system in Stalinist Russia — say anything real and you can have a personal experience that lasts the rest of your (in the Stalinist case rudely shortened) life. President Dwight D. Eisenhower, in his farewell address given in 1960, drew what continues to be an outline figure of part of the basic diagram:

> Today, the solitary inventor, tinkering in his shop, has been overshadowed by task forces of scientists in laboratories and testing fields. In the same fashion, the free university, historically the fountainhead of free ideas and scientific discovery, has experienced a revolution in the conduct of research. Partly because of the huge costs involved, a government contract becomes virtually a substitute for intellectual curiosity. For every old blackboard there are now hundreds of new electronic computers.

> The prospect of domination of the nation's scholars by Federal employment, project allocations, and the power of money is ever present and is gravely to be regarded.

For the last two decades, and now, it isn't just the nation's "scholars," it is our bankers, and businessmen, and bakers — and even our comedians — who have been unable to think about or talk about what is so definitively and obviously wrong with 9/11 as a supposed event and as a story. This will not last forever. At the same time that history in any era will tell odd tales, history does have a certain way of outlasting, over the longer term, suppressive systems of many kinds and relieving some of the inhibitions against speaking and writing about actual facts. Even federal employment, project allocation, and the power of money get re-sorted as succeeding generations come to take the place of their predecessors. Nothing else done, though, it could conceivably be a long time from now that the overburden of nonsense is stripped off and 9/11 is looked at directly and talked about clearly.

If the continued insistence on the fraud — by any means or method — is long, not only will we redouble the failures of the last two decades, but we will be defeated further by the actual challenges (almost all of them having little or nothing to do with "terrorism") that have developed and become more acute in the interval. Every country from the Mediterranean to the Pacific Ocean and down to Cape Horn that has any resources will look rather to China than the United States (not just Afghanistan, not just Congo) and it will not be just about copper or oil.[4] Fraud and suppression solve the apparent problem of disclosure and discussion, but not the more fundamental and important problem of distrust. Distrust doesn't believe the fake stories and knows no borders.

Climate change is real. Storms are more intense and do more damage. Clean fresh water is becoming a trying requirement — for farming, and for industry, and for just drinking and washing and bathing. Many of our proposed "green solutions" in fact now use more hydrocarbon energy in their manufacture and use-life combined than hydrocarbon-based systems. Our total annual use of hydrocarbon energy and the release of carbon emissions into the atmosphere have in fact increased over the last decade in ratio to the adoption of purportedly "green" approaches to technology and uses.

Creating a day of "terrorism" so that we could spend two decades out in the world dropping JDAM ordinance, and driving guns around on Humvees, and surveilling, and shooting rockets from drones, was

4. "… any big project in African cities that is higher than three floors or roads that are longer than three kilometers are most likely being built and engineered by the Chinese. It is ubiquitous… China is now Africa's biggest trade partner, with Sino-African trade topping $200 billion per year. According to McKinsey, over 10,000 Chinese-owned firms are currently operating throughout the African continent, and the value of Chinese business there since 2005 amounts to more than $2 trillion. *Forbes Magazine*, October 3, 2019.

This is not to say that China as a nation doesn't indulge in a set of "created reality" operations unhelpful to the Chinese and not great for other, partner countries. The fact that China is being chosen by African countries, rather that the United States, principally shows American discredit.

an act of misplaced zealotry, a yearning for meaningless violence and, really, just plain idiocy.

By the time 9/11 was staged, as a nation we needed to be already genuinely promised to an entirely different project. It is a project that has much more to do with human life, housing and health, than with killing hundreds of thousands of people in countries on the other side of the world. It is a project that has entirely more to do with living as materially comfortably as we do now while significantly reducing the rate at which we turn the important resources of the earth into the entropic scattering of waste that is the billions of bits of plastic in the Pacific Gyre, everything that is not nitrogen or oxygen in the air over Beijing, or everything in the Olusosun Landfill Site in Nigeria. It is a project by which America exemplifies respect for ourselves and for others, rather than staging destruction in our largest city so that we could claim we are justified to wreak destruction in so many other countries.

The people who contrived and carried out 9/11 will, in their particular cynicism and configuration of anxiety, claim that war is fundamental and that empires, the American empire included, are built on the subjugation of other countries. Realistically, they will say, it takes shooting to subjugate. If the opportunity to make war is not otherwise available, the empire, for its own sake, must create it.

Other people have written — and, God willing, will write more — about the origins and global spread of Covid-19, about the deceptive practices, lies, and about the number and extent of "vaccine" injuries. The "World of Covid" has been remarkably characterized by widely and repeatedly broadcast official instructions for everyone to act in ways distinctly opposite to the actual best interests of human beings. Despite the persistence of official advocacies for jabs that lead, among other injuries, to neurological damage, myocarditis, recurrent cancers, and increased susceptibility to Covid, and despite all of the very heavy-handed propagandizing calling plain medical truth "misinformation" and "disinformation," some significant part of the population, having lived through a multi-year assault on its reasonable interest in health and life, having witnessed the deaths and injuries of valued relatives and friends, now rightfully disbelieves. Officialdom, however, is, at present, repeating its threats about safety and imploring "vaccination."

The entire Covid event, in a certain, quite significant, sense, comes from, and depends upon, prior processes of lies and manipulations, including the 9/11 fraud. This may not be especially obvious to many people, but, particularly in "schematic" terms, it is importantly true. Yes, there are differences between explosive demolitions of buildings (described as from"office fires") and creating a novel virus in a lab and having it spread throughout the world while falsely denying the efficacy of existing, safe anti-virals, inviting the cytokine storm and ventilator dependence in the ICU (and thus fomenting fear-based conformity to administration of an unreasonably dangerous "vaccine"). But there is a deep similarity in the summons to fear and in the many strong kinds of irrationality and harm to society.

Other books desperately need to be written about many of the basic subjects of this book, about how it is that institutions become corrupt, about the use of institutions to practice fraud, about the suppressions of truth, civil proceedings and civil rights, about the disdain for physical and scientific facts in favor of merely socially borne and enforced conforming, about urged social "norms" fostered from indiscipline and fundamental falsities — the list is long. While there is an existing literature, to be plain it isn't "working" in the way it needs to — in order, basically, to save us from ourselves.

Basically, there are two available, opposite, paths that may be taken by an entity (including a government) at any point after having told a set of lies: 1. To tell more and bigger lies tying to keep the lies in place (or to extend them into other lies, become more immediately distracting, newer, bigger, related, or unrelated but apparently useful). 2. To abate or discontinue the lying, even to the extent of acknowledging some, or all, of the falsehood. As between the two, institutional "logic" will always propose having once "sold" the lies, the further course of action can only be to repeat, extend, and supplement them.

Karl Rove's declaration about "the way the world works now" is a really a declaration about what he thinks excessively greedy and aggressive people who are practiced liars can continue to get away with, and have to continue, even in a world that now challenges humanity to develop and evolve from and through what is good about people and our societies, rather than what is corrupt.

Rove's is a "bad is good" world (or at least a "bad is good enough and, by the way, I'll gain some leverage.." world), which he proposes when we profoundly need a "good is good" world. Rove, by proposing to "create [what might as well just be called] his own reality," describes the business of distracting the attention and energy that the regular and good people of this world need and want to give to making the world a less anxiety-ridden and precarious place. The "created reality" in which a scam about airplanes and demolition completely wracks our attention for two decades, during which we waste every form of value, honesty, and all manner of faith or trust in our own country and in countries around the world, to be sure gets "created" and it is "real" enough. But it remains a "reality" that has not, and will never, quite overcome its origins.

The way the world does often work is by amplifying and compounding. But the world will amplify and produce and reproduce according to seeds sown, ideas conceived, acts begun, roads chosen. Particularly "big" lies have their worst effects not as much in the immediate presentation of the lie as they do in continued conduct constrained to trying to maintain the lies and the other lies told to maintain the lies. The 9/11 fraud was first responsible for the destruction of several buildings and the murder of a few thousand people. Over the next two decades the lies have sponsored the deaths of millions, trillions upon trillions of dollars wasted, and the destruction not of a few buildings, but of many cities — even before considering the relationships and other non-material things ruined.

Rove's "created reality" and the 9/11 fraud are ancillaries to ideas about opposition and opponents that, if they indeed belonged to anything (which they may not have), belonged to a world of much less harmful weaponry, much less difficult to control amplificatory technology, and many fewer people than today's world. Models based

upon and featuring hyper-extensive contention and unprincipled com-
petition are now, at this otherwise uncertain moment in the history of
the world, being now more often recognized to be profoundly unsuited
to current needs. In this, our time, we require not a breadth of opposition and deception, but sturdier and more reliable forms of verity and
trust, much of it necessarily based upon joint recognition of common
realities.

Nine: Metonym.

A name for an observed myriad. I don't suppose I have ever met Philip D. Zelikow. Everything I know about him comes merely from public information, posts, news reports, documents, video and so forth, the sources variously available on the internet. I don't intend to be just "grinding an axe" or taking up a "personal cause" in thinking and writing directly about him and what he has done. 9/11 is the direct creation of scores of people, and the further result of what many more have done and not done. But Mr. Zelikow, both by chance and choice, took on a particularly pivotal role, not only in keeping the 9/11 fraud from being subject to scientific or rational thinking and analysis, but in enabling a much greater extension of the political use of the 9/11 fraud than otherwise. There is a lot that can be gained in our understanding of how September 11, 2001 came to be 9/11, and how 9/11 led to the next two decades of failure and waste if we can understand both what Zelikow thought he was doing and what he did.

Like any other factually untrue story, the 9/11 tale was full of holes when told on September 11th, and, of course, for months thereafter (the continuing propaganda blitz notwithstanding). As noted, President Bush explained to school children that he saw the first plane hit the World Trade Center on live TV, a proposition impossible because that supposed "event" was not aired on live TV. People who had some knowledge of airplane flight properties close to the ground knew that Flight 77 (a Boeing 757 — the alleged "Pentagon plane") could not have been flying at 532 miles per hour close enough to the ground to knock over light poles (as claimed in the FEMA report), and that Lloyde England's taxicab would not be upright and shiny if it had. People who had observed any of the three collapses of tall buildings in New York who knew anything about physics and mechanics and structures knew that the airplanes-and-fires-cause-vertical-freefall story couldn't possibly be true. Exactly how the plane-flies-into-building scheme had been worked up wasn't immediately clear, but it was obvious that actual planes could not in fact have flown "right through the building,"

that there was nothing like plane crash wreckage on the streets below, and the immediate man-in-the-street versions of "plane" were extremely inconsistent, ranging from "private plane" to "missile" to "no
plane — a bomb in the building," so the commercial airliner-at-un-
real-high-speed story had more practical reason to be doubted than
credited, televised images and propaganda blitz notwithstanding.

At the time the reasons for demanding an inquiry into 9/11 were
many. Most of them did not have to do with the various shabby stories
about the "terrorists" and whether Mohammed Atta left things in the
rental car from his trip up to Portland, Maine. Yes, there is always
some appetite for "personal interest" pieces about people in the news,
including malefactors, but the media at the time were producing plenty of those, and some of the families of the unfortunates who died
in the collapses in New York reasonably sought accounts somewhat
more genuinely explanatory.

We know something about what Zelikow did. As 9/11 Commission Executive Director he wrote the Report himself, ("even before
the staff got to work") with apparently some consulting with Earnest
R. May.[1] Some comments about the Report were wildly enthusiastic,
particularly about its easy relationship with the reader:

"It Reads Like a Novel"

In July 2004 the 9/11 Commission achieved one of
the most unlikely literary successes in American history.
No one had doubted that the final report of the independent commission would make political and cultural waves.
Few, however, had anticipated the degree to which the
American public would embrace the tone, style, and even
'artistry' of the report's prose. Within hours of the release
of the authorized edition of the 9/11 Commission Report,
published by W. W. Norton and Company, professional and
lay reviewers began an ongoing and vigorous conversation
about the document's literary merits. In no small part, the
celebration of the "engaging" and "readable" narrative

---

1. The Commission: The Uncensored History of the 9/11 Investigation.
Philip Shenon (February2008)

contributed to the Report's astonishing sales.[2]

Other commentators were not so enthusiastic. In a 2004 article titled, "Whitewash as Public Service: How The 9/11 Commission Report defrauds the nation," Harper's Magazine writer Benjamin DeMott said:

> The plain, sad reality – I report this following four full days studying the work – is that The 9/11 Commission Report, despite the vast quantity of labor behind it, is a cheat and a fraud. It stands as a series of evasive maneuvers that infantilize the audience, transform candor into iniquity, and conceal realities that demand immediate inspection and confrontation.

Whoever looks at his manifold effort is compelled to agree that Zelikow did a lot. He did write what is essentially a novel, a work of creative fiction, one that successfully diverted the attention of the entire nation and the world from any form of critical analysis of actual facts and from the evidentiary basis, or not, of particular assertions, to the drama of the story being told.

The artfulness of the presentation is entire, seamless, accentuating, enticing, leading. For just one simple example, among many, Zelikow avoids the whole matter of technologically-not-possible cell phone calls from the plane and just blithely tells us that "Renee May called her mother, Nancy May, in Las Vegas" and that "Barbara Olson called her husband, Ted Olson, the [S]olicitor [G]eneral of the United States." As an audience, we are sufficiently used to the idea of phone calls, that we just move along to the drama: Renee "…said her flight was being hijacked by six individuals who had moved them to the rear of the plane." Barbara "…reported that the flight had been hijacked, and the hijackers had knives and box cutters. She further indicated that the hijackers were not aware of her phone call, and that they had put all the passengers in the back of the plane." From which we move to: "Shortly after the first call, Barbara Olson reached her husband again.

---

2. "It Reads Like a Novel": The 9/11 Commission Report and the American Reading Public, Craig A. Warren, *Journal of American Studies,* Cambridge University Press (2007)

She reported that the pilot had announced that the flight had been hijacked, and she asked her husband what she should tell the captain to do."

Even among these details, something in the telling and something in us gets us not to think about the patent oddities. Renee May and Barbara Olson both say that all the passengers have been moved to the back of the plane, Renee by "six" hijackers. (The otherwise "official" count of "hijackers" for the flight is five: Khalid al-Mihdhar, Majed Moqed, Nawaf al-Hazmi, Salem al-Hazmi, and Hani Hanjour.[3]) But if the passengers were moved to the back of the plane by six of the five hijackers, who was minding the hijacking? If the pilot was still in the cockpit, he nonetheless never had a chance even to squawk 7500 on the plane's transponder? If the pilot / "captain" (Charles Burlingame) was still in the cockpit, how was Barbara Olson, passenger, in the back of the plane going to "tell the captain" what to do? If the pilot was in the back with the other passengers, what was then the point of "announcing" the hijacking, and what instruction to him, passed to her from Ted, would likely be helpful? (The *Report* specifically says Barbara "did not display signs of panic," so the suggestion that Barbara — a lawyer and television commentator — had "lost it" as such doesn't have particular support.)

Zelikow is able to do a kind of narrative "prance" to make details that don't collectively make much sense *seem* to make sense by inducing credence in them put together from pre-existing emotions about the horror of the scheme of the overall depicted 9/11 event. It also takes a certain kind of reader, someone who is willing to have the "story" take over without any excess of evaluation. But Zelikow's

---

3. Two of them, Salem al-Hamzi and Khalid al-Midhar, were reported alive and well, living in Saudi Arabia by the British Newspaper the *Telegraph*, on September 23, 2001. "Saudi officials at the embassy were unable to verify the whereabouts of the fifth accused hijacker, Khalid Al-Mihdhar. However, Arab newspapers say Al-Mihdhar is still alive. " and "Mr Al-Hamzi is 26 and had just returned to work at a petrochemical complex in the industrial eastern city of Yanbou after a holiday in Saudi Arabia when the hijackers struck. He was accused of hijacking the American Airlines Flight 77 that hit the Pentagon."

talents at modulating word choices, using names, reciting the time, and demurely offering "From this and other evidence, we believe…" introductions are those of someone who also had the opportunity for a brilliant career writing "thriller" novels, and chose to employ his skills to turn what needed to be a truthful report into an elaborate work of fiction.

It may be a bit subtler, but his method for handling the alleged unreal behavior of flight personnel is also notable. The *Report* says "About five minutes after the hijacking began, Betty Ong contacted the American Airlines Southeastern Reservations Office in Cary, North Carolina, via an AT&T airphone to report an emergency aboard the flight. This was the first of several occasions on 9/11 when flight attendants took action outside the scope of their training, which emphasized that in a hijacking, they were to communicate with the cockpit crew. The emergency call lasted approximately 25 minutes, as Ong calmly and professionally relayed information about events taking place aboard the airplane to authorities on the ground."

Again, putting aside for the moment more "technical" faults, for example that there appear to exist two not-completely-matching recordings and transcripts of the Betty Ong 27-minute call beginning at about 8:19, that there is no recognizable sound of jet engines or other airplane noise on the phone calls, that there are serious conflicts and contradictions between the Ong and the Madeline "Amy" Sweeny calls (simultaneous, and both supposedly from flight 11), that Ong first says the hijacker is seated in 9B and then later says 10B, that Flight 11 supposedly descended at one point during the flight (and the call) at between 6,000 and 10,000 feet per minute (a big plane dropping *very* rapidly in the sky) and Ong merely comments at odd intervals that the plane is "flying erratically," that Sweeny did not recognize New York out the windows when she was supposedly over New York, that Airphone service usually did not work on those planes, was costly, and that there is at best confusion about how Ong might have paid in order to originate the call, there is something just funny about a flight attendant at 29,000 feet in a plane being hijacked calling the airline *Reservations* Office. (Should we suppose that since this particular trip isn't going so well, the idea would be to get information about seat space on another one?) Did she really not have "operations" or "management" phone numbers to call? Are we to infer somebody who set up the call wanted later to use the recording? The proposition that she "took action outside the scope of [her] training" is another altogether-too-nicely-packaged example of the author at work. Flight attendants receive training as to what to do in the event of a hijack, and it is not to spend 27 minutes on the phone talking about it. In an actual hijacking, the long phone call could be expected to be a way for the flight attendant to be further hostaged, or harmed or killed, or used in other ways that would make the situation worse. The instructions in the event of hijacking, internationally developed and issued by the U.S. FAA, include "keeping a low profile" and as "passively" — but as effectively as possible — delaying any entry into the cockpit or any other acts furthering the hijacking or the loss of control of the plane.

Similarly, the account proposes that there is one guy, supposedly seated in 9B (purportedly Daniel Lewin, a former Captain in the Israeli Sayeret Matkal special forces unit) who has died from having his throat slashed, and that two other flight attendants have been stabbed and are bleeding. (Supposedly, the cabin crew was originally nine.) The flight crew members that most of us plane passengers have known or ever talked with would, in the described event, tend to or manage the bleeding or dead passenger and the two bleeding fellow crew members. Not tell a 27 minute story on the phone.

But Zelikow succeeds in developing the full *drama* while keeping the reader just out of touch with the many and various absurdities of his account. It is "art" of a sort, certainly "artful," and the work of someone who most definitely had a guiding purpose in writing very different from providing considered analysis of clearly impossible and false accounts that had been before circulated, from telling the truth, or finding a legitimate center for a truthful account in reliably correct scientific principles of long standing.

After the *Report* has romped through the dramatics of its hijackings narrative, it goes straight to the dramatics of its "Usama Bin Ladin" narrative, in a chapter called "The Foundation for a New Terrorism," in writing as energetically detailed and moved along, featuring events at which the United States was "singled out … for attack." Even just some of the chapter titles for the rest of the book convey a sense of the tenor and psychological "push" on the reader the *Report* intends. They include: "Al Quaeda Aims at The American Homeland," "From Threat to Threat," "The Attack Looms," "The System Was Blinking Red," and "Heroism and Horror".

Then, at the end, we are led to something sounding more like a feature article in *Foreign Affairs* magazine, if one that's on some steroids. After all of the *sturm und drang* of the stories of the hijackings of the planes, and bin Laden, fatwahs, recruiting Muslim youth, threats, threats, threats, and terrorists, terrorists, terrorists, the message turns to proposed remedy. And we are told, in substance, that we can "Attack Terrorists" and that we can re-organize, re-shuffle bureaucracies — oh — and do better at "sharing information." In a chapter called "What To Do? A Global Strategy" the first section is called "Reflecting on a Generational Challenge." The next chapter is called "How To Do It? A Different Way of Organizing The Government."

Most remarkable to the reader who is not quite fully caught up in the narrative drama, and who would consider the proceedings of the *Report* somewhat analytically, is knowing that in addition to the Executive Director and the ten Commission Members there were about eighty staff people who worked variously from the time the Commission was established to in November 2002, to the time the Report was issued in July, 2004 and not one, not a single one of the obvious contradictions, impossibilities, and anomalies of the 9/11 story that had been theretofore told and re-told by the United States government and media in the period from September, 2001 to the establishment of the Commission a year later was reasonably satisfactorily resolved by the Commission by reference to properly adduced facts. After the *Report* we do not know why a jet engine part that did not in fact match the engines on any of the airplanes that allegedly hit the towers was found on the corner of Murray Street in New York, and we do not know why none of the hot sections of matching, actual jet engines (which are dense and usually found at crash sites) were found in "the Pile."

But, perhaps, that is just a small detail, too small to consider. A question big enough, however, surely must be how those terrorists could possibly have been able to fly a Boeing airplane with an aluminum fuselage (in effect, a soda can with wings) right through a wall of steel box columns much more massive than the plane and much physically stronger. Every other time a passenger plane crashes (at any speed) into a big, hard, strong object, such as a barrier wall, a mountain — or a building — the plane breaks up into pieces, lots of them. If the "terrorists" were really able to get the whole plane to "go right *through* the building" any "Report" regarding the event owes us, the citizens of the United States of America: a) a very accurate recounting of all of the relevant physical facts, the composition and weight of the plane, material and properties of the building, etc. b) an accurate recital of the learning regarding collisions as a matter of mechanical science, and c) a clear admission that those principles applied to those facts would have the plane in many fragments falling to the street. And if, after that, the *Report* wants to make a claim about what the Commission says happened twice in colliding with buildings and four times overall in immediate succession on a certain Tuesday morning in this case, let's have a very full and fair explanation *exactly* how the Commission says those "terrorists" did so many things on that day that are entirely unprecedented and that contradict everything true about mechanics since the beginning of time, and that we have consciously and analytically known about mechanics for hundreds of years. Similarly, one would think the *Report* would tell us at least something somewhat honest about why the NORAD cab in Rome, NY at one point on September 11th, was handling "29 different hijackings." Zelikow simply re-tells the before-told 9/11 tale decorated with more narrative direction to help skip over and past all of the very many obvious deep gaps and hollows in it, and caps the telling with propositions about "A Different Way of Organizing The Government."

One is taught as a trial lawyer not to find yourself casually asking an opposition witness aloud a question "why?" The notion is that to ask is to invite descent into an unhelpful confusion of pseudo-explanation. If you are working on a "case,"as you are supposed to be doing, confusion, particularly of the kind willfully created by your opposite, doesn't usually help. Nevertheless, in real life sometimes trying to assess cause, even societal or personal cause, can become a worthy significant basic effort. For our purposes, it is worth trying to figure out at least some part of why Zelikow did what he did. Just as in other situations we evaluate wrongdoing according to an evaluation of intention (we separate manslaughter from first degree murder by "malice aforethought") the Commission *Report* is an act of singular betrayal of this nation, regarding which we should want to understand something about actual impetus and motivation.

Mr. Zelikow is definitely not stupid. In various YouTube appearances he speaks with consideration and reflection about topics having to do with history, government, diplomacy and policy — all subjects in which he has clearly read very widely, and which he has done a lot of thinking about. He has served in upper level counseling roles in several presidential administrations. He is longstanding close friends (and prior co-author) with Secretary Condoleezza Rice. He is presently a chaired professor at the University of Virginia, where he has been Dean of the Graduate School and Director of the Miller Center. His is a "triple-A" resume.

Governor Thomas H. Kean, co-chairman of the 9/11 Commission, said the Commission was "set up to fail" both aloud in public (including at a National Press Club event) and used the phrase as the title of the first chapter of his book W*ithout Precedent – The inside story...* Even as we might notice that precedent for the failure of verity was ample, and if it be said the story told is "inside," it is deep inside a pile of lies, the various accounts of the activities and the practical history of the Commission suggest that it was Zelikow, more than anyone else, who made sure that the fraud that began with the 9/11 events and was developed then and thereafter in the media was further perpetuated, re-perpetrated and ratified by the Commission *Report*.

Zelikow is poised to be the last person on earth to admit that the whole 9/11 four-part-hijacking/boxcutters and planes/buildings-turned-to-clouds-of-dust isn't true. So there is probably not much point in asking him, either in fact and in person, or as a kind of "thought experiment" and "example," for an answer, why it was that he chose to propagate and extend the lies rather than tell the truth, or even some portion of the truth. The actual or the imagined Zelikow is just going to spout a bunch of nonsense, perhaps including stuff that comes from the FEMA Report or the NIST Report, or media accounts, and he is not going to get interested in the fact that the "crunch down/crunch up" theory specifically contradicts the "falling dominoes" claim about the building collapses, nor recognize as interesting that there is not enough potential energy in the structures as standing to create that much dust, nor recognize that the forensics from steel samples, and ejection of material, and from air samples, and from pile temperature, and so on all fully contradict the "jus' a regular ol' gravitational collapse" story in any form.

Zelikow now says publicly that "friends" told him not to take the job as Executive Director when it was offered to him. The information that is available reasonably puts up: 1) the question why he did take the position, received advice notwithstanding, and 2) somewhat more importantly, why he then acted in that office as he did. Not every Executive Director writes the intended report even before the hearings are held, not every Executive Director works so assiduously to reinforce the "security" claims of the entities being examined and investigated (including especially the obviously most absurdly "stretched" propositions about classification), and not every Executive Director confronted with thoroughly contradictory testimony from, for example, the military, such that only some witnesses can possibly be telling the truth and others must be lying, works as hard as Zelikow did to quash and suppress "the problem."

As in other historical examples of (considered relative to context) "big" lies, the false economic and health "statistics" propagated by the East German government, the business conduct of Bernard L. Madoff Investment Securities, many of the people who "tell the story" according to and in terms of the lies are in some way "representative" as to what they are doing, but that doesn't always make them particularly interesting. Often, they are just lying for the sake of telling the lies. Others, John Paul Vann in Vietnam, for an example (perhaps too complex for simple comparative use), Henry Kissinger (not simple either), Cary Grant or Rock Hudson — fairly taken in the context of their time — (maybe), Lance Armstrong (also maybe), Fitzgerald's Gatsby (fictional but an astute portrayal, maybe fiction more focused than fact) each in their way have a particular relationship with untruth that can be worth learning about and thinking about, even while nothing could be claimed for virtue in it.

The possibility is that Zelikow is such a person we should have thought more about (and continue to evaluate), not so much because he, too, did plenty of lying while forwarding the false 9/11 story, but because he appears to have gone to so much effort to make further decisions about extending and exploiting the false story and to celebrate the extension and exploitation.

There are some simple and somewhat "dismissive" answers we can posit to the basic questions about personal cause. "It was my job" or maybe "I was told to" — and so forth. To anyone who genuinely would like to understand why the bad choices to stage 9/11 and to extend and "defend" and, in distinct sense, "celebrate" the fraud, were made, summary or conclusory propositions about what Zelikow did and for what reason are at best unhelpful, and mostly lead to further wondering about how much someone like Zelikow was lying to himself, how much about the fake stories about he believed, or "taught himself" to believe. At the center of it all, perhaps was he just terribly scared, frightened that if there were to develop apparent cracks in the story, the whole scam would fall apart — and then ... perhaps he thought the country would thereby disintegrate. Maybe he decided that 9/11 having been done, the only thing to do was to keep pedaling. Or has he loyalty to Israel to the extent he was concerned about revelation of the facts of Israeli involvement and thus conceived that further confirming and instituting the fraud was necessary? (I can't say that I have any idea.)

But there is a second aspect to Zelikow that mirrors and replicates a comparable second aspect to 9/11 as a whole, and to the *Report,* and it is something from which we may be able to get a part of explanation. As much as Zelikow is smart and articulate, he also regularly announces logically very "diagonal" propositions, typically by means of the inferential positioning of unwarranted inferences. So, twenty years after 9/11 he boastfully announces that the *Report* and response is "a success scenario at the very upper bound" because in the interval America did not suffer "another major catastrophic terrorist attack from violent Islamist extremists." (Not that we in fact suffered one on September11th, 2001 nevertheless.) He calls the *Report* — the one that helped with none of the outstanding issues and questions — therefore a "triumph of public service and public learning." He also says some other things that have more of the appearance of modesty, but at center, he takes what should have been a matter of evidence, science, forensics, and rational thinking and turns to sanctimony.

To the 9/11 lies thus gets added a thick "triumph" meta-layer, an emotion-rich, celebratory surrounding, that completely diverts attention from and recognition of the facts inside. This self-congratulatory meta-layer has a particular further effect in keeping the 9/11 lies in place and helps make sure they are never evaluated scientifically or rationally.

Even if one believes the 9/11 story, the produced events that could be labeled something/anything (including "successes" — if one wanted to force a label) that one could say were consequent to 9/11, were that the United States both killed thousands of its citizens in rather gruesome fashion behind the locked doors to the stairwells in the collapsing North and South Towers, and created "the Pile" from which ten thousand and more responders and workers and got cancer and serious respiratory ailments, many leading to unpleasant deaths, and after the immediately produced events attacked Afghanistan and Iraq and made further war in other Middle Eastern countries, Syria, Yemen, and that the United States went "Homeland" obsessive, created the TSA, and went "news dramatic" endlessly repeating "fear and fright" memes that showed the Trade Center Towers collapsing straight down, featured the word "terrorist," and later the phrase "since 9/11," and the United States government and media said a lot of things that, even though ordinary thoughtful people have been scared into silence about them, are entirely unreasonable. The subsequent and continuing rhetorical move by which an extended spate of major destruction gets called an achievement at "the very upper bound" should, at the very least, startle us, but Zelikow manages to get a nation (or world) of what are (realistically) "half-readers" fully hypnotized into believing the various and extended damage a high end accomplishment. And he keeps at it — even to this day.

The soul of every political propagandist who has ever lived has to be admiring and very... jealous (?) of Zelikow's manipulative feat. Back down at the level of some connection to reality, however, only if the objective of some other nation or group in staging a "terrorist attack" were to get the United States to begin *another* war somewhere and to *add more* to its domestic portfolio of fearmongering dramatics, surveillance bureaucratizing, and tawdry politics and stupidities, could there be any reason for *another* terrorist attack, whether an actual or another hoax-style attack (including with plenty of real murdering). If the United States will demolish its own biggest buildings, killing its own civilian people in the financial downtown of its largest city, why would any other adverse group or country think it has to do much "provocative attacking" at all?

Even a casual study of the history of "terrorist attacks" shows that, if events such as the Norwegian attack on the Vemork heavy water plant are included, they have their place as a part of armed warfare, and indeed shows that they are used, and by argument are perhaps useful, when the attack is a "false flag" event, blamed on a country or group that did not in fact perpetrate the attack. The Israelis, for but one example already mentioned, dressed as Arabs when they committed the bombing of the King David Hotel, blamed Arabs and, at the time, Jewish leaders pronounced condemnations of the attack. Thereafter, as it became more widely known that the Jews were the perpetrators, they blamed Sir John Shaw, the British Chief Secretary for "causing" the 91 deaths and 46 injuries.

Terrorist attacks arguably can function as demonstrations of anger and protest and, particularly in cultures in which revenge is central, terrorist attacks may also serve as a method of revenge, especially against a more powerful or more organized entity that has committed a besetting wrong or offense. Otherwise, terrorist attacks usually do not in fact have an especially great longer-term level of accomplishment. Killing some members of a civilian population readily makes the civilian population as a whole angry, frustrated, scared (yes), and more concerned and alert. Inflicted civilian deaths can tend to make recruitments to arms easier, increase support even for non-democratic governments, and create ready justifications for control measures, even those inherently oppressive. In conflicts between nations, most of that response is not helpful to the nation recognized as gratuitously inflicting civilian casualties. Even without particular group "terrorism" methodologies as such, consider the role that killing villagers and other civilians clearly had in the defeat of the United States in Vietnam. Similarly, in conditions of small-team "terrorist" penetration and murdering, many of the examples of suicide bombings clearly yield no strategic advantage to an identified perpetrator, while creating a large propaganda and image disadvantage, readily exploited and pressed by the pictures of victim corpses. Not to be unfairly re-writing a history (that a few smart people realize could not do much worse if re-written, no matter how) from and after 1947, arguably the Palestinians more than anything else needed to be a nation of very talented documentary filmmakers. (And, by argument, it might also have helped, if just a little, if they spoke even their native language a little bit more slowly and with intonation cues more readily accustomed to the ears of other nations. Even if you are not crazy, it can only help if you don't —or can't be readily made to —"sound" dangerous to other ears.)

The events of the last two decades taken together, we, the people of the United States of America, have made a particular set of mistakes, some of them particular and unusual. But we made them with a lot of encouragement, almost all of it forceful and very wrongfully urged. Collectively we over-reacted, we accepted claims all of us should have simply rejected and refused, we abetted and participated in covering facts with false labels, and we took on an entirely foolish fascination with narratives, pretending that telling stories, rather than science and rational analysis, was the means to discover facts.

Our over-reaction can be measured in many ways, but perhaps

the most generally illustrative way is to realize, as several commentators have, that, if you take the quadruple-hijack story as true, we, the American people, spent between five hundred million and one billion dollars "responding" to what the hijackers supposedly perpetrated on 9/11 for every single dollar the "terrorists" spent doing it. Put another way, never in the history of terrorism of any kind, both false flag and acts for which perpetrators were correctly identified, has the relationship between the doings of the perpetrators and the ensuing activities of the target country attributed to the things the terrorists did been at a "pay ratio" so large. We ordinary people need to take a measure of responsibility. Including this obligation that should be ours, there is some responsibility that needed to be taken in 2000 to 2001 in preventing the 9/11 that was staged (preventing the scam scheme from being created among the group that created it), but even more in preventing the scale and extent of what was said and done in "response" to 9/11 from and after September 11, 2001.

Indeed, the necessary central point of this chapter, but especially in thinking and discussion about Zelikow, concerns responsibility. It is a fuddy-sounding term, "fiduciary duty," or as the tenets of our law more or less would have it, the "duty to act solely in the interest of another to whom one is responsible" but it is used in the law regarding a wide set of conditions and circumstances and, reasonably understood, it most basically represents the most important idea that we should now be thinking about to understand the failure of the "set up to fail" Commission *Report*, the serious failures of Zelikow, its author, and the consequent national failures of the succeeding decades. Mr. Zelikow is very smart. He worked very hard. He wrote great narrative prose. But nothing that he did was in the interest of the people of the United States of America. Seriously. Nothing. If he had a principal obligation to the United States of America or to our people as the Executive Director it was to tell the truth, not to lie. And, instead, he reveled in the lies, danced with them, dramatized them, dressed them up, saluted them, celebrated and extended the nonsense — oh — and added some "policy choices." Not merely was he irresponsible, he was aggressively and dramatically irresponsible. Nothing he wrote or said about 9/11 was less than very dramatic. Nothing that he wrote or said about 9/11 was true.

As is certain beyond peradventure from uncontradicted physical facts, the 9/11 event in September, 2001 involved flying planes around, any passengers in which we probably have to surmise are no longer with us, demolishing tall buildings and a section of the Pentagon with living people in them, by means of explosive and cutting devices, and telling a whole set of big lies about everything. None of that is in any part in the interest of the American people, in the same way that any premeditated wanton murder in a community is neither in the interest of the victim nor in the interest of the community. But replacing the factual investigation and fair public trial of a murder with extended rounds of false storytelling and strenuous propaganda enforcement of the propositions that not only was the crime the work of supposed foreign terrorists, but that it must be responded to by repression, war, and bureaucratizing is, upon any thoughtful consideration of the matter, an even greater betrayal of public interest and public trust.

In the most blunt practical terms, we haven't yet found any good way to get everyone to promise never to commit crime, and to keep that promise, nor have we found a way to guarantee that we can always intercept or suspend criminal acts. By contrast, the matters of investigating, examining, and legal trial of wrongdoing, to every extent they are done in the clear view of the public, as they should almost entirely be, are all under some semblance of our collective control. We do not easily, and cannot reasonably, permit even the local Sheriff to offer to certain murderers to conduct a non-investigation, or a false investigation or tell a fraudulent story or blame the crime on "Arabs," (or, in Mr. Zelikow's style, fully dramatize the fraud in the effort to keep the whole town confused and supporting the expensive destruction of our country and other nations on the other side of the world), while keeping any sense of self-respect whatsoever or holding and maintaining the respect of others.

Wrongdoing and lying about it will happen, but for society to function reasonably well, we must, as conscientiously as we possibly can, remove wrongdoing from the societal response to wrongdoing.

We have no other good choice as a society. To try to explain the point to President Nixon, we might say: "Actually, it is worse than an ordinary crime if the President does it, because, in a nation of excessive secrecy, in which almost all of the suppression of information is controlled by the President and the executive branch, it is difficult to fairly examine the facts and hold the President responsible for the crime and the consequences of the crime."

If Mr. Zelikow had any one single truly significant obligation in taking his position as Executive Director of the Commission, it was not to lie. Whatever he did, right, left, or center, above all else he had the profound responsibility not to further extend the 9/11 fraud. Indeed, in a decent world, he had at least the obligation to curtail it, to say at least the plain truth that the government and media accounts did not cohere with any possible physical reality.

Our law is not perfect. The principles we hold, and do generally support, regarding the obligations of trustees and similarly responsible people are not perfect, but having them and recognizing them is entirely better than not having them. Unfortunately, we are lacking sufficient similar principles, and the recognition of them — and enforcement of them — regarding those whose job is to find and report and act on behalf of the truth in the government and in public matters.[4]

None of this is part of any form of "censorship." It is not "censorship" to say that people aren't free to write bad checks. That is not "expression;" if intentional, it is just an attempt to steal some money from another person. A Commission Report is not an "editorial" in which

---

4. There does exist the crime, inherited from English law, of "Misprison" or "Misprison of Felony" and "Misprision of Treason " more or less defined as " The criminal offense of concealing, or neglecting to report or prevent, a felony or act of treason" and as "The criminal neglect of duty or wrongful execution of official duties." It is to an extent codified in U.S. Federal law in 18 U.S. Code § 2382: "Whoever, owing allegiance to the United States and having knowledge of the commission of any treason against them, conceals and does not, as soon as may be, disclose and make known the same to the President or to some judge of the United States, or to the governor or to some judge or justice of a particular State, is guilty of misprision of treason and shall be fined under this title or imprisoned not more than seven years, or both."

opinions can, and should, indeed "run free" and statements regarding fact maybe don't matter too much. The duties of the Commission are, or at least are meant to be, investigation or examination and truthful presentation to the country, beginning with a presentation of facts that are, actually, facts — upon which the country can, indeed, rely.

Ours would be a better country if, six months after having published the *Report*, Mr. Zelikow, as its substantially single author, were on the witness stand in Federal Court, answering questions (inquiries not limited by purported "secrecy concerns"). If Zelikow can convince a thoughtful court of law that he is innocent of any attempt willfully to deceive others to whom he was responsible in writing the *Report*, he can also be given a special award as the counsellor to Presidents who is also the most unconsidering, unreflective human being ever to have been given the responsibility of gathering and evaluating evidence regarding a set of physical events that have occurred on planet Earth — and then be sent home to Virginia.

It is not too hard to come to suppose that one understands why Allen Dulles turned the Warren Commission to his purposes and fashioned the results it produced, Arlen Specter's "magic bullet" included. Perhaps why Zelikow did what he did to the 9/11 *Report* should be comparably recognizable. But that is also to propose, in effect, that Zelikow has, his intelligence and accomplishments and position in government and academic society considered, as little genuine self-respect, or respect for other humans, or respect for the United States as a nation as, by the evidence, did Dulles, who, throughout his CIA career made choices that were nothing better or different than the government-institutional equivalent of the doings of a *Mafioso "Capo."*

A number of recent Presidents of varying political announcement have, some attention paid, taught us the American voters that we have a propensity to put assorted narcissists, from William J. Clinton to Donald J. Trump, in office, who have constructed political styles by

---

The problem, of course, is that in a country sometimes theorized to have a "Unitary Executive" and having highly politicized courts and justices, and in which the collapses of buildings in New York show "nothing notable," sending a letter regarding a fraud as fully perpetrated as 9/11, however felonious and treasonous, does not do much good.

and through, among other things, strident personal denials and assertions independent of fact ("I did not have sexual relations with that woman, Miss Lewinsky"). Perhaps the more relevant question, more serious for our country, and despite any efforts to the contrary, would be whether we have given greater institutional place to criminality and to substantively criminal means, methodology, and methods. Agreed, it is criminality that is dressed up. It wears a red white and blue necktie. And yet it makes for the human bones on top of the Deutsche Bank building — that belonged to… who knows who.

This is not about being prissy. In every human society, there has always been a certain amount of crime, and some of it is perpetrated by "officials." On the other hand, we all know what eventually happens when malevolence comes to exceed a certain minimum, and when it becomes "official."

It may just be that Zelikow belongs close to I. Lewis Libby, Richard Perle, and Paul Wolfowitz, that he is just another "gang member," arguably a little bit better "dressed" wearing more academic, and "study of history," and "counselor" clothes, and that his appointment and role as played in the *Commission* is equivalent enough (even if in ways pointedly even worse) to Dulles' wrongdoing in 1963-4. But, again, 9/11 has to be recognized as a departure. After the Kennedy assassination all driving through streets in front of buildings was not halted. Oswald was first used as a patsy and then killed by Ruby (supposedly as his "handler"), but that is still "baseball among the players;" there was no "dramatic" telephone call from the sixth floor of the Texas Book Depository saying that Oswald had overcome the inhabitants with box cutters. Dulles, Meyer, and that group greatly disrespected the country in the sense that they had purpose to change out an elected president by means of murder, and they lied about committing that murder, but not only did they did not demolish huge buildings incidentally to kill occupants, they did not as directly "amplify" the lie to give alleged purpose to major "Wars on such and such" including against the Middle East as a region or against conceptual settings, such as "Terrorism." (Even if they were seeking next to engage in wars. They did very intentionally immediately start war in Vietnam.)

By contrast, arguably they somewhat "minimized" the effect to the extent they claimed Oswald was a "lone assassin" (although capable of firing from several directions and once and of reloading, aiming, and firing a bolt action rifle curiously rapidly).

9/11 disrespects the country entirely more directly and completely. Ordinary Americans are killed only for the sake of doing killing.[5] There is no possible argument (ugly, foul, and very non-democratic though it may be) that the political and diplomatic course of the country will be changed (much less claimed to be redeemed from being insufficiently belligerent toward "enemies") by replacing the murdered in office. The 9/11 lies are not just about who did it; the lies hyper-completely falsify what in fact was done. To take a few frames out of the Zapruder film is intentionally to deceive the country, but four completely synthetic "special effects" airplane "impact" events in one morning is deception of a different order. To add to all of which there is the disrespect involved in propagandizing and insisting on lies that diverge so much from that which is scientifically certain. The high altitude cell phone calls are nonsense, and that's dumb enough, but then we get to the proposition that "the plane went right through the center of the building…" (or the idea that all but a small scattering of other airplane parts that don't match — of the millions of the parts[6] of four planes — became instantly physically unreal / non-existent at the moment of a crash), then on to the final proposition that the plane "impact" started office fires that turned the building to widely strewn sections of structure and huge clouds of dust. (And to disagree with the obvious nonsense is to be shouted at with much, much more nonsense or otherwise to receive retribution.)

By argument, the most grievous offense is the government's, but made much worse by Mr. Zelikow's attraction to and ungodly reliance

---

5. It is not much more than "street rumor," but there have been heard some suggestions that the group who put on 9/11 were at one point concerned that "not enough people were killed" for its purposes.

6. "… 3.1 million parts in a 767 provided by more than 800 international suppliers." (Boeing literature). "In the case of the 757, there are about 3 million parts, held together by about 415,000 fasteners, many of them expensive titanium rivets." (*Seattle Times*)

upon the presumption of entirely unfairly presumed non-facts. Again and again the claim was that there was no need to adduce actual, scientifically cogent, believable evidence regarding airplane hijacking and by whom, because (as the government and media said) they "knew." (And, yes, NIST similarly said a horizontal steel member became unseated from Column 79 due to thermal expansion without a shred of actual, competent evidence that this actually occurred before the collapse or caused the collapse.)

Thoughtlessly common though it may be to intone that "there oughta be a law," 9/11, considered as a whole, rather than indicating the re-re-reorganization of the federal bureaucracy, demonstrates the strong need for effective law, particularly law requiring government to act responsibly and providing specific remedies if it fails to. To make a list, specifically:

a) Genuinely independent forensic investigations should be required by law in every case of significant structural failure, common disaster, or serious crime regarding which the physical details are in in any way possibly uncertain. More particularly, even if some event is alleged to have been staged by "terrorists" or is said to be part of a "war on something," the law should specifically prevent suspension or curtailment of the forensic investigation. (In matters specifically concerning active combat areas during declared war, the investigation of course may be stayed to ensure the reasonable safety of investigators.)

Those charged with conducting a full and fair scientific forensic investigation with full published results should be criminally liable for willfully failing to do so.

b) All of the device data and other information ascertained or developed in a forensic investigation should become a long kept (30 year) permanent record in an independent, non-government library, public access to the information in which should only be restricted if at an evidentiary hearing conducted according to the principles of due process legitimate cause is specifically shown and, even if shown, any restriction, if imposed, must be narrowly tailored in time and extent to the cause.

c) Crucial information identifying and contained in significant forensic devices (including, but by no means limited to, such devices as flight data recorders and cockpit voice recorders) should be assured against tampering including by means of sufficiently unique (all known technologies considered) complementary security "keys" held in escrow by non-government, independent trustees. Keys should only be presented at authentication events. Those presentation events, in full, should be public and become part of the public record.

d) Significant fraud committed in the course of a forensic information being recognized as a serious crime, as with other serious crimes, the government should lose the privilege of suppression of the facts regarding such fraud, whether through classification or imprisonment of people, or other sequestration or by any other comparable means. Intentional tampering with evidence should carry a penalty not less than the penalty for the crimes to which the evidence is material. Any person or entity able to make a showing of probable cause should be entitled to present the case regarding fraud or tampering at a public trial to a jury of citizens who, upon voir dire show understanding and experience required to be unbiased, astute and capable of technical understanding and factual honesty. At such a hearing, questions from the jury, reasonable in nature, should be permitted during the presentation of witnesses and other evidence.

e) Our law should also directly articulate the trust obligation and duty the government has to the nation, and should specifically provide for substantive legal redress in cases of unjustifiable large scale fraud against the nation perpetrated by the government and other entities working under the auspices of the government, or induced by the government, or inducing the government or its agencies, to perpetrate substantial and significant scams, including, but not limited to, news media and other means of announcement and declaration to the public. The right of trial on the facts should be maintained upon a showing of triable facts, and the trier of fact should have reasonable powers to set aside any unwarranted secrecy claims. The law should make provision for injunctive remedies and for protective orders.

In other, simpler, words, from now on, no Phillip Zelikow should ever have the raw opportunity to do what this Philip Zelikow has done, and the law should work as directly and effectively as it possibly can to prevent another instance of the same, or a similar, process. Societal "mythologies" will, undoubtedly, continue to be created. Political campaign speeches will carry on and provide many not-so-real but emotion-stimulating sets of images. But it is most clearly against our interests as a nation to have such "mythologies" created in place of forensic analysis, no matter who or what sponsors them, no matter the auspices invoked.

Ten: In Sum.

As noted, not only is it hard to tell just one lie, but also hard to tell just a few, or not too many. In the instance of 9/11, we could not make do with less than an extensive plethora. At the corners of a web of many lies we usually find at least one very "compromised" person, someone experiencing something like Colin Powell says he did after the Iraq WMD speech at the UN or, sometimes, something in several, various ways worse.

Since 9/11, at every turning in the march of deceits there is at least a small coterie to notice in the procession (and often enough a pretty big mob) carrying bags from which malodorous brown smelly stuff just continuously oozes and drains, false history from one or another on-line "history" channel, "popular" science and mechanics magazines that offer cartoons-in-words articles purporting to explain impacts or collapses, strange explications for late arriving fighter jets, absurd alleged particulars of light poles knocked over in front of the Pentagon, or ridiculous claims about the very blurry contents of the video from the Citgo Station, Hollywood movies that invent many times more wildly than any epic ever made about the Alamo, or a nearly infinite number of high-end "liberal-y" glossy weeklies or monthlies that relentlessly insist on explaining what did or did not happen as physical events by means of purported analyses of described societal and organizational proclivities of bureaucracies and bureaucrats, and without any mention of or reference to any forensics or facts at all.

After two decades, the point at which more lying could possibly, even temporarily, be helpful, is past. Neither do distractions now palliate how used (and worn) we are. Campaigns, as emerge, to the extent they have, hardly entice.[1]

---

1. Mark Twain is said to have explained, "It's easier to fool people than to convince them that they have been fooled." Dictating his autobiography, in an apparently reflective moment, he is recorded saying (including about his own doings): "The glory which is built upon a lie soon becomes a most unpleasant incumbrance. ... How easy it is to make people believe a lie, and how hard it is to undo that work again." (1906)

The memorializations we have made where World Trade Center buildings with people in them were turned to shards and dust, that are now big square black pits in the city ground from which water flows into square black holes set deeper, now present themselves, like the 9/11 events and building demolitions themselves, as things commissioned, and become in their dark open squares an unwitting version of the unreality that can give to us who are even minimally aware a form of re-rendering of the original fraud, while echoing reminders of the wrongs committed by and with the fraudulent story. No, we don't directly see the bodies of the workers who died from working at "the Pile," but in an unhappy and ghoulish moment it is possible to imagine that they are yet before us, being carelessly washed down into the square black holes in the middle of "the monument."

The greatest injustices derive from the largest schemes when their appropriations are, in fact, misappropriations. A certain culture of putative leaders, some self-appointed, some by political deals made, started by talking about "transformational events" and "transforming actions" — and then, by force, by lies, and by great clouds of dust wrought a certain version of them.

Something odd sometimes happens to humans, particularly Americans. As paradigm, we start to get things screwed up on Earth, and we talk about maybe moving to Mars — a trip about three hundred million miles long (a spacecraft jaunt of about 9 months) where the atmosphere is about 1% of the density of Earth's and about 95% carbon dioxide, the temperatures average around -81 degrees Fahrenheit, (and vary on the order of 280 degrees F. between night and day) and the planet's surface is pocked with impact craters, many of them large, the largest one over two thousand miles in diameter. The advertising that the perpetrators of 9/11 preached to themselves and each other and to all of us is similarly dissociated and absurd (a purported "New American Century" from a pretzel-logic of scam and warmongering.)

The obvious more curative thought is that perhaps we should instead make a somewhat more conscientious effort to figure out how to live well on this planet, with its many resources and its multitude of life, before we say that we are a people ready to go to a place where it would in fact be really hard even to grow a single potato. Brought back to 9/11, for but one instance, if indeed the World Trade Center buildings needed to be something else, there are many things the World Trade Center Towers could well have interestingly become rather than a death pile of cancer-causing dust and rubble from which the steel was shipped to China.

It is an oft-volunteered trope, but the Founding Fathers of this country in the eighteenth century, to read the *Federalist Papers* and other similar works of political analysis and government structure of the time, were sincerely and significantly concerned with balancing, and the use of the instruments of state to achieve and maintain certain kinds of complementary and corresponding relationships they viewed as fundamentally important. This can be observed in everything written regarding "faction," or, for further example, in the rejection of State "quotas" in the new Constitution. They clearly expected and anticipated many of the developments and changes that have happened in the intervening two and a half centuries, a country from one ocean to the other, the admission of new States, more people, more commerce, and so on. On the other hand, there are several prominent features of our lives and country at present that they did not anticipate, and they could not be expected to have seen, no matter how hard they looked at what might be recognized of the future at the time. For just one example, given that killing other people required at the time the fact of physical presence and used a simple form of armament, a musket or a cannon (they could choose to shoot from behind stone walls, but there were no missiles for killing whole continents that could be launched from the other side of the planet, or which could, in launch-able number, immediately radically change the further course of the Earth entire) so ideas and conditions we now have to think about (down to the effects that war really would become something other than a distinct condition declared by Congress) did not come to their ken.

In some sense, electricity and its uses were, if obscurely, presaged at the time, but computers or computation, not really. (Even Babbage was not born until the 19th century, and his mechanical "Analytical Engine" more or less the 1840's.) At the founding of our country, words, well written, turned to images in the human mind, and an object held in the light of a lamp would cast a shadow, but "virtual" could mean only "almost" and not "made by software." The field upon which fraud could be played was also thus comparatively smaller and narrower, and fiction for the purposes of theft could be set up, but typically fell down exposed at a soon required physical production. The kind of crazy person who might talk about "creating" one's own "reality" was a different kind of crazy in the 18th century than we have from many of our 21st century examples.

The last fifty years have brought the collective discovery of what can generically be called informational amplifiers and amplifications. Among many other results, we can now create very "full" and very detailed appearances that can seem representationally "perfect" to an observer, but which have no actual, physical existence. Many of these appearances can, at least in theory, continue indefinitely. An extensive realm of "simulation" and entities created and existing by means of simulation now exists that never did before. A part of it is societally valuable. Another part, not small, is dangerous. In many instances, the lack of actuality matters, actually quite a lot — even (especially) when a given observer (or many) can't know, can't distinguish. Informational amplification can be the death of genuineness, even of purely informational things. This is not just about video "special effects." This is also about completely not-scientific descriptions of medical treatments delivered on the Nightly News. Facile simulation also entails that a hacker can access a computer with the same credentials the computer administrator can. (The computer, as it were, doesn't know the difference).

If the problems with 9/11 were just the problems with 9/11, even though the list is long and large (fake planes, demo-ed buildings, murdered / disappeared people, etc.) maybe all the lies, having been told, could — with a deep sigh — just be lies that were told. But 9/11 is an instance and example of events and conditions much more extensive than 9/11, the events, or the story, the policy choices, or the failures. The culture that created 9/11 has a fundamental problem of which 9/11 is but an instance. Technical facility has merged with large scale cultural, political, and legal failures. The problem can be noted and in some part outlined, evidenced, or otherwise described in any of many ways, and a list, that is just a small sampling, might include:

— By the overwhelming prevalence of the notion that any given proposition, including any particular truth, should be understood and rated as a mere "social construct" of the same kind as any other. (Karl Rove's "create our own reality" is another "postmodern" conceit about the purported irrelevance of anything other than mere assertion, without support from evidence or coherence.)

— By the frequently insisted upon lack of distinction between an inductive sequence and a genuinely deduced result.

— By the widespread urging that a falsehood proposed to be supported by another falsehood is the sufficient equal of the correction of a falsehood by a truth. (Otherwise, and similarly common: that many claims, all of them false, can "factually outweigh" actual truths.)

— By the confusion of a statistical result with a logical inference.

— By the very large number of announced "results" of scientific experiments (particularly in medical science) that cannot be replicated when the experiment is repeated, no matter how carefully.

— By news broadcasting that has become a form of low information, high zealotry re-makes even of plain facts.

— By the use of repetition as a intended substitute for verity.

— By news broadcasting that "converts" the news (as when protests in Cuba that, from all the available evidence, are not at all about Covid are converted in the American reporting about them into riots demanding Covid vaccines).

— By "elbowing" editorializing including from gratuitously unnecessarily laden adjectives added into a news report for no purpose other than to push the audience into using the same or similar over-characterizing words when later repeating or discussing that news item.

— By the repetition of "association editorializing," as when a "high-emotion" evaluative adjective, adverb, or noun gets word-paired with a name or other noun by endless repetition. ("Collapse" with "fires" and "terrorist" with "planes" in 9/11 news coverage on the morning of September 11, 2001).

— By distributed "mimicry of the feed" gone mad (as shown when a person with a little extra time on her hands and a video editor assembles a clip portfolio of the newscasters of forty different television stations in different corners of this country saying the exact same "cutesy" lines word-for-word to lead a propagandizing "human interest" story copied from the AP feed) or in which memes proposing the substitution of thoughtless anger for thought, "… terrorist… our values...." are repeated with the same insistence.

— By the collective devaluation of the simple facts, including, for but one example, biological facts regarding the biological sex of particular human beings by means of insistences, enforced by institutional sanctions, including retributions based on treating mis-appelation as "hate speech" or "unlawful discrimination," that people, biologically regular, are entitled to conceive themselves "genderfluid," "third-gender," "amalgagender," "demigender," "bi-gender," "pansgender," or "a-gender" and require others, upon significant penalty, to use one or another invented pronoun "set," including: Ze/Hir (Ze, hir, hir, hirs, hirself), Ze/Zir (Ze, zir, zir, zirs, ze), Spivak (Ey, em, eir, eirs, ey), Ve (Ve, ver, vis, vis, verself), and Xe (Xe, xem, xyr, xyrs, xe).

— By news-media representatives requiring a statement of condemnation for suggested social misdeeds, such as "discrimination" or "harassment," that have nothing to do with any actual occurrence, but are merely offered in respect to an event that did not in fact happen.

— By repeated assertions that Science, actual, genuine, rational hypotheses tested by confirmed experiment, is inherently "colonial" or "sexist" or "racist" or some other similar "ist."

— By the continuing and extended use of the words and language, and some of the lesser methods of actual science in ways not at all scientific, and without any regard to scientific principles.

— By the denial of actual complexity. By thoughtless reductionism. By simplifications that significantly misrepresent the subject being described. By infantilizing.

— By betrayals of the abilities and understandings that are the accomplishments and achievements of the country and among its people, including by manipulations of the economic market directly and specifically contrary to conditions of value.

At present there is no small number of us who characterize the whole of what the government and the media daily say and write as "bullshit." (The slightly gentler word sometimes used is "bamboozle.") These are not crazy people; they are not "radicals." They are well educated. They are not young; nor are they inexperienced. Many of them are former newspaper reporters and broadcasters.

What happened? The discovery of how easy it is to make and sell "synthetic" informational things, arrived together with the recognition that human relationships and institutions in a society which has more connection to cheaply offered synthetics than to anything notably real can be moved arbitrarily long distances away from authenticity. Our present era has been called "post-truth." It is that. It is also a greater assemblage of bad substitutes in ordinary life than has ever been put together before in our history. The worst of these are non-physical, the substitutes of prejudice for knowledge, debt for money, or money for value, press releases for legitimate investigation and caricature for analysis. Were the 9/11 scam in structure abnormal, there is at least a decent chance that the country would have purged or dismissed most of it. Someone who understood the world would have said aloud that airplanes don't fly through buildings and that buildings don't collapse themselves into dust — and not so many legislators would have voted against the interests of the country (and, maybe, the country would have put its attention to its security — necessary — and genuinely to some of the substantial issues of a planet with 7 billion people living on it, using it, and changing it — even more necessary.)

But 9/11, although very much in its own category in many ways, is also in schema like so many other fake and false things recently made, and a syndrome composed from parts copious in our present surroundings. The false stories often come as and from "levels," with isolating "membranes," "fences," between them. The "presentation" level is what is seen on a screen or heard from a "talking head." Across something of a fence in the form of "rules regarding presenting," there is a "created" message, or possibly a form of working at "authorship" level for the presentation ("producers"). But presenters as authors aren't really writing, and certainly not researching and writing. They are, in the immortal words of Jane Standley, BBC Reporter, "just reading from a Teleprompter." Providing the language to the Teleprompter are sections of an organization that, put bluntly, principally conduct a form of "trade" in information. On the other side of that trading are so-called "sources," a certain majority of them "government sources," who are indeed and should also be called "traders"— but "for the house account." And among the significant purposes of the "house" is to control the trade, again across certain fences (or "walls" perhaps as descriptively) in use such as secrecy and classification law, rules, and enforcement choices. From which setup, basic rules regarding controlling the trade emerge. Those yield the "news" that gets (and deserves to be) called "bullshit" by thoughtful and very well educated people.

It is another example from 9/11, but on Fox News a "freelancer for Fox" actor called Mark Walsh (also apparently "Nick Pugh") is interviewed at about 11:55 a.m. on Church Street in Lower Manhattan by reporter Rick Leventhal as two "Men in Black" are attending in the near background. Walsh, very emphatically, says:

> I was watching with my roommate, it was approximately several minutes after the first plane had hit, I saw this plane come out of nowhere and just *cream* right into the side of the twin tower, exploding through the other side and then I witnessed both towers collapse, one first and then the second, mostly due to structural failure, because the fire was just too intense.

In the passing of time, cell phone video, apparently taken by ordinary people and apparently veridical, that shows the explosion and billow of flame from the "Second" (South) World Trade Center Tower, that also shows a copious amount of surrounding sky, and shows no plane descending or hitting the Tower has emerged and circulated to confirm the fact, also ascertainable from physical science, that a

Boeing airliner did not in fact (and could not, would not) go "through" a building constructed as those buildings were. A photograph from photographer and Professor of Photojournalism David Handschuh from nearly directly below, that also gives every indication of being veridical, shows the South Tower explosion pushing out of the building — and no plane. Other than Mark Walsh, the people who were looking at the buildings themselves saw no planes, and are recorded as saying "No second plane — it was a bomb — bomb in the other building, not second plane," and "…it looked to me like a charred piece of metal … and there was an explosion from within the Trade Center" and "… everything I saw told me it was bombs in the building."

David Handschuch, who took the photo that shows the explosion and shows no airplane, is on record saying, "I was underneath it, I was looking at the tower, I had my camera in my hand, I heard the noise, I never saw an airplane." (Underneath, if a real airplane, he would have been showered with many broken-apart pieces of plane.)

The people who were watching TV saw the composited video into which the moving image of the plane had been inserted. But the people looking at the buildings didn't see the airplane that has only ever existed as an inserted video image.

So we get the so-called "witness" Mark Walsh and his very emphatic account of having seen the plane "cream right into" the building and explode "through the other side." To which he adds a confected-to-the-political-purpose theory of the collapses of two buildings "mostly due to structural failure, because the fire was just too intense." No kidding, Mark? Structures collapsing "mostly due" to "structural failure." And that was "…because the fire was just too intense"? How, exactly did you figure that out? No similar steel-framed structure has ever collapsed due to fire in all of building history before, and some of the fires (One Meridian Plaza, Philadelphia, First Interstate Bank, Los Angeles) were much more extensive and burned much longer than any of the 9/11 fires. But you knew, looking out your window, watching these buildings turn to dust and flying debris it was all because the fire "was just too intense." We should be impressed.

Illustrating that it is difficult to tell just one lie, we have the falsehood that is the video composited planes shown hitting the side of the buildings in the much broadcast video. Thoughtful people looking at the footage will realize it's not right and not real, but we have lots of "news" narrators telling people in emotional, credulousness-inducing tones that the composited event just actually happened. We need, and don't get the physical facts in Lower Manhattan and we get, and don't so much need, Mark Walsh's excitement while he tells his emphatic lie about what he "saw" from his apartment window (along with similar stories coached-in by others, including, apparently, Bryant Gumbel's producer's wife).

And from there the show just goes on and on and on. In order to try further to overwhelm dissonance regarding the planes story, over the next 24 hours we get a slew of further composited short video sequences that overlay a plane image on a clip of the explosion on the side of the South Tower from Evan Fairbanks and from Michael Hezarkhani and several others. Most of them contradict possible physical reality in and of themselves (aluminum wings appear to pass unaffected through large steel columns, fireball shows no wake turbulence from the airplane, no airplane parts at all breaking off the plane from among the 3.1 million, etc.). The videos also contradict each other, for example, showing the purportedly same plane arriving from different flight paths and at different angles to the buildings, and so forth. And we soon start to get "experts" telling us how it is possible that airplanes could cause building collapses an hour or two after impact. We get "miracles of fire" stories. Kerosene / jet fuel fire causes steel reinforced concrete floors to heat up and sag, pulling columns inwards, causing the whole building to fall down (at basically freefall speed, creating huge amounts of dust that could only be created by explosive devices…)

Honestly considered, 9/11 isn't about an "attack" on the country, or about America's "resolve" or some such (recognizing, as we should, that many firemen and workers and others suffered in the event and on the Pile). 9/11 is most fundamentally about how aggressively selected and forced and how complete our commitment to falsity can be and has been, about how much our penchant for lying feeds on itself and extends itself. Not just one lie, not just a dozen, not just a hundred. One after another, after another, after another. Lies about physical events, and lies about "debunking" perfectly valid scientific analysis of physical events in order to keep the lies about the physical events, and the lies about the lies, about the lies… apparently in place.

Even more than twenty years later, and without any thought that we can bring back the dead, if we have a thought to cure the damage to our reputation among people who know the difference between real and bogus, or restore some of the resources and opportunities wasted, we are called upon to withdraw from the lies and fraud that created 9/11. As a nation we have not just been telling lies, we have become addicted to lying. Our addiction is not unlike an addiction to gambling, or to opium or heroin. We now live a national daily life that is organized, not just around maintenance of the 9/11 lies (and extensions), but in servicing lies about political events, financial conditions, computer software and software security, medical conditions and hazards, and diplomacy, conflict, agreements, and aid in our relations with other countries of the world. The highest government officials in our country can be counted on to lie, not just as required, or arguably usefully, but copiously, as and when they speak. Media organizations reliably augment and amplify the lies received and developed in their source relationships official and unofficial.

The often commented upon "deep division" in and of the country has become, more than anything else, an extended contest of false propositions, from mere exaggeration to wholesale reversal of full sets of significant facts. The "Steele dossier" is "commissioned" (financed) by the Democratic Party. The Associated Press reports that the Mueller investigation found none of the Steele "charges" true, and also "put to rest four other non-dossier conspiracy charges." The Steele material claimed "…Michael Cohen secretly traveled to Prague in August 2016 to meet with Putin cronies to devise a cover-up of the conspiracy and pay off hackers." The Mueller report says: "Cohen had never traveled to Prague and was not concerned about those allegations, which he believed were provably false."

Examples like this, and in many varieties, some much more serious and some quite frivolous (but some of those fretted about with
much intent) repeated many times, in many different ways, it is not
hard to get the sense that the truth, whatever it is, has indeed sunk
beneath the "bottom of a bottomless pit" beneath a tonnage of lying,
dumped from one big societal/government/media/corporate truck or
another. Disagreements, particularly reasonable disagreements, can
frequently be bridged. Lying and scamming, however, considering
also that lying so readily leads to more lying, characteristically create
irreparable disintegrations, plenty of mistrust and thoroughly intrac-
table conditions. (In theory, one or more parties could possibly "declare" a point at which lying would stop, if others could believe that
such a declaration was not just another propositional lie. The principle
of "once burned twice shy" applies — although usually, and particularly for big lies, the number for the prospective shyness "factor" gets
to be a bit bigger than two. Typically, to reduce lying an amount of
definite factual confirmation several times greater in scope and extent
than the lies that have been experienced in the relationship must be
proffered, examined, and accepted before any useful amount of trust
in factual averments can be, even partly, reclaimed.)

No suggestion is made here that the lying can just be prohibited.
But for our county and our world to succeed in the complicated present and the future, we will need to recover from our addiction. Our
compulsion consumes vital energy and resources, curtails choices and
ruins opportunities. Our addiction to lying as much, and more, than to
drugs or alcohol destroys respect and self-respect (and, of course, that
which cannot exist without dignity, honor, or due regard).

In the end, it is indeed about respect and self-respect. In simple,
practical terms, the first required act of rehabilitation is an act of valu-
ing truth to enable a coming to truth. It sounds "corny" to be sure, and
readers who would like to find more elaborate and technical expression of the same ideas can read instead from the *Journal of Addictive
Disorders*, but treatment professionals regularly say, for example, that
alcoholics begin to recover when they acknowledge their drinking and
what is it is doing to them and to their families. The first of the "twelve

steps" of Alcoholics Anonymous is an admission that "… we were powerless over alcohol—that our lives had become unmanageable." The first of the AA "twelve spiritual principles" is "1. Honesty – Fairness and straight forwardness of conduct: adherence to the facts."

Again, it may seem trite, but the situation is not so different for a nation suffocating itself in "bullshit." To regain enough self-respect to sustain us through a process in which we change from being the victims of our own collective behavior, to the creation of valuable autonomous lives of which we are reasonably in control, we have no choice but to speak truth in exactly those circumstances in which we have practiced the habit of telling a false story to further the false stories and lies we have been telling and re-telling.

We now have no other good option than to recover from what we have done and who we have become, and that recovery begins with honesty and continues with decisions, including implementations in our law, that we are going to have, and act in the name of, respect for others and for ourselves.

We have been kept from recovering by a lack of self-awareness, a lack of genuine self-confidence, and by several types of fear. At first, from the 9/11 event and the media blitz many of us were consumed by the fear of portrayed "terrorism." Some follow-on stories notwithstanding, the last two decades provided enough time for thoughtful people to think. However, our society entire, everything around us, every meme of culture, every bit of doctrine preached, every example of subject and context tells us that truth about the most serious government and media lies is not only discounted and disdained and dismissed with prejudice, but it is very dangerously despised — reprisals can be expected — not just by and from the relatively few people who stand to be convicted of the crimes committed, but by and from the nation that has, for all these years been, collectively, their victim.

The wisest among us have been set aside. The most educated among us have, in too many cases, also succumbed to fear. (They are smart enough to notice the surround of threats.) Raw human intelligence is easily taught to become scared of punitive social isolation and

sanction, for it is obviously true that human beings develop and prosper in groups and according to collective understandings. Yet this is a
truth that should also describe to us the dangers from the enforcement
of collective misrepresentations and misunderstandings.

Biologically, humans embody genetic developments and hormon-
al chemistry that leads to and adapts to conditions of hierarchy and authority, similar to primate species in which the effects can often even
more distinctly be observed (consider societal "ranking"). In humans,
the effects can principally be discerned in "levels" of the being more
basic than "mental." It is not too unfair to call them "instinctual." For
a couple of million years in the progress of evolution, these comparatively "hardwired" properties in our forebears were useful and organizational and lead to survival. And, in plain terms, fear, in self and
others, and the ensuing decisions as to opposing or succumbing or
compelling or avoiding, made on the practical behalf of adrenaline
and epinephrine, dilations of organs and eye pupils, and so forth, was
an effective instrumentality of the societally and evolutionarily useful
ordering.

All of us still have the physiology in us related to that which or-
ganizes colonies of primates. But we have built a world much more
intricate and complicated and extended than one that's mostly about
swinging through the trees and eating fruit. Having developed the facilities of the imagination and intellect to create a world in which humans and the product of humans dominates and determines in ways
that no other species ever has, we have not done much, not only not
in "replacing" fear and other emotions in cases where we have forced
the need to, but to understand what should best be our relationship to
the more primitive parts of us. The emotions, particularly as they are
directly physiological (consider the "mental" roles of adrenaline and
dopamine), are features of personality in the majority of people directly "reactive," and thus readily directly exploited.

We have no other good choice about it, the world we have created requires us especially to confront and experience and consider our
fears with all of the other faculties and strengths of our person and our
soul. The practical point becomes that, although those at engineering

firms with large government contracts who would lose their jobs and be called "stupid truthers" and be "blacklisted" and have a very hard time paying the mortgage were they to say anything about the 9/11 fraud, there are others among us for whom recognition of the facts would not take food from the mouths of their children.

Along with the many comforts of the modern world we receive its requirements and challenges. We cannot now live a meaningful life without much more thoughtful consideration of our nature and place than ever before required, nor without engaging in a "dialogue of fundamental being" with ourselves — and with our fears, and with preoccupied (if not crazy) other people. This is not something anyone else, or any organization, or institution can do for us. When others exploit them, our fears are damaging to us. When we meet with our fears with honesty, our fears become uniquely valuable.

Even to the forces that have acted to create our fears, the things that are truly scary can connect us, create in us awareness, make us more conscious, more comprehending, and more respectful. Some time ago, one or another wit observed, "When they start burning books, they are also telling you what you should make sure you get hold of and find time to read."[2] The more current version might say something about YouTube videos that are nothing like lurid or obscene (not at all about sex, that is for sure) but are said to be in violation of "Community Standards" (or web posts by real, licensed, highly competent doctors or fully accredited medical research professionals that are called "medical misinformation" when they analyze the obviously contradicting and misinforming statements that government spokespersons have made about medical conditions and treatments).

By no means is every person called crazy is a misunderstood genius. But as lying becomes endemic, the world becomes populated

---

2. At which point I, as an author, also interrupt to ask you a favor. If you are ever in the midst of giving this book to another person (which I hope at some time you are), and that person looks at it, and says something like, "I heard that book is just crazy and says bad things about 9/11," I would like you to reply, if you can manage to, "And that is why you should read it — at least give it honest and fair consideration."

with "reversals," (Inversions all the way to the "War is peace. Freedom is slavery. Ignorance is strength." kind). In and of themselves these inspire a certain fear, including in the described "majority," who, no matter what they may outwardly assent to, continue to know in some remaining part of themselves that the "reversals" are nothing like interesting statements of paradox; they are just propagandistic falsities that will not, by turns in their own lives, treat them kindly. The progress of the use of lies (another word for "reversals" more fully set out in language) as it occurs is also inherently terrifying, in that it can be hard to know what or who will be the next victim. (We probably should have conceived that, as the practice of medicine became more and more "corporatized" and made subject to politics, contrivances such as "vaccine mandates" or "vaccine passports" to keep a job you've always worked at, or to cross a national boundary, for a vaccine that evidence clearly shows is neither "safe" nor "effective," either in ordinary or technical terms, would become a substitute for diligence and honesty regarding medical and biological facts and patient treatment — but events as they unfold remain offensively disconcerting.)

As much as we did not ask for, and do not want to have the problem of sheltering our humanity from the onslaught of regularized untruth, or guiding our recognition of truth through a wilderness of amplified nonsense, here we are.

In the end, we need new rules, genuinely much better rules, rules that cope with technique, technologies, and conditions very different than those available and in use when this country was founded. If we are successful, very few or none of those rules will create new opportunities for the perpetration of frauds or other abuse of the people and of the country. Making them will be difficult, entirely challenging, and can be expected to have to be done while groups wielding no small amount of power work regularly to convert the process into a special appropriation for themselves.

Rules and limits will have their place, yet at the center of the change that we have to make for the sake of our country and our sanity have to be us, the people, not the government, not government people, but the reasonably aware human beings who are among us, who have the heart to stand for something better than fraud.

In proposed rebuttal to what is written in this book, it will likely be said by some that lots of lying has been done for a very long time, and yet the population of the world has increased and we have life on this planet that remains. For decades "patent" medical "remedies" that contained just ethyl alcohol and some "flavoring" were sold at the county fair and consumed in answer to everything from gout to kidney failure, and yet human society evolved and, if not individually, collectively learned something about disease, health, and medical practice, enough to have more of us live longer. If we have learned; we have understood, and we have invented despite lying and fraud, why should the future not be an extension of the past, only better and faster and safer and whatever else we'd like?

The well-considered answer to this question notices that we have actually come to a new place in human history. Because our society contains many highly "amplificatory" structures, there are lies and frauds that we now cannot afford to abide. Our lives are still "real life"— glorious even in all of its mistakes and uncertainties and things that just plain go wrong. But as we can still afford to make mistakes absolutely must we be given to realize our mistakes, and fix some of the most wrongfully made of them.

Eleven: And So.

Beyond the arguments made so far, but connected to them, some very abstract and somewhat "technical" discussion that may be helpful comes to mind, despite how hard it is to find words that are simple enough, one the one hand, and accurate and comprehensive, on the other. Events in the world that hew to and come about according to the subjects of this discussion, however, are often powerfully direct and consequential.

The proposition that stability will continue even as yet more and bigger and more unreasonable lies are told, is ever more ready to be proved untrue. Fraud, in general, is inherently and harmfully unstable as a "system," and the instability is usually developed "systemically." The collapse of any given Ponzi scheme is as basic to its structure, its nature and trajectory, as the "first instance" Ponzi process of converting inputs in fact (solicited investments) to alleged output "returns on investment," but it is the continuing process of converting that most particularly and definitively causes the collapse.

That which is lost when systemic failure occurs is predictable in many cases. In others, the nature and extent of loss is uncertain. The facts notwithstanding, beliefs, credit, and credibility (for examples), are often tenaciously enough held onto by people, but then can quickly become not just disbelief, but extended discredit that runs far into innocent adjacent institutions. The change can spread by logic, or by illogic and emotion.

As said, our world, the world of humans, moves toward many real dangers, many of which have been already mentioned and many of which can be read about every day in the news. We could again make another list to repeat other lists set out above and known by everyone, that runs from atomic weapons and waste, to climate instabilities and change, to pathogens and pandemic, to resource depletion, to distributed and unrecoverable commercial and industrial scale toxic pollution, and so on.

Behind those challenges, and coupled to all of them, though, is a circumstance of underlying hazard that is in particular ways greater and more encompassing. It may seem silly when I give it a name, but please stay with me if you possibly can. I would call it "gross information failure." "Information integrity collapse" is probably a better term. Or maybe it should be: "very low visibility conditions in widely extended information fog — leading, randomly, but eventually, to crashes more serious than anticipated."

This can seem impossible in a world of "so much information." How can we not have enough information to know and project the size and scope of what can or will happen? As said though, it is the lying, the bamboozle, the nonsense, the propaganda, the very stupid mythology, the fake, false, absurdly non-real "created" reality also that make ready this failure. It isn't just 9/11. We lie about everything from opiates (Purdue Pharma), to mining cobalt, to censorship. And, as observed, these miscarriages of the facts are "systemic," reinforcing and extending and re-creating the wrongdoings (in the same sense that addiction is a "system"). These things happen in, and by what they do creates, an environment that is complex and non-linear.

It may be fitting to add to what has been said something about systems as such, including the "system" which is "civilized society" in any form to which we can apply the name. Indeed it is, if it is anything, a "complex system." Although even the matter of what constitutes a certain "system" is notional, arbitrary, and formally imprecise, "complexity," as the word is used in discussions of the kind describes something different than being merely "complicated" and says several specific and worthwhile things. First, there is no such thing in a complex system as either a cause or an effect that is exactly single in nature. Complex systems are multiply connected (or "interconnected") and include "feedback loops" to such an extent that states in what might otherwise be an "isolated" part of them are in fact propagated to other parts, and vice versa. The same can be said about whatever is labeled "outside" the system with which it interacts. Valuable analysis of complex systems generally cannot be done simply by means of dissection into "parts." The behavior of complex systems is almost always to be attributed to multiple causes and considered to produce multiple effects. Sheer quantity (including quantity of a particular kind of information) can be close to irrelevant to the operation of the system, and particular features ("matchings," "connections") can be crucial. Complex systems, generically, are also, at the same time, "emergent," adaptive, and, to a greater or lesser degree "self-organizing."

There have been efforts to "mathematize " the properties of complex systems (and of societies), all of them, as far as I know, only limitedly successful, and none of them successful with regard to some of the most crucial or interesting properties of the systems or societies. Commonly, the best that can be done is to offer observations and "rules of thumb" or what might be called "heuristics" (if derisively — but let's refrain from hustling to judgment lest doing so prevent us from understandings, even if partial, that can valuably be gained). There do exist "truths" about complex systems and about societies that, fairly understood and used, reward us with respect for them by leading us to useful and proper, if not formally exact, observations and non-throwaway predictions.

Some of these truths, in briefest statement, are:

— Information is not a physical thing, but is that which exists by representation (by being represented/encoded/detailed in differentiations in physical things). Information does not have the "conservation properties"[1] of physical things.

— Quantity of information can be responsibly measured several ways, including as the entropy of a model that includes (or "reproduces") all of a set of differentiations and, as a different measure of a different kind, as the compound and sum of state changes induced in an entity that receives the information.

— In the context of any particular complex system, a given quantity of information used in the system can usefully be described as "adequate" or, conversely, "inadequate" for the purposes of the performance of a part of the system or the whole.[2]

---

1. Or, otherwise stated, adhere to the same kinds of "symmetry laws" that physical things do.

2. Possibly helpful simplistic metaphors / examples: A "quantity" of information can be enough or not enough in a certain memory stick to

— Information of a given quantity can also be assessed as to its "quality." Although the measures regarding quality do not have even the less-than-truly-complete formal strength of measures of quantity, concepts having to do with the accuracy of correspondence between the information and relevant features of and facts in the universe can be used to assess quality in a way that is not merely subjective or relative. (Another useful word regarding the quality of information is "fidelity," which also can refer to the accuracy with which information does its representing.)

— "Amplification" in its simplest form is the matter of modulating a process "stream" or flow, such as a "current" of electrons, or a flow of hydraulic oil, by an input sequence of "values," or "states" (or the positions of a lever by a hand moving it). Amplifiers which make a one-to-one copy of the input sequence states on the "stream" can be characterized, in terms of information, as "duplicators." Amplifiers that modulate to results that are not a one-to-one duplication and that exist in an extended state space are distinguishable from mere "duplicators," and can be understood to create "new" information, or to be "information amplifiers." (A computer is an information amplifier in this sense. So is a cogent human being.)

— Fidelity or quality in the information contained in, used by, and created by complex systems depends, by no means exclusively, but more often than upon anything else, upon the existence and nature of "feedback" structures or "feedback relationships" in the system. Generically, feedback occurs when one or more "outputs" of the system are also represented as "inputs" to the system.

Some examples are likely to help, even though as described in words they lead to a reasonably accurate intuitive understanding but nothing like a full proof from a formalism. When amplifying an audio signal, for instance, when we have a set of small voltage changes on a wire over here (to the left) that we want to emerge over there from a set of speakers over there (on the right) as a faithful rendering of Handel's

---

contain a given "text"; a quantity of information can be enough or not enough in a set of instructions to go from here to the place where the buried treasure lies.

"Hallelujah Chorus" we need to make a more electrically "powerful" copy of the signal to drive the cones of the speakers, and we want to get "clean" sound that is equal in amplitude across the spectrum of audio frequencies. Most commonly we use a differential amplifier and connect the "input "signal wire to one of its input terminals, and connect a derived sample of the output to the other, making a "feedback loop." We use the properties of the loop, correctly designed, such that the quality of the sound is better than otherwise.

It is not quite "fair" to say the amplifier thus "knows" its output from the input, and thus the sound quality is improved. The simplest feedback loop is just a connection that "provides a copy to help guide the process of copying," most commonly by "modulating" the amplification in relation to output, or being "negative feedback." While the audio is now better, the sound amplifier in toto remains paradigmatically just a duplicator. Information amplifiers, by important contrast, are the structures that more fairly may be said to create what we might begin to say can be "knowledge." (Representation as such. It can be, and be called, "metainformation" — information *about* information. In other, perhaps helpful, words, the output information is "information" that has interesting "informationally dynamic properties" greater than those of the input. Similarly, differences that distinguish informational amplification can be noticed or observed in several ways, including by whether "error" portrayed an a connected feedback loop is non-linear and "semantic" in nature.)

If we advance the notion of "system" just enough to say that there may exist an "objective," similar ideas and principles apply, and these can provide further explication. Suppose a table in front of a person, a surface green, large enough and flat, except for a small blue dot/"bump" somewhere on the surface. A blindfolded person in front of it will have to do a comparatively lengthy search to put an index finger on the blue dot / bump. Eyes open, the person creates a representation of the surface (eyes, brain) and guides the finger accurately and directly, continuously observing and representing the distance and direction to the dot. Again, "feedback" often is fundamental to the properties of the system we would describe as salient. (The "finger the dot" system works as it does from the eye feedback as to finger position.)

Relevant imagination can usefully be applied to situations we can readily conceive that will give us a chance to have a better than primitive understanding not only as to how information regularly works in systems with regard to basic circumstances and conditions. For an example, suppose we ask the person to guide the index finger to the objective ("dot"), but using a television image of the table that we provide. If the television image is fair and accurate and not distorted or corrupted, we can guess that putting the finger on the goal will be not be much harder than it was with the table immediately in front of our subject, looking straight at it (no TV).

Next suppose we corrupt the television image one way or another. Even if we just turn the video image vertically upside down, it will take some time for our subject to figure out what is going on and to land the index finger. But if our manipulation of the image doesn't delete too much information or contain a lot of incorrect information, adaptation can restore the overall system to usefulness.[3]

Next suppose we can corrupt the video properties of the blue dot / bump as shown on the screen by "telling lies" about where the dot is with respect to the image of the finger, even suppose we can have the "lying" move the dot from one false place to another — even as the finger moves. We would make putting a finger on the dot difficult.

Once the system becomes "complex" is that way, the results (from being able to put the finger on the dot or not, to seriously real, seriously large seriously complex systems) become dependent upon what we might call the informational "abilities" of our imaging system, on the one hand (if only to "corrupt" the presentation), and the information "analysis and management" abilities of the person who would put his finger on the dot, on the other.

To say that a system is "complex" is to say many things about it,

---

3. Experiments by Erismann and Kohler, for example, show that a person can fully adapt to an un-obscured but inverted ("upside down") world presented to that person's vision in about ten days (to the point of being able to ride a bicycle.)

many of them quite important to understanding it and working with it, but it is not to say that the system *necessarily* functions with regard to any particular described purpose with any particular amount of fidelity or quality. Tesla cars on "autopilot" crash at high speed into fire engines parked by the side of the road. Honeybees suffer "hive collapse." Despite a variety of financial adversities stock markets create many trillions of new dollars over a decade or two — and then slump. Even highly redundant, high functioning complex systems prosper spectacularly, and fail suddenly.

Informational "ability" of the kind noted above is context dependent and not mensurable by any simple metric or according to any non-complex "factor," but it is real, it is of major consequence, typically more significant to what the system can do, and does, than any other feature of it.

That said, we can also usefully generalize to notice that although complex systems can withstand and recover from corrupted information and continue on despite error and infidelities, that corrupted information in small and large amounts,[4] and by cascades, can entirely defeat the purposes, outcomes, outputs to and for which the transmission of the information in the system is made, and can destroy the functioning of the system as a whole.

Let us then leave list-making just at that for the moment. As the thoughtful reader will be aware, the list begun above can easily be extended indefinitely. (Complex systems, as part of their operation, manage to create new, never before seen, system properties, and once we begin itemizing what might be called "adaptations" and "structural potentials" the list then becomes that much more endless.) Having observed several times earlier that "coherence" and "truth" are inseparably related, that true facts "make sense" with other facts, particularly with regard to scientific facts for which known and very well demonstrated very definite relationships apply, basic valuable understandings

---

4. If it helps, an example of sorts: Once upon a time in a computer lab a game was played to "crack" "protected" software by "patching" the executable. The winner was the successful patch with the least byte count modification. One byte patches won in an interesting percentage of cases.

how to understand and care for human society in a modern world are suggested even by just this small set of basic precepts.

For all of human history until about 1945, toward the center of the organization of society was the fact that groups had practical advantages that individuals did not. A hunting party of several hunter-gatherers could surround and kill the wild boar, taking home meat for dinner, whereas a single human would end up just chasing the beast. As important than anything else, therefore, was keeping the group as a group, a requirement for which the exercise of "authority," including by a "ruling" entity, a government, was usually helpful. Much that was wrong or absurd could be endured for the sake of maintaining the group as a group.

Because it was from multiple processes and events that were multiple, and much of what was happening was profound and hidden until the results multiplied into obviousness, saying that the change happened at one particular time is merely arbitrary but, for most of the Western world, the middle of the twentieth century is as convenient as any time to declare to be the historical stage when many basic societal and political relationships were inexorably altered, no small number of them "transposed" in some way. The extensions of the differences continue to the present. This usual list of factors and causes is as good as any: global interdependence, atomic weapons, semiconductors and high density electronics, computers and networking, large fleets of passenger and cargo airplanes, containerized shipping and large cargo fleets, technology developments and technology transfers, scientific developments in biology and genetics, hyper "digital" monetary systems without underlying precious metals, etc. and so forth. The "size" of every form of government, and of nearly every actual government on Earth, also increased many fold as part of the change.

Collectively we have only half-noticed, but complexity, amplification, and the size of government, taken together, the matter of forming society to the advantage of those living in it reversed. The reasonable primary concern now is no longer whether *by means of government,* society can be organized, it is now whether, *by means of society*, government can be organized, at least to the extent that it is not captured by concepts and interests damagingly adverse in fact to the well-being of the society. If the fundamental issue and question for human society had been, for millennia, the matter of individual people becoming successfully ''grouped,'' the fundamental issue now is corruption among and between the forces and institutions that construct and control a grouping. There are many related, alternate, but comparable and connected ways to say it. If the primary matter for millennia was raw amplification, the essential question now is fidelity of signal. If the way to accomplishment was formerly the application and expression of "raw" power as such, the means to improvement now has instead everything to do with modulation and metainforrmation.

Corruption can be fairly well tolerated in a world in which natural resources are, in practical terms, unlimited, and the weapons in use are bows and arrows. Corruption of all kinds, however, becomes dangerous in a world of a high degree of amplification, whether the amplification is merely mechanical, mechanical and particularly energetic, whether it is essentially a matter of duplications, or "informational amplification." (Informational amplification can, of course, extend and amplify more significantly.) What is here meant by "corruption"? Everything that we ordinarily associate with the word, from "corruption" of an institution, to "corruption" of a message; from "corruption" of an idea or principal to "corruption" of a person in office; from "corruption" of biological or ecological relationships to "corruption" of security arrangements, from corruption of a "sample" of something to corruption of the execution of a computer program.

Put another (somewhat raw) way, if you are going to have major league amplifiers, you need capable and accurate (truthful) feedback loops. Even if we do not have a handy way to formalize this precept, many examples commend it to us. Indeed, there are many other somewhat "sloganizing" ways to say similar and related things that have, at their center, effects that come from the same underlying realities about systems, complex systems, information, amplification, value, and trustworthiness. They all point to an understanding that must become much more widespread if we are not going to destroy ourselves. At the center of that understanding is an ultimately genuine appreciation, a profound esteem, for fidelity, for verity, honesty, truth.

As humans, we will always "make up things", we will always be liars to some degree or another. But then there are big lies that get made up to compel millions and billions of people to be subject to, and governed by, to be plain about it: fraud. The people telling the big lies conceive that they are right, that they must be right, exactly because they have been able to get great multitudes to believe complete bullshit. But those people are actually very wrong because a society having its basic connection to the world around it to be — and to continue to be — lies, nonsense, incoherent politically-concocted stuff, will, one way or another, at one time or another, make titanic mistakes, often unexpectedly, and will therefore also continuously run the risk of self-destruction. Over time, it becomes more likely than not that the continuing risk will turn consequential.

The historically great change that has occurred in the society as a "complex system" (including making it more complex by increased amplification, particularly informational amplification) makes sufficient, accurate, correct, truthful, honest *system* information, especially in high-functioning "feedback loops" the sine qua non for its long-term success.

The 911 fraud, even now, after more than two decades, continues to offer an opportunity to the people of the nation and the world to be very clear in our disavowal and disapproval. Concerning other stories perhaps a group "was trying to do something useful" but "made a mistake." There is no question as to the intent or as to the falsity of the 9/11 story. 9/11 is not about an "accident" or "mistake" or "glitch." Buildings do not get rigged for demolition and collapsed vertically due to an inadvertence. Turning the World Trade Center buildings into a great plume of dust was in every way intentional. Nobody who did it was "confused" about what was happening. Because it can be so fully analyzed and understood in its physical details by Newtonian mechanics, there is no reason to be in the least unsure about what did and did not happen.

What is certain about mechanical facts also enables us to be certain that blaming "Muslim hijackers who stole planes and flew them into buildings" is completely false and fraudulent, not only as to the alleged "hijackers" but as to us, as to our "framing" of the "picture" from a "representational" point of view. (Just for one, moment of "re-frame:" lucky for them, those "hijackers" did not die in suicide plane crashes, but seem to be alive in the Middle East — and not so lucky seem to have been almost all of the people — people more like "us" — sitting in seats on the planes that took off from Dulles, Newark, and Boston the morning of September 11, 2001). The manipulation that is 9/11 inherently does becomes all about fooling ourselves (and, in some metaphorical, but applicable sense, about what we are "sitting in.")

More fooling, of course, even as we can know without reservation that the 9/11 Commission Report is prodigiously untrue. Without intending to, the actual perpetrators of 9/11 thus fortuitously "gave" to us a fully ripe "example" from which it behooves us to learn, to respond, and to change. We fail to do so at our collective peril.

Pipe dreams could have it that Philip Zelikow is someday put before the rest of us to confess and reflect, perhaps even to recognize that putting on the 9/11 scam was a really bad idea, and that the wonderfully novelistic — complete bullshit — Commission *Report* he produced was an icing of wrongdoing atop a cake of malevolence. Even without having those fantasies come true we should anticipate that the society, world, nation we have created will recognize that we require, instead of the S. Shyam Sunders and the John Grosses and the Zelikows, an institutional form in which the citizens who have expertise, understanding and knowledge, who are, yes, as a cohort, genuinely educated scientifically, intellectually and morally, instead take the place of the government "cronies" who do some of the most egregiously corrupt fabricating and falsifying. Whatever way we can get it, we genuinely need those who have the courage, as and when it should be told, to tell the truth.

The changes happening in our society and in the world also compel us to change how we create and use information and how we practice societal shaping (and organizing). For a some time now, considering the world as we have made it, although in some respects we have continued as before, overall we have been working "backward." Events and results taken together, our societal and political systems are now "devolving" rather than evolving. Indeed there once existed the "Paranoid Style in American Politics" as described by Richard Hofstadter, but we have moved from mere "paranoia" as he labeled it in 1964 to what might now be call the current "Style of Maximally Aggressively Mixing Hyper-Anxiety with Thuggery While Belligerently Disrespecting Truth." When a person, entirely thoughtful and well qualified to appraise facts and propose a reasoned opinion, says something that irks government or its relata (from over-size corporate interests to subcontractors) in any form, the plain thinking now gets not only menacingly castigated, condemningly screamed at without evidence or analysis, wrongfully called "conspiracy theory" and "harmful misinformation" but any YouTube / Twitter, etc. account, or license to practice (even professions such as law or medicine), is forcedly canceled or suspended or otherwise interfered with. For a country with a First Amendment, all up we in the United States censor with the avidity of the Chinese Communist Party. (Even as we might claim we are better than the CCP at pretending not to.)

Who or what is doing this and why? What is the thrust and purpose? What "need" does it respond to? In a word we might say: "control." The one word itself is admittedly completely inadequate as an "answer." But it can be useful to use, to cite, because if we pay some attention it immediately points to some of the mechanistic basics of several of the societal failures taking place. One of the first comes from the very idea of "control" as usually conceived or espoused. Societies are inherently more like "ecologies" than they are like "machines." They become more and more complex and "ecological" as they continue. As "complex systems" they do not respond well to the usually wildly simplistic (monomaniacal) ideas about how to "control" them — especially over time. As with the use of "Roundup" (glyphosphate) weed killer; the cancers are ultimately a greater cost and burden than employing other, more modest, ways, to cope with weeds. Correspondingly, measures intended as simple societal "control," applied to complex systems, more often degrade the system rather than develop or improve it. The more complex the system; the more true.

Further, the more such measures are also applied to information and informational structures, the more the mismatch and propensity for failure. Our forefathers more or less understood as much even back in the late eighteenth century. The First Amendment "make no law abridging..." provisions were extended in effect from the time of adoption until the end of the twentieth century. Similarly, we have examples such as the well-known thoughts of Justice Brandeis in 1913, "Publicity is justly commended as a remedy for social and industrial diseases. Sunlight is said to be the best of disinfectants; electric light the most efficient policeman. And publicity has already played an important part in the struggle against the Money Trust." We have steadily been walking realizations of this kind backward, however, in the twenty-first century in favor of claims we now make about the supposed value of imposed restrictions and suppressive mandates, especially in regard to information, the distribution of information, the care of information, and the use of information.

As we should be working to be more articulate and accurate in what we say to each other, rather than less, to speak from connection to the facts, whatever they actually are, rather than while trying to "spin" or pervert or otherwise molest them (so that we can do better than just chew up the only habitable planet we've got), we should also recognize that having institutions too much determine and limit the true information available about them is not good for all of us (including, usually, not good for the great majority of the more "ordinary" people within the institutions or who work with or for them).

As structures become larger and more complex, in order to function well the information flow through and about them must become greater, more extensive, more accurate, more detailed, and more comprehensive — and should be handled by entities and other institutions with more capacity and capability than the subject organizations, not less. Our current practice is ruefully opposite. Governments and businesses now maintain much more secrecy and engage in more suppression as they engage in more and more various doings that change more around and about them more irreversibly and profoundly. The society at large meanwhile gets an increasing stream of lies, distractions and denials.

Many of the things that need to be said about the society are necessarily complicated because they are said about a system complex enough also to be complicated. That complicatedness can make it less easy to see the incoherences in the first place, to understand them, and to recognize which are the most telling and the most consequential. But it doesn't make fidelity any less valuable.

As a set of events, 9/11, uniquely, demands to be truthfully understood and used, worldwide, greatly to improve our understandings of our world, our responsibilities, and the virtues and the failings of our systems of government. 9/11, in terms of the central events that happened, concerns very basic, simple, not complex, mechanical matters — about which we can be a hundred percent sure. Physical objects (of any arbitrary degree of mixed componentry and complication) act according to Newton's principles in collisions. Thus, the surrounding information "mess" created (the lying, the propaganda, the bullshit) by government and media is, in certain sense, set in relief, made clearer, more obvious, and it should provide a "much better than otherwise" opportunity for us to help ourselves. We have a chance to recognize (right in front of us since September 11, 2001); we can fully examine all the "stuff" put up.

(The best way that Richard B. Cheney and David Addington, and I. Lewis Libby could spend the rest of their lives would be answering questions before an investigative committee of the most capable magistrates having a quality research staff and having no ties or connections to government, or military, or spy agency, or federal bureau establishment interests. And if they really don't want to answer any questions, better that they switch places with Julian Assange, being tortured and in long solitary confinement in prison. For the viable future of this country and the world, the scamming and lying of Cheney and Co. is much more reckless and dangerous than showing videos of an American helicopter crew shooting unarmed civilian press reporters on a street in Baghdad.)

The chances are better than even that the next "crisis" of similar kind (whether the mess brought on by "Covid" or by the next (financial de-dollarization/debt/credit death? war with the Russians? war with the Chinese?... malevolent chaos) will leave us an order of magnitude more uncertain as to who did what and to whom and why, and be that much more difficult to unravel. If we have any chance to recognize for ourselves and to explain to each other that synthetic events ("created" reality) followed by bullshit and false "debunking" and ('us experts at NIST didn't hear no explosions') denials are not good for us, not good for our national character, not good for the sake of reasonable trust and understanding among us, not good for our wellbeing, and not good for our future, we are obliged to take that chance. 9/11, oddly perhaps — but it is an "oddly" that does not so much matter — gives us collectively a profoundly needed opportunity to render a true and unambiguous autopsy of fraud of the sort in use for such purposes, and the choice to avoid a similar, but even worse, set of events in our future. For the sake of the people, the ordinary, human people, we should put it up as an example of fundamental wrongdoing and condemn it.

When many bodies wielding shovels were the way that holes that required to be dug were dug, it more or less made sense to have a king who pressed the society, through a certain system hierarchy — and rigidities of doctrine and dictate — to keep digging. Almost nothing we now do is comparably simple, however, nor located in simple collection in the same way. We get the force we employ from many other sources than human hierarchy. The social and political structures that remain with us as "control systems" from a time, not too long ago in years, but very far behind us in its terms and conditions for human life, have the benefit of connecting to and applying to that which remains in us that is "primitive," "the four F's," or "fear and greed," or "the reptilian brain stem at work." They can be used in that way — but in practical terms such use is now, as often as not, abuse. Such structures do *not* have the benefit of quality dynamic functioning in what is now a highly complex system.

The "shape," or the form, or "scheme," in which we organize ourselves matters. The transition from monarchy to representative /

legislature with executive governments that happened in the late eighteenth century (time of the French and the American revolutions, extended and leading to what now gets called a "Western form of government" in many countries in the world) was a complicated and various matter, but near the center of the change was the fact that monarchies were too "narrow" in structure, and thus also insufficiently connected and too constricted in information "flow," accuracy, utility and use. (Admittedly very coarse summary: a given king or queen and the immediate "Court" came to the point to which they struggled adequately to model and understand the lands and people they were putatively governing, which, of course, led to stupid decisions, which then led to harshness and further irrationality and, in some cases, revolution; in others major political resettlement.)

The schematic "shape" of our current American government suffers from a somewhat analogous problem, whether we have the wits to recognize this or not. Obvious to a significant portion of us, the relationship between government and the people of the nation is suffering significantly and is breaking down. Approval ratings for Congress as a whole are low, as are approval rates for the President, and for many federal agencies and entities. This, even after money in large aggregate amounts has been spread around the society for several years (with the effect, among many others, that about a million Americans are now homeless, many of them drug addicted and living in makeshift "blue tarp" tents alongside garbage-strewn freeway exit ramps.)

Why the discredit and the antipathy despite the largesse? At core, it is for reasons some of us have been thinking of, but many of us have not yet come to terms with. The two word answers, or a few of them, are "structural corruption" and "brute relationships," "displaced relationships," "artificial ingredients," "political money," "corporate lobbying," "promoted ignorances," "non-nutritious fundings," "substituted-in primitivisms" — and so on. The public is not ultimately sophisticated, but people and groups among us often manage to come up with a developed collected set of ideas that are not completely wrong. Even the people who do not understand much about finance have the (reasonable) sense that the supposed "solution" to the financial crisis of 2007-8 was just to make the problem bigger and worse. Even the people who haven't quite figured out the 9/11 hoax, live with a form of recognition that too much was made of supposed "terrorism" for the good of nation or its people, and they are well aware that the wars in Afghanistan and Iraq, etc. were major failures.

For the relatively more "bandwidth rich" and complex "connections" government needs to make in order to be successful in the present environment, the relationships that have so far been created are much too crude, too "mafia-like," spend too much time and resources servicing one or another few members of a "Plutocratic Exploiters Club," to work well.

Even though the better "shape" to be created in order to invoke success is not a plain box, it is not impossible to outline well enough to be observed. Rules can help. In the particular area of information in the form of news and reporting, for example, news media can be treated to standards under which only corroborated facts are reported as news; rumors and the like get called rumors. Raw opinions are offered only on the opinion page or in the "editorial" segment. Sources, even when not specifically identified, are, reasonably in the circumstances, accurately enough described. Government should not be permitted to blackmail, bribe, or otherwise coerce any media outlets, should have no prerogative of "prior restraint" (or "prior anything" — or "subsequent anything," really).

Entities and actors practicing fraud on behalf of the government or any of its multiple extensions can be discovered and sanctioned. Those who have no secrecy agreement with the government should not be subject to any "Espionage Act" criminal claims as a result of disclosure in honest reporting. True reports of fact should be immune from censorship, unless the publication is directly calculated to wreak destruction (in other words, such as — extreme case — the publication of nuclear launch codes). No more "Operation Mockingbird" (CIA "active role" in "influencing" news media). And so forth.

One can further envisage that a society which has had the bad experiences with "created reality" that we have had would collectively want to bring into existence an entity that might be called the "Auditors of the United States" — a non-government "fourth" branch of governing comprised of citizens of knowledge, experience, and ability forty-five (say) years old and up who serve for approximately 90 days at a time and who convene in a panel of fifty (one from each state) to ascertain veritable fact regarding matters of substantial national concern in which such facts are missing or buried beneath assertions entirely incoherent. No government "Commissions" — no Warren (Dulles) Commission, no 9/11 (Zelikow) Commission. No corrupted media, depending upon the brokerages of self-serving propagandizing officialdom. Engineers of the highest reputation for understanding and honesty, doctors, medical scientists, biologists similarly able and truthful, entrepreneurs of similar character, mathematicians (the Bertrand Russells of the world), statisticians, designers, people who actually understand programming and modeling, etc. would join a kind of common "roster" / or "database" and be summonsed for periods of approximately three months to investigate impartially and answer the reasonable questions and interests of the nation truthfully. Much of the time we cannot afford to have most (or many) of the people who are drawn to the politics of government comprise the institutions of society, governmental or otherwise.

9/11 and the "response" did not in fact "prevent further Muslim hijacking of planes." Indeed, as noted, Muslims did not actually hijack planes on September 11, 2001 in the first place. The 9/11 fraud stands out because it is so definitely, thoroughly false; there is no fuzziness, no coloring, no shading to be drawn about the collapses, no "maybes" suggesting misunderstanding as cause. There is no possibility that those who detonated the charges that brought the buildings down thought something else was going to happen. There is no possibility that the people who did the video fakery didn't understand they were making fake video.

The unhappy likelihood is that the nation will come to understand how important it is to take a common position against institutionalized fraud just *after* a set of consequences takes place even more damaging than the erosion of the trust environment, and the resources wasted on wars in the Middle East, and the economic dislocations, and the harm to a population of soldiers, and to the sense of well-being in the country to which they returned, than ensued from 9/11. (Perhaps the "years of Covid" — with all of the misrepresentations about the virus and the "vaccines" and the suppressions of medical facts as alleged "misinformation" will possibly bring us collectively closer to an understanding of what we are capable of doing when the applied interests are neither those of the people nor the nation but, as this it written, national self-rescue is easier to hope for than to predict.)

It is, of course, best to cure the syndrome before it further spreads and does more destruction. Again, even after two decades, 9/11, for all the harm and wrong it has done, also offers the country and the world a chance. Not just a chance, but a useful chance having the benefit of completely simple, completely incontrovertible science being at the center of the refutation.

Similarly, it is (or should be) stunningly clear that there were many skilled people involved in creating the 9/11 hoax, but they, and the nation, and world that followed them, acted entirely without self-respect. There were no adults either in the room, nor in the world beyond. No one trusted to any honesty of any kind or form. The ensuing degradation has been comparatively slow, but corrosive and continuing. It is time, even now, to gather together enough self-respect from among us all as a nation to come to the plain facts about what happened. Our children really will be better off if we can have at least some decent regard for plain facts.

Even those among us who conceive of themselves as "realistic" often believe in a "realism" that is less than helpfully, or reasonably, real. It is actually more like just another "flat earth" claim than like the round, rotating and orbiting truth, and it again credits immediate appearances entirely too much. Like Richard Nixon's "...not a crime if the President does it..." a part of supposedly "realistic" ideas, for example, often is that wrong is only that which is sentenced to a prison term. In other words, whatever is done, it is not wrongdoing if societal mechanics are organized such that it happens to escape sanction. Sanction becomes the sole measure of detriment. Again, too much credit is given to social constructs and not enough appreciation gets directed to facts and truths more real than what is merely "constructed." Understandable though it may be that humans, indeed too many of us, have a fondness for what we concoct and administer — especially when it can be used to control and manipulate other humans — ideas that connect deeply to fundamental facts and conditions are inherently much stronger than those that rely merely on manipulative opportunity.

Allen W. Dulles, and those with whom he consulted and those whom he directed, also entirely avoided responsibility for the murder of President Kennedy. People in the United States Government and military worked unremittingly by a series of maneuvers that included multiple arrivals at Parkland Hospital, armed refusal to permit the Texas Coroner from conducting an examination, even though doing so was specifically his duty and responsibility by law, by moving the President's body surreptitiously from one casket to another, by separate autopsies, including xrays and photography of a brain that was not Kennedy's, and so forth, all to create the appearance that Kennedy, who was in fact blasted from the front, had been shot only from behind (by Oswald). Thereafter, as in the case of 9/11, an accordingly thoroughly false account of events was published in the form of an official report created by and on behalf of the same general group that had decided upon and perpetrated the murder.

Much of the public, the otherwise uninvolved public, without thinking a lot about what it is doing, falls quickly to the role of believer in the false story, to the role of creditor, assents to and adopts the false and unreal model that celebrates propaganda tales and diktat and avoids or suppresses fact. The "realism" of reference to social construct, although false as to the facts, if we just consider the realities of contagion, by its terms, is so far "accurate" in the sense that it correctly generalizes about the progress of duplicities.

Comes then the question whether that can change. While further to the question whether we ordinary people can stop believing lies, particularly stop giving credit to the mendacities of government, there are added ancillary questions regarding how this can be done and what resources will be required. The change needed is not something which any installed government will ever help. On the other hand, considering the number of people not in government, and the number of people whose lives would be improved by discrediting the discreditable, and the particular abilities and awareness in subjects from science to economics to history in people among the overall ordinary population, if the government's opportunities to maintain a huge excess of secrecy, and to select against and suppress and punish statements of true facts can be curtailed, there is a reasonable chance that the conversation may at least re-balance in favor of less nonsense and bamboozle and fraud.

Since the middle of the twentieth century, many considerate people have recognized that information has been corrupted and suppressed in ways that are deeply damaging the wellbeing of the United States. At the same time, our country — especially before the expansion of things informational — enjoyed a distinct freedom, unique in much of history, from either the actual or supposed need for several kinds of bad behavior, suppression, scam or other forms of government or official wrongdoing. Not to say the country, even the 18th Century land of our Founding Fathers, didn't practice a certain share of evils, but in the longer history of the world prejudicial tax collection, punitive draft for military service, confiscations of household / estate assets from livestock to boats and ships and cargo, sudden appropriation of lands, and possible restoration only upon payment of bribes were regular features, not to mention slavery as the means for the regular provision of labor. Yet we had the great good fortune to find ourselves, nationally, in circumstances in which several kinds of the usual "bad acting" were not necessary to the anything like the degree prevalent in many countries of the world for centuries.

On the other hand, we developed (and extended and re-developed) something of a rather exploitive system of our own. Societal entities, both business and government, were made large, often abusively large, by accumulation, agglomeration, consolidation and merger, by selectivities of exploitation and enforcement. By the turn of the Twentieth Century, oil and steel and railroads came to be managed by corporate "trusts." As some of these particular business combinations were then disassembled into parts, after an interval, we created other assemblages, an army to fight in and "decide" first World War 1 and then World War 2, and thereafter a worldwide corporate empire from Coca-Cola to Boeing, and from hundreds of military bases to schematics imposed upon the world as to everything from soda branding to reserve currency management. By the turn of the Twenty-first century the federal budget was in the several trillions of dollars. We have made beasts, gargantua. They have made some of us again into rulers — of technologies and markets and populations. By and large, however, they stand out for just having rather bad manners.

Dominion inherently brings problems of its own, and erratically practiced, creates even more demands hard to respond to — except clumsily, crudely, and forcibly. Our country thus engaged in a sequence of policies that entailed fundamentally counterproductive malevolence. A few episodes of Senate hearings (the "Watergate" hearings of 1973, the Church Committee hearings of 1975, the "Iran-Contra" hearings of 1987) have questioned — although not especially deeply, nor with lasting effect — whether the overbearing schemes, including the secrecy and the false stories are, to say the least, unbefitting or, saying just a bit more, manyfold unwise. The few episodes of review and examination are the surfacings of an otherwise continuing awareness that has been submerged and avoided, that notices that we, as and by the forms we have developed, have been acting badly for bad reasons, managing to deceive ourselves about our wrongdoing and deception to our collective detriment, and not actually to any advantage.

We lived well enough through the mistakes we were making, more or less, until 2001. The 9/11 scam and hoax, however, as noted, enacted against this country, represents an extended and larger culmination of a history of doing distinctly wrongful things to others that are wasteful, and counterproductive while claiming to serve this nation.

As such, 9/11 isn't all that huge. Three skyscrapers, and a couple of other assorted buildings in New York? There are lots of buildings in New York, and in lots of other cities in this country and around the world? Compared to the damage readily done by an earthquake, the

9/11 "Pile" is just another, maybe not so huge, cleanup job. What's the problem?

Okay, and our Declaration of Independence was written on one piece of parchment. It couldn't possibly have said much. (And, by argument, it wouldn't have said much if events had happened to come out otherwise; if Washington hadn't been able to sneak the army across the water from Brooklyn without getting caught, or been able to lead the army across the Delaware December 25th, 1776 to the surprise of some drunk Hessians.) Very salient events can be greatly dependent for their salience upon other events, but nonetheless be every bit as signal and significant as indeed they are.

Unhappily, 9/11 is so much more important to our history and our country because the other schemes / scams / "dark side" manipulation projects, particularly those of the Dulles era 1) happened almost entirely across wide oceans, in countries on continents most of us have never even been to, and to which most of us will never go, 2) although some news (content tailored to United States interests) was typically provided, to the most considerable extent, all possibly inconvenient facts were well suppressed, kept secret (entirely a different schematic from the often repeated broadcast of the 9/11 building collapses on network TV that insistently contemporaneously embodied the complete mis-description of recorded video), 3) did not compress into a whole set of adverse actions on a single day, from "hijacking" airplanes to destroying buildings and killing thousands; the "scam sequence" often, in other political manipulations in other countries, was distributed over events days, weeks, months or even years in extent, 4) were schemes not only done far away from us, and to other populations than us, other governments we wanted to change or control or displace, but weren't ours, and most often the assaults were styled as "liberation" from customs, ideas, and concepts "distant" (and often already understood to be "alien from and harmful to" us, e.g. "communism," 5) didn't in the same way specifically kill "innocents" — people who got on an airplane intending to fly to California or who went to work in a downtown office building on a Tuesday — Americans who did not deserve to be crushed in a building collapse, and 6) not only were the other "dark side" projects not brought to Americans "on live TV," but by 9/11 the United States and the whole world was "brought to a halt" while the story was narrated and re-narrated, and commented upon and re-narrated again, while the video and the "talking heads" were on a seemingly infinite loop.

As and when the lies are then amplified and extended, and re-used for other governmental and institutional mis-managements at world and national scale, the lies take over. The lies become the then replicated essence of the original event and all that follows.

Again, it is not as if no one noticed. Many did. However their honest and accurate observations and plenty clear discussion of what they observed have in every instance burned to but a thin smoke then blown away in an insistent wind. This has so far happened so continuously that it should be described as having become fundamental. The structures that in fact put in place the exploitive and detrimental choices are not overt. Nobody stands up and says, "You should all support me while I co-opt the resources of the nation and subvert what should be our good purposes." Yet it happens reliably. And it is reliably carried along by gross misrepresentations. 9/11 is every way a fraud, all on its own terms, but, again, it is also an enormously overgrown descendant and relative of a once often repeated schematic. 9/11 has been extended, transferred, and amplified.

For just one, early, example of "noticing," President Truman was soon thereafter profoundly uneasy (to say the least) about having founded the CIA in 1947 and regarding the scope of the 1949 "National Security" / CIA Act.[5] and is reported as, at one point, saying:

> Those fellows in the CIA don't just report on wars and the like, they go out and make their own, and there's nobody to keep track of what they're up to. They spend billions of dollars on stirring up trouble so they'll have something to report on. They've become ... it's become a government all of its own and all secret. They don't have to account to anybody. ... That's a very dangerous thing in a democratic society, and it's got to be put a stop to.

(President Kennedy is reputed to have said he had a mind

---

5. Truman to biographer Merle Miller, as reported.

to "splinter the CIA into a thousand pieces and scatter them to the winds.") Noted, the Dulles brothers, by contrast, (at least outwardly) thought they were geniuses and heroes. Allen took a kind of "victory lap" tour of Agency stations around the world at the close of his career as Director.

We who now live are, however, inevitably responsible for our own lives, the life of our country, and our own destiny. Whatever else is made clear by our now current condition, by our inheritance and by the circumstances in which we live, only the most committedly blind can fail to observe that our wrongdoing and our dishonesties have been useful (especially financially) to but a small number of people, and they have distracted and cheated many. (Metaphorically, what we have been doing may be said to have gouged out the eyes and chopped off heads and limbs of the nation.) Clear understanding cast on this history, although it shows certain forms of plotted "economic growth," shows technological progress, and most recently shows some particularly pretentious devotion domestically to the claims of grievance politics, should let us know we have become entirely careless of substantive human and national values, from all of the rights enumerated in the Bill of Rights to all of our international treaty obligations (upon so many of which we have reneged), to the ethics and precepts of honest and independent news reporting. We have meanwhile cultivated some of the ugliest proclivities we could manage to acquire, from the widespread misuse of digital surveillance data, to wracking unrecoverable injury to principles of medical practice and public health policy, to the use of purported economic "rescues" among other things, to destroy both the life of our homes (never mind the now-labeled "Homeland") and the reasonable market for housing humans can afford and live in.

Much of the adherence to (and offered belief in) the 9/11 hoax over the last two decades has been the consequence of the fear of thinking, of considering upon first principles, on the one hand, and fear of independence itself, making the lesser choice just to follow cues and instructions, on the other. Much of the rest of what has continued the fraud has been the continued devaluation of what once had been valued. To say that the United States as a county has a "right" to wrongdoing and to cheat and lie, whether because we say we are "exceptional" or that "we are an empire now [and can] create our own reality" is at the same time to say, implicitly, that we lack the requisite meaningful confidence or self-confidence to live and work in the world of some measure of reality and truth, reasons for which we neither trust ourselves nor each other.

Over time, our lack of respect for facts, for the bona fides of people and nations in the world, and thus our lack of self-respect, has been reflected and reproduced around us. At some further stage, the schemes we have played and leveraged not only will no longer be in our control, even diagonally, but also will no longer work for us. We will then no longer have good choices to repair our circumstances and our relationships. We will have destroyed too much of the fidelity and trust required.

Afterword: A Note from the Author

Because this book will best serve all of us to every extent that the interest and attention it receives is directed specifically to the book and the issues it raises, I offer it just as the considered thoughts of an American citizen. I was born here; I have traveled, but I have lived here all my life. I have reasons good enough, as do all of us, to appreciate this nation's successes and to be disappointed in and concerned by its failures.

It would be published in an ordinary way but for the range of censorship and suppression now in the United States and other countries. No matter what they tell you, "editors" in various well-known organizations, and those who "guide" them, work to prevent books having to do with the facts of 9/11 (for just one example, among many) from seeing the common light of day.

This book is about things I believe we all should think about, and in the presence of which we should reflect and consider very thoughtfully. It is not about me. Many other people could have – should have – written it. Rather than beget remarks about its author then, best it become its own subject for reading and discussion.

Express permission is given to copy from this book, electronically, on digital media, or on paper as print, provided the copy is unaltered. Posting or distribution is encouraged, again only with the restriction against any alteration of the original, and a humble entreaty to make every effort to be honest. As any author, I write hoping that you also communicate to everyone you know (or don't know very well) and ask that they, and their friends, read it. They don't have to agree with all that it says; and they don't particularly have to like it, however, every person who reads and who does some clear thinking will, in the end, one way or another, be helping all of us.

I wrote this book, but now it belongs, in every important sense, to everyone. Commentary of all kinds is welcomed. That said, the more informed, more thoughtful, wiser, and more deeply considered the comments, the more my purpose will have been met.

I accept that some commentary may be vehemently critical, hostile, wildly intemperate, just offer ridicule and hatred. No matter how vituperative what may be said, however, I suggest that we listen to all, but that we proceed in all events by crediting as factually true only what is actual truth. If the book is about anything, it is written to say that we must be (and are) collectively capable of knowing what is true, and separating out falsity.

The 9/11 "story" includes, and has been has been accompanied by, more utterly unreal, fake, absurd, and unworthy propositions about readily knowable physical facts that any other purported "news account" of any other public occurrence. Whatever else may now be said, proposals to the effect that all of the sham and lies were, despite themselves, something else, do not, could not, offer to us what honesty now can.

Often enough we think we know, or saw, something very different from what happened. We didn't. But, not wanting to be wrong, or at a social margin, we talk ourselves into beliefs that mistake the plain facts. We have every reason to be interested in our experiences and our thoughts about them but, as this book proposes, very well established actual science deserves, at the same time, thorough credit for the verified factuality it provides. We should forgive ourselves for any mistake we may have made, but we should also promise every rightful correction and amnesty to ourselves and to each other.

These things said, as much as this book is about facts, it is intended to be yet more about the possibility for remedy and about the remedies we can achieve. My thought is that even the people who cannot come to accept the extent of the hoax that is 9/11 will nonetheless support rules in the law that end secrecy about serious criminal acts, that require scientific forensic investigation conducted openly and honestly regarding collapses and other failures, whether from accidents or from other causes, and that provide recognition and the possibility of remedy in cases of serious breach of public trust.

- An American Citizen

(September, 2021 / March, 2023)

www.ingramcontent.com/pod-product-compliance
Lightning Source LLC
Chambersburg PA
CBHW020122180726

47992CB00020B/1720